The Book of Essential Islam

THE BOOK OF ESSENTIAL ISLAM

Ali Rafea
With Aliaa and Aisha Rafea

THE BOOK FOUNDATION
BRISTOL, ENGLAND AND WATSONVILLE, CALIFORNIA

THE BOOK FOUNDATION
www.thebook.org

Special Thanks to Talal and Nadia Zahid for their support.
Publication Design by Threshold Productions.
Cover Design by Kabir Helminski & Ahmed Moustafa.
First Book Foundation edition published 2005.

British Library Cataloguing in Publication Data
A catalogue record of this book is available from The British Library

Library of Congress Cataloging-in-Publication Data
The Book of Essential Islam / by Ali, Aliaa, and
Aisha Rafea.
Watsonville, California: The Book Foundation.
ISBN 1-904510-13-2
BP 161.R
Includes bibliographical references.
1. Islam. 2. Islamic teaching & beliefs
I. Ali, Aliaa, and Aisha Rafea II. The Book Foundation

Contents

About the Authors

Ali, Aliaa, and Aisha are the children of **Master Rafea M. Rafea** (1903-1970); a Muslim spiritual guide whose earthly life was a living expression of love to all humanity. Despite his physical absence, his spiritual presence is deeply felt, continuously inspiring them while they carry on his mission. This mission stems from the conviction that people need to correct their views about themselves, thus realizing their humanity. Fulfilling the meaning of being human is a never-ending process. Yet when Man takes the path towards that ultimate goal, he fulfills God's purpose of his creation. Rafea believed that man has always sought that goal and was supported in realizing it by Revelations and all forms of wisdom. As such, he was open to all spiritual knowledge; old and new, from the East and the West.

Ali Rafea is the spiritual guide of the Egyptian Society for Spiritual and Cultural Research (ESSCR)[1]. He does not see himself as a teacher or a *shaykh* but a seeker of truth and the symbol of the study circle. This attitude in itself is a breakthrough in spiritual teaching. It marks a new approach to the guide-disciple relationship, for it implies a request from the disciples not to be dependent on outside guidance alone. Rather, a disciple has to struggle in order to derive and understand truthful knowledge from within and through his own experiences. Ali Rafea's sincerity and straightforwardness, his devotion and simplicity are striking. His enlightened soul shines within clean hearts in the circle's members. His words echo in their hearts, springing from within their souls. He guides their steps all along the way. Ali Rafea is also a prominent scholar in Computer Science. He obtained his Ph.D. in France and is now a professor at Cairo University.

Aliaa is an anthropologist and a professor at an Egyptian university. She obtained her Ph.D. from Ain Shams University and her M.A. from the American University in Cairo. She has partici-

[1]http://www.esscr.org

pated in a number of international conferences and is the author of several academic publications in which she used her knowledge of anthropology to address spiritual issues and their impact on man. For the spring semester of 2002, Aliaa was a visiting Professor at Randolph and Macon Women's college in Lynchburg where she lectured mainly on Islam and where she also gave a public lecture and a number of public addresses all touching on various aspects of Islām. Under the spiritual umbrella of Ali Rafea, Aliaa gathers regularly with a group of women who are interested in spiritual knowledge and leads their discussions on spiritual experiences and the path to spiritual growth.

Aisha is a writer and journalist. She has written several books and numerous articles in the field of spiritual culture. She currently contributes articles to the prominent weekly Egyptian magazine *October* under the title of *"Moments of Realization."* In all her writings, she focuses on the spirituality of Islamic teaching and its role in freeing humans from the enslavement of matter. Without spirituality, she believes, people turn Holy Scripture into literal, lifeless, and dogmatic commandments. They then become stagnant, arrogant, and inclined to dominate others, which is contradictory to the true spirit of religion.

Aisha and Aliaa translated into English *Memoirs of Khabarides: The Future of Spiritualism,*[2] a piece of fiction that their father Master Rafea wrote in the 1960s in Arabic. It foretells that the 21st century will witness the revival of spiritual awareness, eliminating religious conflicts based on prejudices and misunderstandings.

[2]Rafea Mohamed Rafea, *Memoirs of Khabarides*, Vantage Press, New York, USA, 1990.

Acknowledgments

We wish to thank Peter Orr for his contribution in editing this book.

Being part of the spirit of love motivating the writing of this work, Ahmad Abdel-Azeem, Ibrahim Abdel-Khalek, Akram Abdel-Al, and Ali Abdel-Azeem exerted a great effort in documenting the Prophetic Hadiths. Sameh El-Ansary and Khaled El-Adawi volunteered to format and carry out the production of this book.

Notation and Conventions

Abbreviations

HC *Hijrī Calendar*

HQ *Ḥadīth Qudsī*[1]

PH *Prophetic Ḥadīth*

Matt. *Gospel of Matthew*

John *Gospel of John*

Deut. *Deuteronomy*, the fifth book of the Pentateuch, "the first five books of the Old Testament," also known as the Law of Moses, or Torah.[2]

Ex. *Exodus*, the second book of the Torah

Notes

1. Unless mentioned otherwise, the translation of the Holy Qur'ān used in this book, with small changes in some cases, is that of the Holy Qur'ān (Electronic Version 7. 01), Harf Company for Information Technology, Egypt, 1998. (Translation by A. Yusuf Ali.) XXXXXX
القرآن الكريم ، الإصدار السابع، شركة حرف لتقنية المعلومات، القاهرة ١٩٩٨.

2. All Prophetic and Divine *Ḥadīths* in English are the authors' translations.

---

[1] A *Ḥadīth Qudsī* is a saying in which the Prophet Muḥammad quoted Allāh in His exact words, but which is not part of the Holy Qur'ān.

[2] According to the *Oxford Dictionary of the Bible*, W. R. F. Browning, Oxford University Press, Oxford, New York, 1966.

Preface

In all of human history, man has never witnessed the immediacy of communication that is available now. Distances do not count for much anymore; it is now easy to explore the world via the Internet or other media. Yet this vastly increased proximity has not ended clashes and conflicts on either the ideological or the cultural level. On the one hand, there is an attempt by the more powerful to invade the world culturally, provoking resistance, even enmity, in many areas of the world. On the other hand, dogmas and fanaticism widen the gap between peoples and create obstacles to cultural communication.

In order to bridge these gaps, the world needs to build a dialogue based on assumptions different from those that currently prevail. There is no reason to accept clashes between civilizations merely as facts, nor that only one way of progress must be dominant. Instead, the world should search for common ground, where each nation or civilization can enrich the others and be enriched by them. There is a need for a very special dialogue, one that would bring people together without attempting to impose uniformity. We need a dialogue that deeply penetrates cultures and understands our struggle to discover the purpose of our existence. We need a dialogue that goes beyond diversities in order to see the oneness of humanity and the purpose of existence.

This book represents the authors' reflections on a Call that seeks to gather the world to "a common term, a reconciling principle," *al-kalimah as-sawā'*. It is the Call that the Divine commanded the Prophet Muḥammad (Peace be upon him) to convey; a Call that introduced to humankind a method and a way to realize the purpose of existence; a Call that clarified that all Revelations are representations of the same Truth.

This Call, however, dates from the beginning of humanity's existence on earth; it was revealed in various places, and expressed in diverse terms, languages, and symbolic behavior. Enveloped in darkness and veiled from the authentic state of being, humanity was deceived by fallacy, mistaking it for reality and truth. As such, humanity shut out the face of our inner messenger and turned a deaf ear to the divine voice inherent in our own existence. Humanity then continued to create an illusory world in which we compete, fight, and kill, while concealing the conflict taking place within ourselves.

As human beings, we share the fact that we like to give meaning to our lives, to look beyond simply satisfying our physical needs. In short, we—directly or indirectly, consciously or unconsciously—experience ourselves as more than physical matter. Yet we do not allow this natural tendency to emerge and develop. We suffocate the divine inner voice; we allege that we do not need a metaphysical outlook or that we already know everything, thanks to this or that teaching. Thus we are materialistic or dogmatic, antagonistic or atheist. In each case, we evade our inner guidance.

The authors of this book suggest that if any human being, wherever he or she may be, would listen to their inner guidance, he or she would be directed to a path that all Revelations guide us to take. Here we refer to this path as the "common term" or a "common unifying message." Its commonality is not ideologically imposed or socially invented. This path is "common" because it stems from the nature of the human being as human. In Arabic it is called *fiṭrah*. To take this path requires and leads to complete inner freedom. Therefore it cannot be indoctrinated or imposed, but must be continuously discovered and individually experienced.

Beyond the diversity of revelations, each with a different name, there is that One Truth, One Wisdom, One Way.[1] It is required now, as it was required through the ages, that we probe into the revelations' shared meanings and go beyond their various names. Humanity is asked to go beyond this diversity and search for that common Truth. We are challenged to dig deep within so that we can discern between fallacy and reality.

This challenge is not new. Fifteen centuries ago, the Prophet Muḥammad guided people from various creeds to come to this "common term" or "reconciling principle" that can unify their goals,

[1]The authors discuss the basic themes of Revelations in their book: *Beyond Diversities: Reflections on Revelations*, Sadek Publications, Cairo, Egypt, 2000.

allowing them to discover that they belong to one another and to the Oneness that has taken varied shapes. That realization is intrinsically related to the Call for peace as one of humanity's primary goals. Even the word Islam connotes and is derived from the same roots as peace, *salām*. Islam as revealed to the Prophet Muḥammad points to the One Truth that stands beyond diverse names. It focuses on the main principles with which the other Revelations had constructed their calls.

By discussing the Islamic Call as revealed to the Prophet Muḥammad, the authors would like to share their ideas with all those interested in searching for the "common term." By focusing on the meaning of the Islamic Call, the confusion about Islam that has prevailed in the minds of Muslims and non-Muslims may be untangled. The challenge lies in showing how that Call was addressed to the whole world while respecting diversity and freedom of choice; how its universal nature does not seek to abolish variations or impose uniformity. It will become increasingly clear that Islam is based on spreading peace, not waging wars. Islamic teachings focus on how to support each human being in the process of inner transformation so that our very existence might convey love and peace.

Re-examining this Call today opens new channels for religious debate and interfaith dialogue and paves the way toward establishing a world community. Our contention, therefore, is not just theological; it has practical dimensions, as did the original Islamic Call. It was that Call which liberated people from living false lives and on whose principles Islamic civilization flourished.

Introduction

Out of our conviction that the Islamic Call as revealed to the Prophet Muḥammad (Peace be upon him) was a continuation of all previous revelations,[1] we will show how that Call explains the core of all revelations. By confirming and clarifying the lessons of previous revelations, the Islamic teachings provide comprehensive guidance which integrates a system of spiritual training and a process of coping with mundane life.

What we present herein is in full harmony with what we understand to be the Islamic Call. It is our aim to demonstrate that Islām as revealed to the Prophet Muḥammad transcends names and creeds and directly explores the main mission of all revelations. The Prophet Muḥammad said,

> *God considers not your appearances, He rather considers your hearts and your deeds. (PH)*[2]
>
> إن الله لا ينظر إلى صوركم وأموالكم ولكن ينظر إلى قلوبكم وأعمالكم

The Holy Qur'ān, on the other hand, addresses those who are fooled by illusions:

> *You worship nothing but names. (Qur'ān 12:40)*
>
> مَا تَعْبُدُونَ مِنْ دُونِهِ إِلَّا أَسْمَاء

In a world full of ethnic conflicts and battles in the name of religion, the Call conveyed through the Prophet needs to be addressed once more. It teaches that no privilege should be based on religious affiliation, race, or gender, and that submitting oneself to Allāh is the main principle that brings people closer together.

---

[1]The word "revelation" as used throughout this book points to all revelations, natural or Prophetic. When capitalized, "Revelations" points to those of the Prophets, from Abraham to Muḥammad.

[2]Narrated by Muslim, Ibn Mājah, and Aḥmad.

And they say: None shall enter Paradise unless he be a Jew or a Christian. . . . Nay, whoever submits his whole self to Allāh and is a doer of good will get his reward with his Lord; on such shall be no fear, nor shall they grieve. (Qur'ān 2:111, 112)

وَقَالُوا لَنْ يَدْخُلَ الْجَنَّةَ إِلَّا مَنْ كَانَ هُودًا أَوْ نَصَارَى تِلْكَ أَمَانِيُّهُمْ قُلْ هَاتُوا بُرْهَانَكُمْ إِنْ كُنْتُمْ صَادِقِينَ. بَلَى مَنْ أَسْلَمَ وَجْهَهُ لِلَّهِ وَهُوَ مُحْسِنٌ فَلَهُ أَجْرُهُ عِنْدَ رَبِّهِ وَلَا خَوْفٌ عَلَيْهِمْ وَلَا هُمْ يَحْزَنُونَ

To submit one's whole self to Allāh is the core meaning of Islām. As simple as that may sound, knowing how to surrender to Allāh is a complex process. This submission is the purpose of creation. All revelations have pointed to this submission, using different terms and different means.

The word "Islām" in the Holy Qur'ān points to that one Religion that has appeared in all revelations. However, the use of the word "Islām" was confused over the centuries, so that it gradually lost its broad meaning. Instead it has become a reference to certain cultural identities. These distortions have accumulated over time, leading to the present situation in which confusion prevails and the use of the word "Islām" is linked to behaviors and concepts which are alien to the original meaning uncovered by the Revelation to the Prophet Muḥammad. The Islamic Call that transformed people during the time of the Prophet Muḥammad needs to be rediscovered. It can empower us to create a new world, one full of peace and love.

Just as the use of the word "Islām" has been confused with meanings alien to its original intent, the term "Islamic Call" is also unclear and subject to certain stereotypes. When it is used, several questions are raised: Does it imply that Muslims see themselves as superior? Does it attempt to convert others to Islām? Is it the right of Muslims to judge the followers of other revelations? Do Muslims have the right to wage wars against non-Muslims until they convert to Islām? Do Muslims consider followers of all other revelations to be "non-believers"? Do Muslims have the right to fight others simply because they are "non-believers"? Do Muslims insist that the whole world should be Muslim?

Various groups wearing the label of Islām have given very different answers to these questions. This is not the forum in which to present a critique of the various conceptions of the "Islamic Call"; instead, we introduce our own reading, supported by the main ideas of the Islamic Call that were developed during the life of the Prophet.

From our perspective, the Islamic Call is not linked to a certain creed; nor does it merely belong to history. It is still alive and relevant today. While the life of the Prophet represents for humanity an example of how the Call can be fulfilled. The continuation of that Call shows that there is a method that is as valid and as credible now as it was long ago, because it is related to the "pure nature of things," *al-fiṭrah*. Each of us is required to revive the call for Truth within our own heart and to strive to liberate ourselves from illusions and dogmas.

We can safely say that uncertainty about the meaning of the Islamic Call prevails because politics are confused with religion. The role of Muḥammad as a statesman has attracted the attention of historians, analysts, and even those who claim to be his followers, to the detriment of the core meaning of the Call that he conveyed. Such observers view Islamic history with the assumption that Islām's main goal was to establish a strong community and that the Prophet was first and foremost a political leader. Accordingly, they overlook the spiritual guidance that was the root of all the social changes that followed.

From our perspective, the primary objective of the Islamic Call has always been to guide humankind to realize the goal of our existence and to reach the highest rank that human beings can achieve. The path of Islām offers a way to maximize the spiritual gain that an individual can reap during their short earthly life. Following this way, a person's spiritual struggle is reflected in their ordinary work and in their relationship with nature, with other individuals, and with the whole world. The Call to witness the oneness of God had a great impact on the lives of the first disciples of Muḥammad, radically changing the social environment of Arabia. It can still bring change today, this time to the entire world.

The Islamic Call is universal in the sense that it is imbued with love for all people. And it is universal in that it reveals the law of spiritual growth revealed in previous revelations. The Prophet Muḥammad said,

I was sent to ALL human beings. (PH)[3]

أُرسلت إلى الناس كافة

I was sent to all human beings including the red and the black. (PH)[4]

بُعثت إلى الناس كافة الأحمر والأسود

Speaking of the Prophet Muḥammad, the Holy Qur'ān says:

We have not sent you but as a universal (Messenger) to men. (Qur'ān 34:28)

وَمَا أَرْسَلْنَاكَ إِلَّا كَافَّةً لِلنَّاسِ

This Call does not force those of different creeds to abandon their teachings. On the contrary, Islām as revealed to the Prophet Muḥammad confirmed the teachings of the previous Revelations and even explained them to their followers. The followers of other Revelations are invited to learn, through Islām, more about the teachings that they already have. Those who follow Muḥammad are guided to see that the teachings of Islām had their roots in all previous revelations. The "common term" that all these revelations share is how to believe not only theoretically, but practically, in the oneness of God. This belief leads to the fulfillment of the purpose of our creation. The Prophet Muḥammad articulated the ethics of a debate that can take place among followers of various creeds that adhere to the one Religion as expressed in those creeds. These ethics were feasible then and remain so today.

In order to eliminate the confusion that has prevailed for more than fourteen centuries, certain preliminary requirements must be met, such as clarifying certain issues that have distorted the meaning of the Islamic Call. For example, when it is said that Islām has universal dimensions, certain implications have been wrongly

[3]Narrated by Aḥmad.
[4]Narrated by Aḥmad.

attached. Some Muslims seem to dream of converting the whole world to the Islamic creed, even forcing people to become Muslim. Similar confusion veils our ability to receive the guidance of the Islamic Call. We have tried to address these issues below.

Multiplicity versus Unity: Relativity versus Universality

Variation is an intrinsic principle in nature. We are asked in the teachings of the Holy Qur'ān to observe nature in order to comprehend how the world is ordered. Science is the offspring of this observation, but the target of contemplation transcends scientific knowledge. It is inspiring as it gives both heart and mind the means to observe certain principles of creation. By observing the natural world, we can learn that variation is in the nature of things:

> *. . . We* ***produce vegetation of all kinds****: from some We produce green (crops), out of which We produce grain, heaped up (at harvest); out of the date palm and its sheaths (or spathes) (come) clusters of dates hanging low and near: and (then there are) gardens of grapes, and olives, and pomegranates,* ***each similar (in kind) yet different (in variety)****. (Qur'ān 6:99)*[5]
>
> وَهُوَ الَّذِي أَنْزَلَ مِنَ السَّمَاءِ مَاءً فَأَخْرَجْنَا بِهِ نَبَاتَ كُلِّ شَيْءٍ فَأَخْرَجْنَا مِنْهُ خَضِرًا نُخْرِجُ مِنْهُ حَبًّا مُتَرَاكِبًا وَمِنَ النَّخْلِ مِنْ طَلْعِهَا قِنْوَانٌ دَانِيَةٌ وَجَنَّاتٍ مِنْ أَعْنَابٍ وَالزَّيْتُونَ وَالرُّمَّانَ مُشْتَبِهًا وَغَيْرَ مُتَشَابِهٍ
>
> *And the things on this earth which He has multiplied in* ***varying colors*** *(and qualities). (Qur'ān 16:13)*
>
> وَمَا ذَرَأَ لَكُمْ فِي الْأَرْضِ مُخْتَلِفًا أَلْوَانُهُ

[5]The stress on this and the following verses is added by the authors.

And in the mountains are tracts white and red, of ***various shades of color****, and black intense in hue. And so among men and crawling creatures and cattle, are they of* ***various colors****. (Qur'ān 35:27-28)*

وَمِنَ الْجِبَالِ جُدَدٌ بِيضٌ وَحُمْرٌ مُخْتَلِفٌ أَلْوَانُهَا وَغَرَابِيبُ سُودٌ، وَمِنَ النَّاسِ وَالدَّوَابِّ وَالْأَنْعَامِ مُخْتَلِفٌ أَلْوَانُهُ

And among His Signs is the creation of the heavens and the earth, and the ***variations in your languages and your colors****; truly in that are Signs for those who know. (Qur'ān 30:22)*

وَمِنْ ءَايَاتِهِ خَلْقُ السَّمَوَاتِ وَالْأَرْضِ وَاخْتِلَافُ أَلْسِنَتِكُمْ وَأَلْوَانِكُمْ إِنَّ فِي ذَلِكَ لَآيَاتٍ لِلْعَالِمِينَ

If your Lord had so willed, He could have made mankind one Nation: ***but they continue in their differences****. (Qur'ān 11:118)*

وَلَوْ شَاءَ رَبُّكَ لَجَعَلَ النَّاسَ أُمَّةً وَاحِدَةً وَلَا يَزَالُونَ مُخْتَلِفِينَ

If the Holy Qur'ān stresses that variation is a part of the nature of things, it is unlikely that people should be expected to follow a unique creed or only one way of thinking. However, as human beings we share the fact that we are all created for a purpose. Therefore our goal is one, but it is very natural that our ways to achieve that goal will vary. Each person even has their own unique way to develop spiritually. The Islamic teachings address all people and reveal the unity behind this diversity without attempting to deny the varied nature of things.

To each among you have We prescribed a Method and an Open Way. If Allāh had so willed, He would have made you a single Nation, but (His plan is) to test you in what He has given you; so strive as in a race in all virtues. The goal of you all is to Allāh. (Qur'ān 5:48)

لِكُلٍّ جَعَلْنَا مِنْكُمْ شِرْعَةً وَمِنْهَاجًا وَلَوْ شَاءَ اللَّهُ لَجَعَلَكُمْ أُمَّةً وَاحِدَةً

وَلَكِن لِّيَبْلُوَكُمْ فِي مَا ءَاتَاكُمْ فَاسْتَبِقُوا الْخَيْرَاتِ إِلَى اللَّهِ مَرْجِعُكُمْ جَمِيعًا

Because there is this unifying goal underlying our differences, the Prophet's mission is universal. Once man is aware that he is to devote himself to Allāh, he will search for that which makes him closer to Him.

From this perspective, multiplicity and unity are two categories used to express different ways of seeing the same phenomenon. Therefore they do not contradict each other, but integrate in a higher level of perception. Within this context, relativity refers to the way that each revelation expresses the one truth according to humankind's awareness of spiritual realities and the cultural languages that different groups employ. The universality of the Islamic Call lies in the fact that the main themes by which human life spiritually evolves are the same in all revelations and are clearly defined and explained in the Islamic teachings.

Dynamism versus Stagnation: Belief versus Dogma

From certain perspectives, religion and dogma are somehow linked. The simple logic behind this linkage posits that religion offers realities assumed to be beyond space and time. According to this view, the person of faith should adhere to those so-called realities regardless of the actuality of human life in a changing world. There are numerous examples in history where religious institutions confirmed this link between religion and dogma when they played a role in fighting innovation and scientific discovery.

Religious teachings that seek to establish dogma are a common feature of religious institutions and are a phenomenon shared among nations, but such dogmatic tendencies are surely alien to the authentic teachings of revelations. All revelations came to encourage man to think for himself, to discover realities through experience rather than through blind obedience. It is a mistake, then, to focus on religious institutions, thinking that they represent authentic heavenly teachings. What applies to revelations in general applies to Islām in particular. Islām, like all heavenly Revelations, encourages dynamism and innovative thinking, and highlights inner individual experiences.

The belief in one divine origin of life does not conflict with our continuous growth in knowledge, be it scientific or other. That belief helps human consciousness acknowledge a manifested order in the universe. On the basis of that assumption, scientific achievements are being made continuously. As humans discover the world and themselves, they realize their own limitations as imperfect beings and realize, too, that perfection is attributed to a power that transcends their knowledge. Revelations came to assert to humanity that the spontaneous realization of the Unseen, Unknown Supreme is well-founded.

These beliefs stand unshaken for a believer regardless of circumstances. Faith in a Divine Power means that the person affirms this Power's existence and rejects the notion that Divinity is a human invention. For the person of faith, this Truth does not even require proof; he is sure of what he considers to be the Truth. To ask him to prove his faith is like asking him to prove that he exists.

A person's faith reflects a vision of the heart, an insight, rather than a result of the mind and logic. A faithful person's behavior is evidence of and describes his faith. One does not absolutely need to codify those beliefs in the form of doctrine. Rather, a believer should be open to learning in an ongoing way. We are challenged to purify our hearts continuously, to improve our ability to decode the secret of our own existence.

The rule of spiritual development is not rigid and cannot be judged outwardly. For example, it is not *what* one does that will move one to a higher spiritual status, but *how* and *why*. Faith in the Divine opens channels for knowledge. This knowledge belongs to the realm of the heart but does not contradict that of the mind. Such knowledge cannot turn into dogma, simply because it cannot be imposed logically, but is revealed only through spiritual experiences and communicated to those who share similar experiences.

Due to the nature of this knowledge, the rate and speed of acquiring it and the spiritual evolution that accompanies it cannot be measured. While the grace of God is not necessarily measured proportionally to man's deeds, the first step in asking for His grace comes from man. This inner feeling of yearning for Allāh is in itself His grace. Those who are spiritually awake and alive have the responsibility to call for those who remain spiritually blind, knowing that there is no guarantee of a response. But the responsibility of those who call does not extend to attacking, insulting, or even judging those who reject the call. The only task of the former is to remind the latter of the call and then leave them to their own unique experiences.

In short, faith in the Divine opens up a realm of spiritual knowledge and spiritual transformation. This faith can be awakened, not imposed, and as such it is not part of a dogma but is the language of the soul.

This understanding explains the difference between a dogmatic call, according to which people claim to know the absolute Truth, and a call in which people believe in the Divine as an unattainable Truth. The former pays much attention to forms, names, and rituals. The latter focuses on purity of the heart, life experiences, and the meanings of all religious symbols. For the first group, calling others means indoctrinating them with certain teachings and orders. For the second group, calling means reminding those who are ready to open themselves to the Truth.

The inner experience is free of the names of specific religions, worship systems, and rites. The Islamic Call focuses on how to awaken people spiritually, regardless of creed. It does not stoop to judging or humiliating people who are different.

It may be clear now that we do not approach Islām from a superior standpoint or with prejudice; our task is to convey what we believe is best for our humanness. If we unify our goals to achieve the highest possible rank of humanness, we will realize how close we are, regardless of various heritages and religious practices.

We present our ideas in six chapters:

The **first chapter** considers the use of the word "Islām" in the Holy Qur'ān, showing that it is not limited to the Revelation to the Prophet Muḥammad alone; rather it is used to describe all Revelations. As such, "Islām" is the One Religion that has appeared and that has been explained by various Prophets and Messengers of God.

In a similar vein, the **second chapter** discusses how the teachings received by the Prophet confirmed previous teachings. Islām as it was revealed to the Prophet is a continuation of other Revelations. In confirming their teachings, the Revelation to the Prophet Muḥammad clarified them and explained them anew.

In order to guide humankind to a clear path, the Revelation to the Prophet established some basic concepts; the **third chapter** explains these. In order to be effective, these concepts move us from the mental sphere to our very core as human beings and can radically change our outlook on life.

In order for man to cultivate his own existence, he should become aware of his primary mission on earth. The spiritual training system in Islām, commonly known as the worship system, functions as a constant reminder of that mission. The **fourth chapter** explains how this spiritual training system is a coherent discipline that maximizes spiritual awareness if approached correctly, not only in the form of rites or rituals, but as meaningful expressions of our longing for the Divine.

It is a common tendency to seek short-cuts for what should and should not be done in order to travel a straight path. Our approach to the recommendations of Islamic teachings and the instructions of Islamic law, *Sharī'ah,* is different. We argue that without the basic concepts that form the core of Islamic teachings, the guidance of the Prophet and the legal system of the Call cannot be comprehended or implemented in order to serve their true purposes. The **fifth chapter** explores this in detail, arguing that Islām as revealed to the Prophet Muḥammad links living on earth and cultivating oneself for heaven.

Acting on an essential principle in Islām that one is not a person of faith unless one loves people to the same degree that one loves oneself, Muḥammad called his community and the world to Islām, but never used violence to impose it. The **sixth chapter** clarifies many misconceptions related to the Islamic Call and the Prophet's teachings in this regard.

We conclude our work by emphasizing the great need to understand and solve the problems of the modern world from a spiritual perspective that focuses on uncovering the oneness of revelations and coming to a "reconciling principle." The oneness of life and the oneness of humanity are derived from our faith in the Oneness of the Creator.

Ali, Aliaa, & Aisha Rafea

1
One Religion, Many Revelations

In the Revelation to the Prophet Muḥammad (Peace be upon him), the term "Islām" is used to point to the One Primordial Religion, the *Dīn al-Fiṭrah.* To clarify this statement, we will explore how the Holy Qur'ān uses the words "Islām" and "Muslim." Three points will be covered. First, it is obvious that in the Holy Qur'ān as well as in the Prophet Muḥammad's teachings, "Islām" points to the Primordial Religion that was revealed to Abraham and to all the Prophets who followed. Second, Islām is expressed through the behavior and beliefs of those called Muslims in the Holy Qur'ān. Third, to be a Muslim is to live in harmony with the Divine Order. The Prophets are exemplars of how this can be accomplished and their teachings guide man to that end.

There Is Only One Religion Revealed to Humanity

The Holy Qur'ān speaks of One Religion that is "Islām":

> *The Religion that was revealed by Allāh is Islām. (Qur'ān 3:19)*[1]
>
> إِنَّ الدِّينَ عِنْدَ اللَّهِ الإِسْلَامُ

"Islām" within this context points to all revelations, as the verse explains:

> *People who were given the Book differed after they received the knowledge, for they were unjust to each other. (Qur'ān 3:19)*

---

[1]Our translation.

وَمَا اخْتَلَفَ الَّذِينَ أُوتُوا الْكِتَابَ إِلَّا مِنْ بَعْدِ مَا جَاءَهُمُ الْعِلْمُ بَغْيًا بَيْنَهُمْ

The People of the Book "differed" among themselves not because their Revelations were different but because they were not following the straight path. Despite the fact that they received the knowledge of Religion through that one "Book" as revealed at various times, they continued to live in conflict. This is because they "were unjust to each other" as the phrase *baghyan baynahum*[2] indicates.

To elaborate, it is interesting to observe that the word "Islām" is derived from the root *s-l-m*. From this root are also derived the noun *salām* "peace," the verb *sallama* "to surrender," and the adjective *sālim* "the saved one." *Baghyan* is derived from *b-gh-y*. Used alone, *baghy* means an unjustified attack. Those who disagree cannot coexist with each other; they quarrel without justification. Such conflict is in itself an indication of deviation from holy guidance. In this way, people lost the ability to discern between what is true and what is false. In contrast, Muslims (in the broadest sense of the word) are those who surrender to the holy and therefore live in inner peace and manifest peace outwardly. The following verse, in which the Holy Qur'ān addresses the Prophet, explains:

> *So if they dispute with you, say: "I have submitted my whole self to Allāh and so have those who follow me." And say to the People of the Book and to those who have not received holy guidance: "Do you (also) submit yourselves?" If they do, they are in right guidance, but if they turn back, your duty is to convey the Message; and in Allāh's sight are (all) His servants. (Qur'ān 3:20)*

فَإِنْ حَاجُّوكَ فَقُلْ أَسْلَمْتُ وَجْهِيَ لِلَّهِ وَمَنِ اتَّبَعَنِ وَقُل لِّلَّذِينَ أُوتُوا الْكِتَابَ وَالْأُمِّيِّينَ ءَأَسْلَمْتُمْ فَإِنْ أَسْلَمُوا فَقَدِ اهْتَدَوْا وَإِن تَوَلَّوْا فَإِنَّمَا عَلَيْكَ الْبَلَاغُ وَاللَّهُ بَصِيرٌ بِالْعِبَادِ

[2]*Baghyan* is an Arabic word that implies all forms of injustice and dishonest competition. *Baynahum* means "among themselves."

The Prophet was asked to convey the Message of Allāh by being an exemplar, not by imposing anything on others. Peace, not conflict, was what he manifested. He said of himself,

> *O People, I am Mercy that is presented to you (by Allāh).* (PH)[3]
>
> يا أيها الناس إنما أنا رحمة مهداة

He called for the One Religion by uncovering the oneness of the Revelations to the Prophets who had come before him:

> *The parable of the Prophets who preceded and myself is like a building that someone had beautifully and perfectly constructed. But a single brick was missing in one of its corners. So, whenever people passed by that building, expressing their fascination in it, they used to say, "The missing brick has to be laid." I am (like) that brick. And I am the Seal of the Prophets.* (PH)[4]
>
> إن مثلي ومثل الأنبياء من قبلي كمثل رجل بنى بيتا فأحسنه وأجمله إلا موضع لبنة من زاوية فجعل الناس يطوفون به ويعجبون له ويقولون هلا وضعت هذه اللبنة قال فأنا اللبنة وأنا خاتم النبيين

---

[3]Narrated by Dārimī.

[4]Narrated by Bukhārī and most *ḥadīth* scholars. The Prophet, said in another *ḥadīth, The Prophets are (like) half brothers to one father. They have several mothers, but their Religion is one.* (Narrated by Bukhārī)

الأنبياء أخوة لعلات، أمهاتهم شتى ودينهم واحد

Stressing the oneness of the Prophets and the revelations, the Prophet tells his followers, *Do not ever try to show the superiority of one Prophet over another.* (Narrated by Abū Dā'ūd and Aḥmad)

لا تخيروا بين الأنبياء

The Prophet also said, *A servant of Allāh should not say that I, the Messenger of Allāh, am better than Jonah, the son of Matthew.* (Narrated by Muslim and Abū Dā'ūd)

ما ينبغي لعبد أن يقول أنا»«أي رسول الله»» خير من يونس بن متى

Thus the Prophet explained to his followers that believing him implied believing in all previous Prophets and Revelations. The Holy Qur'ān expresses this truth:

> *The Messenger believes in what has been revealed to him from his Lord, as do the faithful. Each one (of them) believes in Allāh, His angels, His Books, and His Messengers. We make no distinction between one and another of His Messengers. And they say: "We hear, and we obey, (we seek) Your forgiveness, our Lord, and to You is the end of all journeys. (Qur'ān 2:285)*
>
> ءَامَنَ الرَّسُولُ بِمَا أُنزِلَ إِلَيْهِ مِن رَّبِّهِ وَالْمُؤْمِنُونَ كُلٌّ ءَامَنَ بِاللَّهِ وَمَلَائِكَتِهِ وَكُتُبِهِ وَرُسُلِهِ لَا نُفَرِّقُ بَيْنَ أَحَدٍ مِّن رُّسُلِهِ وَقَالُوا سَمِعْنَا وَأَطَعْنَا غُفْرَانَكَ رَبَّنَا وَإِلَيْكَ الْمَصِيرُ

The Holy Qur'ān states that Allāh revealed the same truth to all the Prophets, those who are mentioned and others who are not mentioned in the Holy Qur'ān:

> *We have sent you inspiration, as We sent it to Noah and the Messengers after him: We sent inspiration to Abraham, Ismā'īl, Isaac, Jacob, and the Tribes, to Jesus, Job, Jonah, Aaron, and Solomon, and to David We gave the Psalms. Of some Messengers We have already told you the story; of others We have not, and to Moses Allāh spoke directly. (Qur'ān 4:163-164)*
>
> إِنَّا أَوْحَيْنَا إِلَيْكَ كَمَا أَوْحَيْنَا إِلَىٰ نُوحٍ وَالنَّبِيِّينَ مِن بَعْدِهِ وَأَوْحَيْنَا إِلَىٰ إِبْرَاهِيمَ وَإِسْمَاعِيلَ وَإِسْحَاقَ وَيَعْقُوبَ وَالْأَسْبَاطِ وَعِيسَىٰ وَأَيُّوبَ وَيُونُسَ وَهَارُونَ وَسُلَيْمَانَ وَءَاتَيْنَا دَاوُدَ زَبُورًا، وَرُسُلًا قَدْ قَصَصْنَاهُمْ عَلَيْكَ مِن قَبْلُ وَرُسُلًا لَّمْ نَقْصُصْهُمْ عَلَيْكَ وَكَلَّمَ اللَّهُ مُوسَىٰ تَكْلِيمًا

Because there is only One Religion, God asks those who follow the Prophet to say,

We believe in Allāh, and the revelation given to us, and to Abraham, Ismā'īl, Isaac, Jacob, and the Tribes, and that given to Moses and Jesus, and that given to (all) the Prophets from their Lord: we make no difference between one and another of them: and to Him we surrender (become Muslims). (Qur'ān 2:136)

قُولُوا ءَامَنَّا بِاللَّهِ وَمَا أُنْزِلَ إِلَيْنَا وَمَا أُنْزِلَ إِلَى إِبْرَاهِيمَ وَإِسْمَاعِيلَ وَإِسْحَاقَ وَيَعْقُوبَ وَالْأَسْبَاطِ وَمَا أُوتِيَ مُوسَى وَعِيسَى وَمَا أُوتِيَ النَّبِيُّونَ مِنْ رَبِّهِمْ لَا نُفَرِّقُ بَيْنَ أَحَدٍ مِنْهُمْ وَنَحْنُ لَهُ مُسْلِمُونَ

Guidance to believe in the one Religion revealed to all the Prophets was first directed to the Prophet Muḥammad by the Divine:

Say: "We believe in Allāh, and in what has been revealed to us and what was revealed to Abraham, Ismā'īl, Isaac, Jacob, and the Tribes, and in (the Books) given to Moses, Jesus, and the the Prophets, from their Lord: we make no distinction between one and another among them, and to Allāh do we bow our will (in Islām)." (Qur'ān 3:84)

قُلْ ءَامَنَّا بِاللَّهِ وَمَا أُنْزِلَ عَلَيْنَا وَمَا أُنْزِلَ عَلَى إِبْرَاهِيمَ وَإِسْمَاعِيلَ وَإِسْحَاقَ وَيَعْقُوبَ وَالْأَسْبَاطِ وَمَا أُوتِيَ مُوسَى وَعِيسَى وَالنَّبِيُّونَ مِنْ رَبِّهِمْ لَا نُفَرِّقُ بَيْنَ أَحَدٍ مِنْهُمْ وَنَحْنُ لَهُ مُسْلِمُونَ

In the language of the Holy Qur'ān, the Prophets are called Muslims, as were their followers. This serves as a sign of the One Religion:

Abraham was not a Jew nor yet a Christian; but he followed the Primordial Religion and hence was a Muslim, and he took not gods with Allāh. (Qur'ān 3:67)

مَا كَانَ إِبْرَاهِيمُ يَهُودِيًّا وَلَا نَصْرَانِيًّا وَلَكِنْ كَانَ حَنِيفًا مُسْلِمًا وَمَا كَانَ مِنَ الْمُشْرِكِينَ

It is the faith of your father Abraham. It is He Who has named you Muslims, both before and in this (Revelation). (Qur'ān 22:78)

وَمَا جَعَلَ عَلَيْكُمْ فِي الدِّينِ مِنْ حَرَجٍ مِلَّةَ أَبِيكُمْ إِبْرَاهِيمَ هُوَ سَمَّاكُمُ الْمُسْلِمِينَ مِنْ قَبْلُ

Jesus' disciples are recorded in the Holy Qur'ān as calling themselves Muslims, when Jesus said,

"Who will support me in the Message of Allāh?" "We are supporting Allāh's message with you, we believe in Allāh, and you bear witness that we are Muslims," said the disciples. (Qur'ān 3:52)

فَلَمَّا أَحَسَّ عِيسَى مِنْهُمُ الْكُفْرَ قَالَ مَنْ أَنْصَارِي إِلَى اللَّهِ قَالَ الْحَوَارِيُّونَ نَحْنُ أَنْصَارُ اللَّهِ ءَامَنَّا بِاللَّهِ وَاشْهَدْ بِأَنَّا مُسْلِمُونَ

And behold! I inspired the Disciples to have faith in Me and My Messenger; they said, "We have faith, and do you bear witness that we bow to Allāh as Muslims." (Qur'ān 5:111)

وَإِذْ أَوْحَيْتُ إِلَى الْحَوَارِيِّينَ أَنْ ءَامِنُوا بِي وَبِرَسُولِي قَالُوا ءَامَنَّا وَاشْهَدْ بِأَنَّنَا مُسْلِمُونَ

Moses addressed his people saying,

"O my people! If you do (really) believe in Allāh, then in Him put your trust if you submit (your will to His and become Muslims)." (Qur'ān 10:84)

وَقَالَ مُوسَى يَاقَوْمِ إِنْ كُنْتُمْ ءَامَنْتُمْ بِاللَّهِ فَعَلَيْهِ تَوَكَّلُوا إِنْ كُنْتُمْ مُسْلِمِينَ

The Pharoah's Magicians who followed Moses called themselves Muslims:

"Our Lord! pour out on us patience and constancy, and take our souls unto You as Muslims (who bow to Your Will)!" (Qur'ān 7:126)

رَبَّنَا أَفْرِغْ عَلَيْنَا صَبْرًا وَتَوَفَّنَا مُسْلِمِينَ

Noah said,

"But if you turn back, no reward have I asked of you; my reward is only due from Allāh and I have been commanded to be among (the Muslims) those who submit to Allāh's Will." (Qur'ān 10:72)

فَإِنْ تَوَلَّيْتُمْ فَمَا سَأَلْتُكُمْ مِنْ أَجْرٍ إِنْ أَجْرِيَ إِلَّا عَلَى اللَّهِ وَأُمِرْتُ أَنْ أَكُونَ مِنَ الْمُسْلِمِينَ

Solomon said,

". . . and knowledge was bestowed on us in advance of this, and (that is because) we have been Muslims." (Qur'ān 27:42)

وَأُوتِينَا الْعِلْمَ مِنْ قَبْلِهَا وَكُنَّا مُسْلِمِينَ

Joseph asked the Lord to bless him by making him submit to Allāh's will as a Muslim till the end of his life on earth:

"O my Lord! You have indeed bestowed on me some power, and taught me something of the interpretation of dreams and events, O You creator of the heavens and the earth! You are my Protector in this world and in the Hereafter. Bless me by ending my journey (on earth) as a Muslim, and unite me with the righteous." (Qur'ān 12:101)

رَبِّ قَدْ ءَاتَيْتَنِي مِنَ الْمُلْكِ وَعَلَّمْتَنِي مِنْ تَأْوِيلِ الْأَحَادِيثِ فَاطِرَ السَّمَوَاتِ وَالْأَرْضِ أَنْتَ وَلِيِّي فِي الدُّنْيَا وَالْآخِرَةِ تَوَفَّنِي مُسْلِمًا وَأَلْحِقْنِي بِالصَّالِحِينَ

Islām as Seen Through the Behavior of Muslims

It is obvious by now that the word "Islām" as used in the Holy Qur'ān is the description of the "path" or the "method" that the Prophets followed. Islām is revealed through the behavior, attitude, and belief of those who were called Muslims in the Holy Qur'ān. In each use of the word "Muslim" in relation to the Prophets and their followers, there is a semantic dimension that reveals various aspects of what being a Muslim implies.

Preparing Oneself to Receive Allāh's Grace

By sincere struggle and searching for Truth, a Muslim is one who prepares himself to receive Allāh's Grace. The greatest grace of all is to realize the one origin of all and to open oneself to receiving the guidance of Allāh from within. That is the way Abraham realized the Oneness of God; he called this realization God-given "knowledge." Abraham is quoted in the Holy Qur'ān as saying:

> *"O my father! To me has come knowledge which has not reached you." (Qur'ān 19:43)*
>
> يَاأَبَتِ إِنِّي قَدْ جَاءَنِي مِنَ الْعِلْمِ مَا لَمْ يَأْتِكَ

This knowledge was God's grace to all the Prophets. The Prophet Muḥammad clarified that God's grace is to be sought by man ceaselessly. As an exemplar of a Muslim he says,

> *"O my Lord! Advance me in knowledge." (Qur'ān 20:114)*
>
> وَقُلْ رَبِّ زِدْنِي عِلْمًا

Over and above that knowledge, when reflecting upon the narrated stories of the Prophets in the Holy Qur'ān, we find that Allāh's grace takes various forms. Moses was commanded by Allāh to show His support to Him by the use of supernatural signs. Solomon learned the language of birds and animals, and Joseph could interpret dreams. Allāh's grace to Abraham revealed to him the Primordial Religion within his heart.

The verse in which the Holy Qur'ān called Abraham a Muslim—and not a Jew or a Christian (Qur'ān 22:78)—was a response to a dispute taking place between Jews and Christians (the People of the Book), as described by the following verses:

> *You People of the Book! Why do you dispute about Abraham, when the Torah and the Gospel were not revealed until after him? Have you no understanding? (Qur'ān 3:65)*
>
> يَاأَهْلَ الْكِتَابِ لِمَ تُحَاجُّونَ فِي إِبْرَاهِيمَ وَمَا أُنْزِلَتِ التَّوْرَاةُ وَالْإِنْجِيلُ إِلَّا مِنْ بَعْدِهِ أَفَلَا تَعْقِلُونَ

The question posed at the end of the verse shows that there was something very obvious that the People of the Book did not recognize: that Abraham did not gain his knowledge from a Holy Book, but was inspired because he prepared himself to receive Allāh's Grace. When he did not allow the illusory ideas of his people to suppress his inner quest, his insight began to illuminate his way. He could thereby find the Primordial Truth. As such, those verses which ascribe Abraham to Islām rather than to Judaism or Christianity do not compare Islām to other religions, nor do they humiliate another for being Jewish or Christian. They simply emphasize that Abraham is part of Islām as a primordial religion, and thus he should not be named by creed; nor, from this perspective, should any other Prophet.

The knowledge given to Joseph was of a different sort; he could interpret dreams and events, deducing from them messages that others could not. His ability to decode those messages was bestowed upon him as a result of a righteous life in which he observed ethical values and divine teachings.

> *When Joseph attained his full manhood, We gave him power and knowledge: thus do We reward those who do right. (Qur'ān 12:22)*
>
> وَلَمَّا بَلَغَ أَشُدَّهُ ءَاتَيْنَاهُ حُكْمًا وَعِلْمًا وَكَذَلِكَ نَجْزِي الْمُحْسِنِينَ

Joseph said,

". . . That is what my Lord has taught me. I abandoned the ways of a people that believe not in Allāh and that (even) deny the Hereafter." (Qur'ān 12:37)[5]

ذَٰلِكُمَا مِمَّا عَلَّمَنِي رَبِّي إِنِّي تَرَكْتُ مِلَّةَ قَوْمٍ لَا يُؤْمِنُونَ بِاللَّهِ وَهُم بِالْآخِرَةِ هُمْ كَافِرُونَ

Joseph explained his way:

"And I follow the ways of my fathers, Abraham, Isaac, and Jacob; and never could we attribute any partners whatever to Allāh: that (comes) of the grace of Allāh to us and to mankind: yet most men are not grateful." (Qur'ān 12:38)

وَاتَّبَعْتُ مِلَّةَ آبَائِي إِبْرَاهِيمَ وَإِسْحَاقَ وَيَعْقُوبَ مَا كَانَ لَنَا أَن نُّشْرِكَ بِاللَّهِ مِن شَيْءٍ ذَٰلِكَ مِن فَضْلِ اللَّهِ عَلَيْنَا وَعَلَى النَّاسِ وَلَٰكِنَّ أَكْثَرَ النَّاسِ لَا يَشْكُرُونَ

Solomon's knowledge and power derived from his being a Muslim:

We gave knowledge to David and Solomon and they both said, "Praise be to Allāh, Who has favoured us above many of His believing servants." (Qur'ān 27:15)

وَلَقَدْ آتَيْنَا دَاوُودَ وَسُلَيْمَانَ عِلْمًا وَقَالَا الْحَمْدُ لِلَّهِ الَّذِي فَضَّلَنَا عَلَىٰ كَثِيرٍ مِّنْ عِبَادِهِ الْمُؤْمِنِينَ

Solomon acknowledged the grace of Allāh and called the Queen of Sabā' to believe in Allāh who bestowed on him such knowledge. He says,

"I found her and her people worshipping the sun besides Allāh; Satan has made their deeds seem pleasing to their eyes and has kept them away from the path, so they receive no guidance." (Qur'ān 27:24)

وَجَدتُّهَا وَقَوْمَهَا يَسْجُدُونَ لِلشَّمْسِ مِن دُونِ اللَّهِ وَزَيَّنَ لَهُمُ الشَّيْطَانُ أَعْمَالَهُمْ فَصَدَّهُمْ عَنِ السَّبِيلِ فَهُمْ لَا يَهْتَدُونَ

---

[5]Our translation.

His mission was fulfilled; she followed his path and became a Muslim:

> *She said: "O my Lord! I have indeed wronged my soul. I do (now) submit (in Islām), with Solomon, to the Lord of the Worlds." (Qur'ān 27:44)*
>
> قَالَتْ رَبِّ إِنِّي ظَلَمْتُ نَفْسِي وَأَسْلَمْتُ مَعَ سُلَيْمَانَ لِلَّهِ رَبِّ الْعَالَمِينَ

She understood that there was an unseen power that ordered everything. With this realization, she submitted to that power and abandoned her previous illusions.

Respecting Reason, Fearing Nothing, and Realizing Complete Freedom

All the Prophets in the Holy Qur'ān show respect for reason by rejecting stagnant traditions that humiliate reason and bestow undue respect on dogmas. Because of their respect for reason, the Prophets refused blind imitation. They were not like the people of their times, who would say,

> *"We found our fathers following a certain religion, and we guide ourselves by their footsteps." (Qur'ān 43: 22)*
>
> إِنَّا وَجَدْنَا ءَابَاءَنَا عَلَى أُمَّةٍ وَإِنَّا عَلَى ءَاثَارِهِم مُّهْتَدُونَ

The Prophets realized that to be completely spiritually free is to be devoted to God and not to any man-made dogma. Their refusal to worship false deities was an expression of their search for spiritual freedom and their awareness that a person is deprived of that freedom when they bestow divinity on what is not really divine. They were fully aware that the worship of idols is not merely an outward practice; it is an inner attitude of rigidity and stagnation that blocks a person's capability to be spiritually free. It is an attitude that traps the soul in illusions created by a limited existence. In the Holy Qur'ān, Abraham says to his father,

> *"Do you take idols for gods? For I see you and your people in manifest error." (Qur'ān 6:74)*
>
> أَتَتَّخِذُ أَصْنَامًا ءَالِهَةً إِنِّي أَرَاكَ وَقَوْمَكَ فِي ضَلَالٍ مُبِينٍ

> *"O my father! Why worship that which hears not, and sees not, and can profit you nothing?" (Qur'ān 19: 42)*
>
> يَاأَبَتِ لِمَ تَعْبُدُ مَا لَا يَسْمَعُ وَلَا يُبْصِرُ وَلَا يُغْنِي عَنْكَ شَيْئًا

Joseph also says,

> *"If not Him, you worship nothing but names which you have named—you and your fathers—for which Allāh has sent down no authority." (Qur'ān 12:40)*
>
> مَا تَعْبُدُونَ مِنْ دُونِهِ إِلَّا أَسْمَاءً سَمَّيْتُمُوهَا أَنْتُمْ وَءَابَاؤُكُمْ مَا أَنْزَلَ اللَّهُ بِهَا مِنْ سُلْطَانٍ

Abraham is not afraid of his father's threat to punish him for insulting his practices and beliefs. When his father tells him,

> *"O Abraham, if you forbear not, I will indeed stone you" (Qur'ān 19:46)*
>
> يَاإِبْرَاهِيمُ لَئِنْ لَمْ تَنْتَهِ لَأَرْجُمَنَّكَ

he simply tells him,

> *"Peace be on you. I will pray to my Lord for your forgiveness, for He is to me Most Gracious. And I will turn away from you (all) and from those whom you invoke besides Allāh. I will call on my Lord; perhaps my prayer to my Lord will not go unaswered." (Qur'ān 19:47-48)*
>
> قَالَ سَلَامٌ عَلَيْكَ سَأَسْتَغْفِرُ لَكَ رَبِّي إِنَّهُ كَانَ بِي حَفِيًّا وَأَعْتَزِلُكُمْ وَمَا تَدْعُونَ مِنْ دُونِ اللَّهِ وَأَدْعُو رَبِّي عَسَى أَلَّا أَكُونَ بِدُعَاءِ رَبِّي شَقِيًّا

In the Holy Qur'ān, the Pharaoh's magicians are also examples of being Muslim. They followed Moses when they realized that there was a higher power that ordered the seen and unseen aspects of life. They knew through experience that Moses was not performing magic, but exploring the manifestation of the Unseen, Supreme Power. Faith in Allāh sprang forth in their hearts intuitively and they did not fear the power of the Pharaoh; nor did they change their faith in the face of his threat. They submitted completely to Allāh's will. The story of the magicians demonstrates how people differ in their reactions in the face of the same event. The Pharaoh and his magicians witnessed the same phenomenon, yet while he denied its miraculous aspect, they received Allāh's message wholeheartedly. To be a Muslim in the way they were means that a person fears nothing and realizes complete freedom. Submission to God's will empowers man's will with determination. When Moses spoke to his people, he stressed that aspect; he wanted them to be courageous enough to face the tyrant with faith and confidence. When they were not sure what to do, fearing the power of the Pharaoh who said,

> *"Their male children will we slay" (Qur'ān 7:127)*
>
> قَالَ سَنُقَتِّلُ أَبْنَاءَهُمْ

Moses advised them to place their trust in Allāh alone:

> *"Pray for help from Allāh, and (wait) in patience and constancy: for the earth is Allāh's, to give as a heritage to such of His servants as He pleases; and the end is (best) for the righteous." (Qur'ān 7:128)*
>
> قَالَ مُوسَى لِقَوْمِهِ اسْتَعِينُوا بِاللَّهِ وَاصْبِرُوا إِنَّ الْأَرْضَ لِلَّهِ يُورِثُهَا مَنْ يَشَاءُ مِنْ عِبَادِهِ وَالْعَاقِبَةُ لِلْمُتَّقِينَ

Defending One's Belief and Supporting the Word of Truth

A Muslim in the Holy Qur'ān is one who has enough inner power to uphold faith strongly and substantively. The disciples of

Jesus serve as examples. Jesus' call was part of a recurring theme; he called people to the straight path and few followed him. Those who did were his disciples, calling themselves Muslims (Qur'ān 3:52), while the majority rejected his call. For Jesus' disciples, being a Muslim required responsibility on their part; they felt obligated to support Jesus' message. To be a Muslim is to defend one's belief and to support the word of Truth. In another part of the Holy Qur'ān we read:

> *And behold! I inspired the Disciples to have faith in Me and My Messenger; they said, "We have faith; bear witness that we bow to Allāh as Muslims." (Qur'ān 5:111)*
>
> وَإِذْ أَوْحَيْتُ إِلَى الْحَوَارِيِّينَ أَنْ ءَامِنُوا بِي وَبِرَسُولِي قَالُوا ءَامَنَّا
> وَاشْهَدْ بِأَنَّنَا مُسْلِمُونَ

Being a Muslim enables one to be supported by Allāh through inspiration or any other means.

The Holy Qur'ān clarifies that all the Prophets and devotees to Allāh were models of strong defenders of faith:

> *How many of the Prophets fought (in Allāh's way), and with them (fought) large bands of godly men? But they never lost heart if they met with disaster in Allāh's way, nor did they weaken (in will) nor give in. And Allāh loves those who are firm and steadfast. (Qur'ān 3:146)*
>
> وَكَأَيِّنْ مِنْ نَبِيٍّ قَاتَلَ مَعَهُ رِبِّيُّونَ كَثِيرٌ فَمَا وَهَنُوا لِمَا أَصَابَهُمْ فِي
> سَبِيلِ اللَّهِ وَمَا ضَعُفُوا وَمَا اسْتَكَانُوا وَاللَّهُ يُحِبُّ الصَّابِرِينَ

Expecting No Reward, nor Seeking to Please People; a Muslim Relates Directly to Allāh

In the Holy Qur'ān, Noah is a model Muslim as he did not expect any reward from his people, nor did he seek to please them. His primary concern was to follow the straight path; thus he was guided to be a Muslim and was saved.

> *They rejected him, but We delivered him, and those with him, in the Ark and We made them inherit (the earth), while We overwhelmed in the Flood those who rejected Our Signs. Then see what was the end of those who were warned (but heeded not)! (Qur'ān 10:73)*
>
> فَكَذَّبُوهُ فَنَجَّيْنَاهُ وَمَنْ مَعَهُ فِي الْفُلْكِ وَجَعَلْنَاهُمْ خَلَائِفَ وَأَغْرَقْنَا الَّذِينَ كَذَّبُوا بِآيَاتِنَا فَانْظُرْ كَيْفَ كَانَ عَاقِبَةُ الْمُنْذَرِينَ

The Holy Qur'ān reveals that all the Prophets, when calling their people to the straight path, are motivated by love and mercy, seeking no personal gain of any kind. The Prophets Noah, Hūd, Ṣāliḥ, Lūṭ, and Shuʿayb say,

> *"No reward do I ask of you for it: my reward is only from the Lord of the Worlds." (Qur'ān 26:109, 127, 145, 164, 180)*
>
> وَمَا أَسْأَلُكُمْ عَلَيْهِ مِنْ أَجْرٍ إِنْ أَجْرِيَ إِلَّا عَلَى رَبِّ الْعَالَمِينَ

The Prophet Muḥammad was also guided by the Divine to say,

> *"No reward do I ask of you for it but this: that each one who will may take a (straight) path to his Lord." (Qur'ān 25:57)*
>
> قُلْ مَا أَسْأَلُكُمْ عَلَيْهِ مِنْ أَجْرٍ إِلَّا مَنْ شَاءَ أَنْ يَتَّخِذَ إِلَى رَبِّهِ سَبِيلًا

Respecting Earthly Laws and Praying For Divine Support

To surrender to Allāh (i.e., to be Muslim) requires continuous prayers for Allāh's support, accompanied by using every possible way to achieve one's goals. This is a common feature among the Prophets.

Noah built the Ark, realizing that it was the way to save his people from the flood. Moses went to the Pharaoh and spoke to him, using logic to convince him to free the Children of Israel and allow them to leave the land of Egypt. Yet, at the same time, he asked

Allāh for support and would not face the Pharaoh unless Allāh assured him that He was with him and his brother, watching over and protecting them. The Prophet Muḥammad endured humiliations and resistance in Mecca. He did not depend on miracles to come and rescue him and his followers; rather he used his human capabilities to reach people and awaken their consciousness. When he migrated, he again used reason, for he knew of the Qurayshi leaders' determination to kill him.

The Holy Qur'ān demonstrates clearly how the Prophet Joseph respected earthly laws while at the same time praying for God's support. When the Pharaoh gave him the responsibility of solving Egypt's coming economic woes, he told the Pharaoh that he would manage the problem pragmatically:

> *"Set me over the store-houses of the land: I will indeed guard them, as one that knows (their importance)."* (Qur'ān 12:55)

قَالَ اجْعَلْنِي عَلَى خَزَائِنِ الْأَرْضِ إِنِّي حَفِيظٌ عَلِيمٌ

In the meantime Joseph expressed his devotion to Allāh and his awareness that it was with His support that he would gain the straight path. He says:

> *"O my Lord! You have indeed bestowed on me some power, and taught me something of the interpretation of dreams and events, O You Creator of the heavens and the earth! You are my Protector in this world and in the Hereafter. Take my soul (at death) as one submitting to Your Will (as a Muslim), and unite me with the righteous."* (Qur'ān 12:101)

رَبِّ قَدْ ءَاتَيْتَنِي مِنَ الْمُلْكِ وَعَلَّمْتَنِي مِنْ تَأْوِيلِ الْأَحَادِيثِ فَاطِرَ السَّمَوَاتِ وَالْأَرْضِ أَنْتَ وَلِيِّي فِي الدُّنْيَا وَالْآخِرَةِ تَوَفَّنِي مُسْلِمًا وَأَلْحِقْنِي بِالصَّالِحِينَ

The Holy Qur'ān also clarifies that one way of surrendering to Allāh, to be a Muslim, is to make use of everything with which God has endowed us and thus to improve all aspects of life. It is when we use all our capabilities that we really live in harmony with the Divine Law. In doing this we are considered grateful to Allāh. Hence the Holy Qur'ān praises followers of Prophet Solomon for striving in that sense:

> *They worked for him as he desired, (making) arches, images, basins as large as reservoirs, and (cooking) cauldrons fixed (in their places): "You work, Sons of David, with thanks! But few of My servants are grateful!"* (Qur'ān 34:13)
>
> يَعْمَلُونَ لَهُ مَا يَشَاءُ مِنْ مَحَارِيبَ وَتَمَاثِيلَ وَجِفَانٍ كَالْجَوَابِ وَقُدُورٍ رَاسِيَاتٍ اعْمَلُوا آلَ دَاوُودَ شُكْرًا وَقَلِيلٌ مِنْ عِبَادِيَ الشَّكُورُ

The guidance to respect earthly laws and at the same time seek God's support is mentioned in various ways in the Holy Qur'ān, when it urges people to work, to seek knowledge of all kinds, and to search for the secrets of creation.[6]

To Be a Muslim is to Live According to the Divine Law

Despite the Prophets' varied experiences as Muslims, they were similar in their surrender to the Unseen Exalted Power. This surrender freed them from fear of any temporal authority and led them to the path of complete inner freedom. When they directed themselves to God, they were inspired to do different things and acquired different capabilities and knowledge. They were following the Divine Law.

When man was created, he was endowed with Divine knowledge. The individual must then search for it within; otherwise, he risks being attracted to illusion and forgetting his age-old commitment. Illusion can divert him from the innate tendency embedded within his heart that urges him to find meaning and goals in this life and to then attempt to fulfill them by being in harmony with the purpose of his own existence. This is the very meaning of surrender, Islām. Once man searches for the true meaning of life, he will

[6]More details of this aspect will be discussed in Chapter Five.

be answered by the Unseen Supreme Power. Alas, human beings can easily be drawn away from that direction. Out of Allāh's Mercy, the Prophets were sent, not only to guide people's way, but also to remind them of the embedded Truth within each person's heart and to demonstrate how anyone can seek it. All the Prophets began their mission searching for the Truth and struggled to find answers to their questions about the meaning and the ultimate goal of life. In seeking to serve the purpose of their existence, they were also guiding people, supporting them to awaken their souls, and providing them with striking evidence of the history of humankind on earth. They realized that the highest rank a human being can achieve is to be a servant of God. This servanthood liberates us from illusion, so that we will not be deceived into giving absolute value to what is only transient.

The Human Being is Endowed with the Divine Knowledge from the Time of His Creation

The Holy Qur'ān points to the fact that we are endowed with knowledge of our Lord:

> *When your Lord drew forth from the Children of Adam their descendants, and made them testify concerning themselves, (saying) "Am I not your Lord?" They said: "Yea! We do testify!" (This), lest you should say on the Day of Judgment: "Of this we were never mindful." (Qur'ān 7:172)*
>
> وَإِذْ أَخَذَ رَبُّكَ مِنْ بَنِي آدَمَ مِنْ ظُهُورِهِمْ ذُرِّيَّتَهُمْ وَأَشْهَدَهُمْ عَلَىٰ أَنْفُسِهِمْ أَلَسْتُ بِرَبِّكُمْ قَالُوا بَلَىٰ شَهِدْنَا أَنْ تَقُولُوا يَوْمَ الْقِيَامَةِ إِنَّا كُنَّا عَنْ هَٰذَا غَافِلِينَ

Allāh addresses the Prophet Muḥammad in the Holy Qur'ān, saying:

> *So set your face towards the Primordial Religion, the Divine Order (Divine Nature) innate in human beings. There is no distorting (the nature of) Allāh's creation. This is the au-*

thentic religion: but most among mankind do not understand. (Qur'ān 30:30)[7]

فَأَقِمْ وَجْهَكَ لِلدِّينِ حَنِيفًا فِطْرَةَ اللَّهِ الَّتِي فَطَرَ النَّاسَ عَلَيْهَا لَا
تَبْدِيلَ لِخَلْقِ اللَّهِ ذَلِكَ الدِّينُ الْقَيِّمُ وَلَكِنَّ أَكْثَرَ النَّاسِ لَا يَعْلَمُونَ

Reading this verse in Arabic, one notes the interesting word *ḥanīf*, which may be used as either an adverb or an adjective. Within the context of the verse, *ḥanīf* can be interpreted as a description of the One Religion and can also be understood as a description of the Prophet's approach. There is no one word in English that conveys the whole range of meanings condensed in the word *ḥanīf*, among which are correct, direct, pure, authentic, and original. When describing religion, it may be translated as the Primordial Religion. On the whole, one may conclude that in order to receive knowledge from the higher source, man needs to take the correct approach; that is, he must prepare himself by awakening his innate inner quest.

Call on me; I will answer you. (Qur'ān 40:60)

وَقَالَ رَبُّكُمُ ادْعُونِي أَسْتَجِبْ لَكُمْ

For those who recognized the Divine source of the Message to Muḥammad, their hearts were endowed with that knowledge:

. . . those on whom knowledge has been bestowed may learn that (your guidance) is the Truth from your Lord, and that they may believe therein, and their hearts may be made humbly (open) to it: for truly Allāh is the Guide of those who believe, to the Straight Way. (Qur'ān 22:54)

وَلِيَعْلَمَ الَّذِينَ أُوتُوا الْعِلْمَ أَنَّهُ الْحَقُّ مِنْ رَبِّكَ فَيُؤْمِنُوا بِهِ فَتُخْبِتَ
لَهُ قُلُوبُهُمْ وَإِنَّ اللَّهَ لَهَادِ الَّذِينَ ءَامَنُوا إِلَى صِرَاطٍ مُسْتَقِيمٍ

[7] Our translation.

Some People Do Not Follow the Divine Knowledge Embedded in Their Hearts

To follow the Primordial Religion requires more than observing mere scripture. To have a holy text and heritage without using the correct approach is misleading. In the Holy Qur'ān, those who did not respond to the Prophetic guidance say:

> *"We already know how much of them the earth takes away. With us is a Book (that provides the complete knowledge)." (Qur'ān 50:4)*
>
> قَدْ عَلِمْنَا مَا تَنْقُصُ الْأَرْضُ مِنْهُمْ وَعِنْدَنَا كِتَابٌ حَفِيظٌ

Because they did not interact with the Law of Life by awakening their insight, those who rejected the Revelations adhered to a limited way of understanding and could not, therefore, discern the truth. What needs to be followed is the inner guidance, which is in harmony with the Law of Life:

> *Truly it is not their eyes that are blind, but their hearts, which are in their breasts. (Qur'ān 22:46)*
>
> فَإِنَّهَا لَا تَعْمَى الْأَبْصَارُ وَلَكِنْ تَعْمَى الْقُلُوبُ الَّتِي فِي الصُّدُورِ

Following the Primordial Path, *Fiṭrah*, the Divine Order Leads to the One Religion, "Islām"

The Holy Qur'ān describes the Primordial Religion as *Fiṭratullāh*, which can be translated as "the Divine Order." "Islām," "the Primordial Religion," and "the Divine Nature" convey the same meaning and can be used interchangeably. The Prophet Muḥammad was advised to follow the Religion that is the Divine Order.

> *"So set your face towards the Primordial Religion, the Divine Order (Divine Nature) innate in human beings. There is no distorting (the nature of) Allāh's creation. This is the authentic religion: but most among mankind do not understand." (Qur'ān 30:30)*[8]

[8]Our translation.

فَأَقِمْ وَجْهَكَ لِلدِّينِ حَنِيفًا فِطْرَةَ اللَّهِ الَّتِي فَطَرَ النَّاسَ عَلَيْهَا لَا
تَبْدِيلَ لِخَلْقِ اللَّهِ ذَلِكَ الدِّينُ الْقَيِّمُ وَلَكِنَّ أَكْثَرَ النَّاسِ لَا يَعْلَمُونَ

The word "Islām" is not mentioned explicitly, but Islām in its broadest meaning is implicit. It is clear that one who follows the Divine Order is a Muslim. The Law of Allāh is the that which orders everything in the seen and unseen worlds, in the spiritual and physical existence of man. Allāh created an ordered world. Without faith in this Order, life would be meaningless. Spiritual growth, like physical growth, follows a law. To surrender to the Law, which is the core concept in the Primordial Religion "Islām," is to make oneself accessible to the law of spiritual growth.[9] Violation of the Law of spiritual attainment is a choice that can lead to the destruction of one's spiritual being.

When Man Struggles to Find the Truth, He Will Be Answered

The Prophet explained the process of attaining knowledge and the way to continue along the path. He said that Islām is the religion of innate purity, *fiṭrah.*[10]

By the time people reach adulthood, purity is a goal, for by that time they are polluted by society's illusions; without any spiritual nourishment, they go astray, allowing their desires and lusts to direct them. They become so involved in illusory values that they may lose the ability to regain their purity.

When their hearts and their insights are ready, the guidance given by Holy Books will light their way. The following verse explains:

> *Do you not see that Allāh has subjected to your (use) all things in the heavens and on earth, and has made His bounties flow to you in exceeding measure, (both) seen and unseen? Yet there are among men those who dispute about Allāh, without*

---

[9]See Chapter Four for further elaboration on this point.

[10]According to a Prophetic *ḥadīth* narrated by Bukhārī and Muslim: *Every newborn is given the religion of fiṭrah, whether his parents give him the name of a creed, so he may become a Jew, a Christian, or a Magian.*

ما من مولود إلا يولد على الفطرة فأبواه يهودانه أو ينصرانه أو يمجسانه

knowledge and without guidance, and without a Book to enlighten them! (Qur'ān 31:20)

أَلَمْ تَرَوْا أَنَّ اللَّهَ سَخَّرَ لَكُمْ مَا فِي السَّمَوَاتِ وَمَا فِي الْأَرْضِ وَأَسْبَغَ عَلَيْكُمْ نِعَمَهُ ظَاهِرَةً وَبَاطِنَةً وَمِنَ النَّاسِ مَنْ يُجَادِلُ فِي اللَّهِ بِغَيْرِ عِلْمٍ وَلَا هُدًى وَلَا كِتَابٍ مُنِيرٍ

Those who follow that inner guidance and realize the existence of the Supreme are able to recognize the truth that is given in Revelations, as the following verses indicate:

Those to whom We gave the Book before, and when it is recited to them, they say: "We believe therein, for it is the Truth from our Lord: indeed we have been Muslims from before this." (Qur'ān 28:52-53)

الَّذِينَ ءَاتَيْنَاهُمُ الْكِتَابَ مِنْ قَبْلِهِ هُمْ بِهِ يُؤْمِنُونَ، وَإِذَا يُتْلَى عَلَيْهِمْ قَالُوا ءَامَنَّا بِهِ إِنَّهُ الْحَقُّ مِنْ رَبِّنَا إِنَّا كُنَّا مِنْ قَبْلِهِ مُسْلِمِينَ

(Being) those who have believed in Our Signs and became Muslims. (Qur'ān 43:69)

الَّذِينَ ءَامَنُوا بِآيَاتِنَا وَكَانُوا مُسْلِمِينَ

In the Holy Qur'ān, the Lord addresses the Prophet Muḥammad:

Say: "Truly, my Lord has guided me to ***a Way*** *that is straight, and correct, a precious religion, the path of Abraham, true in faith, and he (certainly) joined not gods with Allāh." (Qur'ān 6:161)*[11]

قُلْ إِنَّنِي هَدَانِي رَبِّي إِلَى صِرَاطٍ مُسْتَقِيمٍ دِينًا قِيَمًا مِلَّةَ إِبْرَاهِيمَ حَنِيفًا وَمَا كَانَ مِنَ الْمُشْرِكِينَ

[11] The stress on this and the following verses is added by the authors.

The Prophets as Exemplars Following the Primordial Path

Abraham did not blindly adhere to his people's beliefs; he sought the truth sincerely, as did the Prophet Muḥammad. Neither began with a text to be read fanatically, nor with a creed to be followed blindly, but from an authentic cry for the Truth and a sincere quest to understand the meaning of life within themselves and in their surroundings. By so doing, their quests were answered. They received guidance through inspiration and revelation from the Unseen Supreme Power, Allāh.

The way that was adopted by Abraham and Muḥammad demonstrates a relationship between the human and the Unseen. If we search for truth, we will be guided to find it. This has always worked and always will.

The way that they sought truth also explains the relationship between the human and our inner messenger, the heart. While support comes from the higher source, the quest comes from the inner self. Knowledge is revealed to the soul and expressed through the joy that we experience as when Abraham cried:

> *"Unless my Lord guide me, I shall surely be among those who go astray." (Qur'ān 6:77)*
>
> لَئِنْ لَمْ يَهْدِنِي رَبِّي لَأَكُونَنَّ مِنَ الْقَوْمِ الضَّالِّينَ

That was a real discovery for Abraham, who was at that moment in the midst of confusion, looking at the moon, trying to establish a relationship between what he was seeing and the Lord he was seeking. That discovery sprang from within; he was not yet sure who was his Lord. The realization that there is a Lord who guides put Abraham on the right path to receiving knowledge about the Transcendental Unseen Supreme. About the path of Abraham, the Holy Qur'ān says:

> *Who can be better in religion than one who submits his whole self to Allāh, does good, and follows* ***the Way*** *of Abraham the true in faith? For Allāh bound Abraham to Him closely. (Qur'ān 4:125)*
>
> وَمَنْ أَحْسَنُ دِينًا مِمَّنْ أَسْلَمَ وَجْهَهُ لِلَّهِ وَهُوَ مُحْسِنٌ وَاتَّبَعَ مِلَّةَ

إِبْرَاهِيمَ حَنِيفًا وَاتَّخَذَ اللَّهُ إِبْرَاهِيمَ خَلِيلًا

The Way of Abraham is the righteous, correct, straight Way. In Arabic, the Way is *Ṣirāṭ*, followed by the word *Mustaqim* as an adjective. *Mustaqīm* connotes a range of meanings, such as straight, right, correct, proper, direct, harmonious, etc. *Aṣ-Ṣirāṭ al-Mustaqīm* can be a synonym of the Law, as well as the outcome of surrendering to the Law. In the wording of the Holy Qur'ān, *aṣ-Ṣirāṭ al-Mustaqīm*, the correct way, is

> ***The Way of Allāh**, to Whom belongs whatever is in the heavens and whatever is on earth. Behold (how) all affairs tend towards Allāh! (Qur'ān 42:53)*
>
> صِرَاطِ اللَّهِ الَّذِي لَهُ مَا فِي السَّمَوَاتِ وَمَا فِي الْأَرْضِ أَلَا إِلَى اللَّهِ تَصِيرُ الْأُمُورُ

Following Abraham's path, the Prophet Muḥammad's guidance was intended to lead humanity to the right Divine Way:

> *A Book which We have revealed unto you, in order that you might lead mankind out of the depths of darkness into light—by the leave of their Lord—to **the Way** of (Him) the Exalted in Power, Worthy of all Praise! (Qur'ān 14:1)*
>
> كِتَابٌ أَنْزَلْنَاهُ إِلَيْكَ لِتُخْرِجَ النَّاسَ مِنَ الظُّلُمَاتِ إِلَى النُّورِ بِإِذْنِ رَبِّهِمْ إِلَى صِرَاطِ الْعَزِيزِ الْحَمِيدِ
>
> *But truly you call them to the Straight Way. (Qur'ān 23:73)*
>
> وَإِنَّكَ لَتَدْعُوهُمْ إِلَى صِرَاطٍ مُسْتَقِيمٍ

To be on the straight way is the ultimate goal for man, which he must seek. For that reason, in the first *sūrah* (chapter) of the Holy Qur'ān we read the following:

Show us the straight way, the way of those on whom You have bestowed Your Grace, those whose (portion) is not wrath, and who go not astray.(Qur'ān 1:6-7)[12]

اهْدِنَا الصِّرَاطَ الْمُسْتَقِيمَ، صِرَاطَ الَّذِينَ أَنْعَمْتَ عَلَيْهِمْ غَيْرِ الْمَغْضُوبِ عَلَيْهِمْ وَلَا الضَّالِّينَ

Striking Evidence to Awaken People's Insight

Because it is not easy for people who have veiled themselves in darkness to recognize that Law, they need striking evidence so that their eyes may open and they may become aware of the fatal destiny that awaits those who violate that Divine Law. The word *Sunnah* (plural: *"Sunan"*), in referring to the Law, relates to people who perished because they violated it. The Prophets were asked to draw people's attention to what happened to previous nations who failed to follow heavenly guidance. From this observation, they could learn about the Eternal Divine Law. That there is no change in the Divine Law is repeatedly emphasized in several places in the Holy Qur'ān:

(This is Our) Law (as revealed) to the Messengers whom We sent before you: you will find no change in Our Law. (Qur'ān 17:77)[13]

سُنَّةَ مَنْ قَدْ أَرْسَلْنَا قَبْلَكَ مِنْ رُسُلِنَا وَلَا تَجِدُ لِسُنَّتِنَا تَحْوِيلًا

That is Allāh's (Divine) Law that worked among those who lived aforetime: no change will you find in Allāh's (Divine) Law. (Qur'ān 33:62)

سُنَّةَ اللَّهِ فِي الَّذِينَ خَلَوْا مِنْ قَبْلُ وَلَنْ تَجِدَ لِسُنَّةِ اللَّهِ تَبْدِيلًا

---

[12]It is worth mentioning that the ritual prayers, *aṣ-ṣalāt*, that the Prophet Muḥammad taught his followers, according to the Divine commandment, includes this *sūrah* as an essential part, without which the ritual is not complete and valid.

[13]This and the following three verses are our translations.

Allāh does wish to make clear to you and guide you to the Law that was revealed to those before you. (Qur'ān 4:26)

يُرِيدُ اللَّهُ لِيُبَيِّنَ لَكُمْ وَيَهْدِيَكُمْ سُنَنَ الَّذِينَ مِنْ قَبْلِكُمْ

But their professing the Faith when they (actually) saw Our Punishment was not going to benefit them. (Such has been) Allāh's Law which has been working among His servants. Accordingly, the ungrateful shall be lost. (Qur'ān 40:85)

فَلَمْ يَكُ يَنْفَعُهُمْ إِيمَانُهُمْ لَمَّا رَأَوْا بَأْسَنَا سُنَّةَ اللَّهِ الَّتِي قَدْ خَلَتْ فِي
عِبَادِهِ وَخَسِرَ هُنَالِكَ الْكَافِرُونَ

What It Means to Be a Servant of Allāh

In a very general sense, the Straight Way is the Divine Law. To surrender to that Law is to realize one's purpose of existence. As the Holy Qur'ān explains, man is created to be God's representative:

Behold, your Lord said to the angels: "I will create a representative on earth." (Qur'ān 2:30)

وَإِذْ قَالَ رَبُّكَ لِلْمَلَائِكَةِ إِنِّي جَاعِلٌ فِي الْأَرْضِ خَلِيفَةً

The Holy Qur'ān clarifies that to serve Allāh and to be on the Straight Way are one and the same thing. Jesus said,

"Truly Allāh is my Lord and your Lord. Therefore serve Him: this is a Way that is straight." (Qur'ān 19:36)

وَإِنَّ اللَّهَ رَبِّي وَرَبُّكُمْ فَاعْبُدُوهُ هَذَا صِرَاطٌ مُسْتَقِيمٌ

The Lord says,

I created the jinn and humankind only that they might serve Me. (Qur'ān 51:56)[14]

وَمَا خَلَقْتُ الْجِنَّ وَالْإِنْسَ إِلَّا لِيَعْبُدُونِ

[14]Our translation.

And that you should worship Me, (for) this was the Straight Way. (Qur'ān 36:61)

وَأَنِ اعْبُدُونِي هَذَا صِرَاطٌ مُسْتَقِيمٌ

Worshipping God is not merely the performance of certain rites, but an awareness of the existence of the holy, an awareness that reflects on our way of life. Those rites carry within them meanings which can be uncovered through practice. Our life will thus be directed to a certain purpose, i.e., to become a tool in the hand of the Supreme. That is the Straight Way, *aṣ-Ṣirāṭ al-Mustaqīm*. To achieve that goal requires "knowledge." Abraham said to his father:

"O my father! To me has come knowledge which has not reached you, so follow me; I will guide you to a Way that is even and straight." (Qur'ān 19:43)

يَاأَبَتِ إِنِّي قَدْ جَاءَنِي مِنَ الْعِلْمِ مَا لَمْ يَأْتِكَ فَاتَّبِعْنِي أَهْدِكَ صِرَاطًا
سَوِيًّا

Summary

The word "Islām," as used in the Holy Qur'ān and the Prophet Muḥammad's teachings, does not point to a creed that was meant to parallel or compete with existing creeds. "Islām" in its original sense pointed to the eternal call from Allāh to surrender to the Divine Law of Life. "Islām" is a synonym for the One Religion that all the Prophets brought to humanity. Thus we can interpret "Islām" as *ad-Dīn al-Ḥanīf*—"the pure, Primordial Religion." *Taslīm* (surrender), *salām* (peace), and *sallamah* (salvation) are interrelated. The core concept is that man needs to be in harmony with the Divine Law; the act of achieving that harmony is *Taslīm*. Once we surrender to the Law, we will be at peace with ourselves and with everything in the universe. That is the real salvation. All revelations came to support man in achieving that purpose. Islām is inherent within man's soul; that is the meaning of *Ḥanīfiyyah*.

Accordingly, the word "Muslim" in the Holy Qur'ān points to a person who seeks full surrender to Allāh by adhering to a straight path. Because the Prophet Muḥammad revived that Religion, the Revelation that he received took the name of the original message: "Islām." The Holy Qur'ān and the Prophet Muḥammad's teachings use several ways to assert that all Revelations manifested One Eternal Law and guided people to surrender to it. Because the Law is One and Eternal, there is a common Way taken by all the Prophets, despite their divergent experiences. In the Holy Qur'ān that Way is referred to as *ad-Dīn al-Ḥanīf* "the Primordial Religion," *aṣ-Ṣirāṭ al-Mustaqīm* "the straight Way," and *Sunnatullāh* "the Way of Allāh."

Surrender to the Law is possible because the human being is endowed with an inner, pure potentiality that longs for his or her Lord. It is when we respond to that inner urge that we learn how to live in harmony with the Law. The Prophets lived that experience. By so doing, their quests were answered; they received guidance through inspiration and revelation from the Unseen Supreme Power, Allāh. And they taught people that surrender to the Law frees them from fear of any earthly authority and leads them to the path of complete inner freedom. It is part of the Law that the human being cannot know his or her Way except by an authentic longing for the truth and a sincere quest to understand the meaning of life within and in his or her surroundings. While following that path, the human being needs support, knowledge, and guidance from a higher source. Revelations equip us with that guidance through versatile means and tools.

2
Confirmation Through Clarification

The Revelation to the Prophet Muḥammad (Peace be upon him) confirmed the previous revelations' guidance, correcting distortions of the authentic teachings.

As has become obvious from the discussion in the first chapter, the Holy Qur'ān uses the word "Islām" to describe all previous revelations. From this standpoint, a "Muslim" is a person who adopts an approach to life in which the ultimate goal in life is to surrender to the Supreme Law; that is the meaning of *taslīim*. Although they shared that approach, each Prophet expressed his surrender in a particular way.

The Revelation to the Prophet Muḥammad uncovered this oneness of Religion, stressing the main concepts that had guided humanity to realize the purpose of existence and the complete freedom implicit in surrendering to the Supreme. Accordingly, the Prophet Muḥammad did not create a *new* Religion, but came to confirm the teachings of the previous revelations and to re-introduce them. The Revelation to the Prophet not only stressed what other Prophets brought but also revealed what the followers of other revelations overlooked or distorted. As such, the Revelation to the Prophet Muḥammad deepened the understanding of the previous messages. As the Holy Qur'ān and the life of the Prophet demonstrate, the Call that the Prophet conveyed relates to the other messages in a profound way.

The following points will be discussed in order to show how the Holy Qur'ān related the Call of the Prophet Muḥammad to other Revelations through confirmation and clarification.

First, the guidance of the Holy Qur'ān shows that every Prophet came to confirm the teachings of previous Prophets.

Second, in confirming the teachings of previous Prophets, a Revelation clarifies the misunderstandings prevalent among the followers of those previous Revelations and corrects the way and the approach that people take. By revealing the essential concepts and beliefs of the Primordial Religion, our understanding and awareness deepen and develop.

Confirmation of the Teachings of Previous Revelations

Several verses in the Holy Qur'ān reveal that every Prophet came to confirm the teachings of previous Prophets.

> *And in their footsteps We sent Jesus the son of Mary, confirming the Law (Torah) that had come before him. We sent him the Gospel; therein was guidance and light, and confirmation of the Law that had come before him: a guidance and an admonition to those who fear Allāh.* (Qur'ān 5:46)
>
> وَقَفَّيْنَا عَلَى ءَاثَارِهِمْ بِعِيسَى ابْنِ مَرْيَمَ مُصَدِّقًا لِمَا بَيْنَ يَدَيْهِ مِنَ التَّوْرَاةِ وَءَاتَيْنَاهُ الْإِنْجِيلَ فِيهِ هُدًى وَنُورٌ وَمُصَدِّقًا لِمَا بَيْنَ يَدَيْهِ مِنَ التَّوْرَاةِ وَهُدًى وَمَوْعِظَةً لِلْمُتَّقِينَ

> *Jesus, the son of Mary, said: "O Children of Israel! I am the Messenger of Allāh (sent) to you, confirming the Torah (which came) before me."* (Qur'ān 61:6)
>
> وَإِذْ قَالَ عِيسَى ابْنُ مَرْيَمَ يَابَنِي إِسْرَائِيلَ إِنِّي رَسُولُ اللَّهِ إِلَيْكُمْ مُصَدِّقًا لِمَا بَيْنَ يَدَيَّ مِنَ التَّوْرَاةِ وَمُبَشِّرًا بِرَسُولٍ يَأْتِي مِنْ بَعْدِي اسْمُهُ أَحْمَدُ فَلَمَّا جَاءَهُمْ بِالْبَيِّنَاتِ قَالُوا هَذَا سِحْرٌ مُبِينٌ

The holy verses of the Qur'ān agree with the Gospel where Jesus said:

> *Think not that I am come to destroy the Law, or the Prophets; I am not come to destroy, but to fulfill.* (Matt. 5:17)

The Prophet Muḥammad conveyed a Call that came to clarify previous Revelations and explain what was misunderstood.

To you We sent the Book in truth, confirming the Book that came before it, and guarding it in safety. (Qur'ān 5:48)

وَأَنْزَلْنَا إِلَيْكَ الْكِتَابَ بِالْحَقِّ مُصَدِّقًا لِمَا بَيْنَ يَدَيْهِ مِنَ الْكِتَابِ وَمُهَيْمِنًا عَلَيْهِ

By the same token, the Holy Qur'ān respects previous Revelations:

It was We who revealed the Law (to Moses); therein was guidance and light. By its standard have been judged the Jews, by the Prophets who bowed to Allāh's Will, by the Rabbis and the experts of Law; for to them was entrusted the protection of Allāh's Book, and they were witnesses thereto. (Qur'ān 5:44)

إِنَّا أَنْزَلْنَا التَّوْرَاةَ فِيهَا هُدًى وَنُورٌ يَحْكُمُ بِهَا النَّبِيُّونَ الَّذِينَ أَسْلَمُوا لِلَّذِينَ هَادُوا وَالرَّبَّانِيُّونَ وَالْأَحْبَارُ بِمَا اسْتُحْفِظُوا مِنْ كِتَابِ اللَّهِ وَكَانُوا عَلَيْهِ شُهَدَاءَ

As is obvious from the preceding verses, it is repeatedly stated that the teachings of each Prophet are included in a "Book." Within this context, the "Book" is not necessarily a certain Scripture. When the Holy Qur'ān speaks of Jesus, it says that Allāh,

*will teach him the Book (**Kitāb**) and wisdom, Torah and Bible. (Qur'ān 3:48)*[1]

وَيُعَلِّمُهُ الْكِتَابَ وَالْحِكْمَةَ وَالتَّوْرَاةَ وَالْإِنْجِيلَ

"O Yaḥyā! Take hold of the Book with might." And We gave him Wisdom even as a youth. (Qur'ān 19:12)

يَا يَحْيَى خُذِ الْكِتَابَ بِقُوَّةٍ وَآتَيْنَاهُ الْحُكْمَ صَبِيًّا

[1]The brackets and boldface in this and the following verses have been added by the authors for emphasis. We have to be alert in how the word *"Kitāb"* is used, because it changes its meaning according to context. Sometimes the Book *"Kitāb"* is used to point to a specific Scripture while other times it is used as a general term.

In addressing Jesus, the Holy Qur'ān quotes God as saying:

> *"I taught you the Book and Wisdom, the Torah and the Gospel." (Qur'ān 5:110)*
>
> وَإِذْ عَلَّمْتُكَ الْكِتَابَ وَالْحِكْمَةَ وَالتَّوْرَاةَ وَالإِنْجِيلَ

Similarly, there is a differentiation between the Holy Qur'ān, which is called *Furqān* in the following verse, and "the Book":

> *He revealed the Book unto you, confirming what is in hand, as He revealed the Torah and Gospel before, guidance for people, and He revealed the Furqān. (Qur'ān 3:3, 4)*
>
> نَزَّلَ عَلَيْكَ الْكِتَابَ بِالْحَقِّ مُصَدِّقًا لِمَا بَيْنَ يَدَيْهِ وَأَنْزَلَ التَّوْرَاةَ وَالإِنْجِيلَ. مِنْ قَبْلُ هُدًى لِلنَّاسِ وَأَنْزَلَ الْفُرْقَانَ

Within other contexts, the word "Book" points to a specific Scripture, as in the following verse:

> *We gave Moses the Book and made it a Guide to the Children of Israel, (**commanding**): "Take not other than Me as Disposer of (**your**) affairs." (Qur'ān 17:2)*
>
> وَءَاتَيْنَا مُوسَى الْكِتَابَ وَجَعَلْنَاهُ هُدًى لِبَنِي إِسْرَائِيلَ أَلَّا تَتَّخِذُوا مِنْ دُونِي وَكِيلًا

In an explicit statement, the Holy Qur'ān explains that the "Book":

> *... is clear signs within the hearts of the knowledgeable, and none but the unjust reject Our Signs. (Qur'ān 29:49)*
>
> بَلْ هُوَ ءَايَاتٌ بَيِّنَاتٌ فِي صُدُورِ الَّذِينَ أُوتُوا الْعِلْمَ وَمَا يَجْحَدُ بِآيَاتِنَا إِلَّا الظَّالِمُونَ
>
> *That which We have revealed to you of the Book is the Truth, confirming what was (**revealed**) before it, for Allāh is assuredly, with respect to His servants, fully aware and All-Seeing. (Qur'ān 35:31)*
>
> وَالَّذِي أَوْحَيْنَا إِلَيْكَ مِنَ الْكِتَابِ هُوَ الْحَقُّ مُصَدِّقًا لِمَا بَيْنَ يَدَيْهِ إِنَّ اللَّهَ بِعِبَادِهِ لَخَبِيرٌ بَصِيرٌ

The "Book" and "Wisdom" correlate in many verses in the Holy Qur'ān:

> *We have sent among you a Messenger, reading for you Our Signs, purifying you and teaching the Book and Wisdom, and you know what you did not know before. (Qur'ān 2:151)*
>
> كَمَا أَرْسَلْنَا فِيكُمْ رَسُولًا مِنكُمْ يَتْلُو عَلَيْكُمْ ءَايَاتِنَا وَيُزَكِّيكُمْ وَيُعَلِّمُكُمُ الْكِتَابَ وَالْحِكْمَةَ وَيُعَلِّمُكُمْ مَا لَمْ تَكُونُوا تَعْلَمُونَ

We may conclude that the word "Book," *Kitāb*, when mentioned as a general term, refers to the "knowledge" and "teachings" of the Prophets, which correspond to the Truth, *al-Ḥaqq*, as opposed to illusion, *bāṭil*. This truth can also be revealed to those with pure hearts. This knowledge, as part of the Prophets' teachings, appears in the form of a distinct Book such as the Torah, the Gospel, or the Holy Qur'ān. Irrevocably, the Prophets confirm "knowledge" of each other.

The following verse uses the word "Book," *Kitāb*, to refer to the "knowledge" revealed by all the Prophets:

> *For We had sent unto them a Book that was revealed gradually to convey knowledge. It is a guide and a mercy to all who believe. (Qur'ān 7:52)*[2]
>
> وَلَقَدْ جِئْنَاهُمْ بِكِتَابٍ فَصَّلْنَاهُ عَلَى عِلْمٍ هُدًى وَرَحْمَةً لِقَوْمٍ يُؤْمِنُونَ

The revelation of knowledge had, with time, been fulfilled, culminating with the Revelation to the Prophet Muḥammad, who came after the other Prophets. The "Book" to be read is more than a collection of words that are written or recited; it is the inherent truth of the universe that can be uncovered to pure hearts. This knowledge is gradually revealed and taught to humanity. This Truth is what we call the Divine Law. The Prophets are those who provide examples as to how to surrender to Allāh, so as to receive that knowledge and to follow the Divine Law.

[2]Our translation.

Reading is undertaken "in the name of the Lord," because it is only when one abandons one's ego and removes the veils of illusion that one is able to see and to know (to read):

> *Proclaim! (or Read!) In the name of your Lord, Who created, created man, out of a (mere) conecting cell: Proclaim! And your Lord is Most Bountiful, He Who taught (with) the Pen, taught man that which he knew not. (Qur'ān 96:1-5)*
>
> اقْرَأْ بِاسْمِ رَبِّكَ الَّذِي خَلَقَ. خَلَقَ الْإِنْسَانَ مِنْ عَلَقٍ. اقْرَأْ وَرَبُّكَ الْأَكْرَمُ. الَّذِي عَلَّمَ بِالْقَلَمِ. عَلَّمَ الْإِنْسَانَ مَا لَمْ يَعْلَمْ

According to this view of the relation among Revelations, there is no contradiction in the Holy Qur'ān when Allāh says to the Prophet Muḥammad:

> *Say: "I was ordered to surrender fully to Allāh with devotion to be his servant and I am meant to be the first of the Muslims." (Qur'ān 39:11, 12)*
>
> قُلْ إِنِّي أُمِرْتُ أَنْ أَعْبُدَ اللَّهَ مُخْلِصًا لَهُ الدِّينَ. وَأُمِرْتُ لِأَنْ أَكُونَ أَوَّلَ الْمُسْلِمِينَ

It may now be clear why the Holy Qur'ān also says:

> *Abraham was not a Jew nor yet a Christian, but he followed the Primordial Religion and hence was a Muslim, and he took not gods with Allāh. (Qur'ān 3:67)*
>
> مَا كَانَ إِبْرَاهِيمُ يَهُودِيًّا وَلَا نَصْرَانِيًّا وَلَكِنْ كَانَ حَنِيفًا مُسْلِمًا وَمَا كَانَ مِنَ الْمُشْرِكِينَ

The word "first," then, does not refer to chronological order, but to a qualitative aspect whereby Islām is confirmed through the life of the Prophet, his guidance, and his ethics.

This is another meaning of "confirmation." The Holy Qur'ān reveals how the Prophet symbolizes Islām:

> *Behold! Allāh took the Covenant of the Prophets, saying: "I give you a Book and Wisdom; then comes to you a Messenger, confirming what is with you; believe him and render him help." Allāh said: "Do you agree, and take this My Covenant as binding on you?" They said: "We agree." He said: "Then bear witness, and I am with you among the witnesses."* (Qur'ān 3:81)
>
> وَإِذْ أَخَذَ اللَّهُ مِيثَاقَ النَّبِيِّينَ لَمَا ءَاتَيْتُكُم مِّن كِتَابٍ وَحِكْمَةٍ ثُمَّ
> جَاءَكُمْ رَسُولٌ مُّصَدِّقٌ لِّمَا مَعَكُمْ لَتُؤْمِنُنَّ بِهِ وَلَتَنصُرُنَّهُ قَالَ
> ءَأَقْرَرْتُمْ وَأَخَذْتُمْ عَلَىٰ ذَٰلِكُمْ إِصْرِي قَالُوا أَقْرَرْنَا قَالَ فَاشْهَدُوا وَأَنَا
> مَعَكُم مِّنَ الشَّاهِدِينَ

To understand clearly what "confirmation" means, as used in the Holy Qur'ān and as related to the Revelation to the Prophet Muḥammad, we need to focus on how confirmation and clarification are interrelated and interdependent.

Clarification of the Teachings of the Previous Prophets

The oneness of God is the basic concept that is revealed through all the Prophets' calls and confirmed by all revelations. Not because God needs acknowledgment from His creatures, but because knowing that there is One Creator and One Originator, Who is unlike any of His creatures and beyond the multiplicity of the physical world, helps man understand who he is and for what purpose he was created. Faith in God is faith in the Supreme Divine Law, according to which everything takes place in the universe. This knowledge is not only to be understood mentally, but should also be experienced existentially. In other words, faith in the One God reveals to man how the laws of spiritual development work. The Prophet Muḥammad called for the oneness of Allāh from various perspectives in order to clarify the Call that previous Revelations had conveyed.

Faith in the One God Enables Man to Follow a Straight Way

The Call that Muḥammad was charged to transmit was a resurgence of that which the Divine commanded Abraham to convey. If we trace the Islamic Call to Abraham, we find that the basic knowledge revealed to him in his search for his Lord lay in his discovery that there is One Originator of the universe. His faith in Allāh was so strong that he sat peacefully in the middle of the fire. That was enough to prepare him for the Mercy of God.

> *O Fire! Be cool, and (a means of) safety for Abraham! (Qur'ān 21:69)*
>
> قُلْنَا يَا نَارُ كُونِي بَرْدًا وَسَلَامًا عَلَى إِبْرَاهِيمَ

That story indicates that faith in Allāh could be so powerful that it might bring about miracles and transform a person to a higher level of existence.

A person who takes false deities deviates from the path that leads to their own salvation; they value the finite, thinking that it is eternal, or miss the way to the Truth by sanctioning the unreal. Such people lose their direction, waste their lives, and go astray. Believers pray to God to save them from this path and lead them to the straight path, as the first *sūrah* in the Holy Qur'ān indicates:

> *Show us the straight way, the way of those on whom You have bestowed Your Grace, those whose portion is not wrath, and who go not astray. (Qur'ān 1:6-7)*
>
> اهْدِنَا الصِّرَاطَ الْمُسْتَقِيمَ ۝ صِرَاطَ الَّذِينَ أَنْعَمْتَ عَلَيْهِمْ غَيْرِ الْمَغْضُوبِ عَلَيْهِمْ وَلَا الضَّالِّينَ

In the Holy Qur'ān, all the Prophets came to remind people of the oneness of God. Existentially, this knowledge means that man will free himself from all illuions and egoistic distortions, and hence achieve his ultimate goal of spiritual realization. Belief in God provides us with the criteria according to which we can observe our actions and correct our mistakes. Yet people tend to forget and deviate from the straight path, destroying each other and even themselves.

> *Truly Allāh will not deal unjustly with man at all; it is man who wrongs his own soul. (Qur'ān 10:44)*
>
> إِنَّ اللَّهَ لَا يَظْلِمُ النَّاسَ شَيْئًا وَلَكِنَّ النَّاسَ أَنْفُسَهُمْ يَظْلِمُونَ

In *Sūrah al-Aʿrāf* (Qur'ān 7:59-100),[3] the Holy Qur'ān surveys the calls of several Prophets, beginning with that of Noah and mentioning those of Abraham, Hūd, Ṣāliḥ, Lūṭ, and Shuʿayb, and then proceeds to explain Moses' call in detail. All these Prophets began by calling their people to believe in God, yet each had different advice to give. The Holy Qur'ān elucidates that the core meaning of the Prophet's call is to clarify the relationship between believing in God and leading a worldly life guided by that belief. In other words, man's life may be spiritually fruitful if he does not violate the ethical law. The Holy Qur'ān shows that the people who go astray share one common attribute—they cannot find an ultimate goal for their existence.

> *Say: "Shall we tell you of those who lose most in respect of their deeds? Those whose efforts have been wasted in this life, while they thought that they were acquiring good by their works? They are those who deny the Signs of their Lord and the fact of their having to meet Him. Vain will be their works, nor shall We, on the Day of Judgment, give them any weight." (Qur'ān 18:103-105)*
>
> قُلْ هَلْ نُنَبِّئُكُمْ بِالْأَخْسَرِينَ أَعْمَالًا. الَّذِينَ ضَلَّ سَعْيُهُمْ فِي الْحَيَاةِ الدُّنْيَا وَهُمْ يَحْسَبُونَ أَنَّهُمْ يُحْسِنُونَ صُنْعًا أُولَئِكَ الَّذِينَ كَفَرُوا بِآيَاتِ رَبِّهِمْ وَلِقَائِهِ فَحَبِطَتْ أَعْمَالُهُمْ فَلَا نُقِيمُ لَهُمْ يَوْمَ الْقِيَامَةِ وَزْنًا

Moreover, those people tend to harm others and to make mischief, such as the people whom Shuʿayb came to guide, who cheated

---

[3]*Al-Aʿrāf* is the name of the seventh *sūrah* in the Holy Qur'ān. There are many interpretations of what *al-Aʿrāf* means. However, it is generally said to be a symbol of a certain "place" or "rank" in the Afterlife of people who are not spiritually evolved enough to be in Heaven, yet are not bad enough to be in Hell.

in their measures. In the Holy Qur'ān, each Prophet called for belief in God and at the same time corrected the way of his people.

The story of Moses, being very special, is mentioned here in further detail. He went to the Pharaoh, following God's command to both Moses and Aaron:

> *"Go, both of you, to Pharaoh, for he has indeed transgressed all bounds. But speak to him mildly; perchance he may take warning or fear (Allāh)." (Qur'ān 20:43-44)*
>
> اذْهَبَا إِلَى فِرْعَوْنَ إِنَّهُ طَغَى. فَقُولَا لَهُ قَوْلًا لَيِّنًا لَعَلَّهُ يَتَذَكَّرُ أَوْ يَخْشَى

The explicit mission of Moses was to save the Children of Israel from the tyranny of the Pharaoh, but the implicit mission was to call Pharaoh to follow the right path. God tells Moses and his brother the following:

> *"So go you both to him, and say, 'Truly we are Messengers sent by your Lord; send forth, therefore, the Children of Israel with us, and afflict them not; with a Sign, indeed, have we come from your Lord! And Peace to all who follow guidance!'" (Qur'ān 20:47)*
>
> فَأْتِيَاهُ فَقُولَا إِنَّا رَسُولَا رَبِّكَ فَأَرْسِلْ مَعَنَا بَنِي إِسْرَائِيلَ وَلَا تُعَذِّبْهُمْ قَدْ جِئْنَاكَ بِآيَةٍ مِنْ رَبِّكَ وَالسَّلَامُ عَلَى مَنِ اتَّبَعَ الْهُدَى

As a savior, Moses was not a politician, but a messenger from God. Moses said:

> *"O Pharaoh! I am a Messenger from the Lord of the Worlds." (Qur'ān 7:104)*
>
> وَقَالَ مُوسَى يَافِرْعَوْنُ إِنِّي رَسُولٌ مِنْ رَبِّ الْعَالَمِينَ

Moses acted with a dual purpose. On the one hand, he called the Pharaoh to abandon the attitude of an absolute dictator and to think of the higher power of God. On the other hand, he defended the rights of the Children of Israel who were suffering from unjust rule. Moses was demonstrating how belief in God could free man from false deities. The Pharaoh, deceived by his power, thought that he was a god. The Children of Israel, fearing his tyranny, were unable to defend their rights; Moses' call stimulated their faith and empowered them. Moses was courageous enough, with God's support, to face the Pharaoh and to try to guide him to the straight path. We can see in this story how the impact of faith in God depends on a person's position. The power of faith culminates in the story of the magicians, who did not fear the earthly power of the Pharaoh; they preferred to be killed rather than to be hypocrites.

> *They said: "Never shall we regard you as more than the Clear Signs that have come to us or than Him Who created us! So decree whatever you desire to decree, for you can only decree the life of this world." (Qur'ān 20:72)*
>
> قَالُوا لَنْ نُؤْثِرَكَ عَلَى مَا جَاءَنَا مِنَ الْبَيِّنَاتِ وَالَّذِي فَطَرَنَا فَاقْضِ مَا أَنْتَ قَاضٍ إِنَّمَا تَقْضِي هَذِهِ الْحَيَاةَ الدُّنْيَا

By recalling the story of Moses in various parts of the Holy Qur'ān, the Prophet Muḥammad confirmed Moses' call, stressing the practical aspect of faith and the interrelationship between the mundane and the spiritual. In other words, the power of faith can be a great incentive for helping, serving, and searching for channels to pursue good deeds. The believer is known by his good deeds rather than by his words alone. By confirming the message revealed to Moses, the Prophet Muḥammad focused on how the Prophets came to awaken man's awareness of the existence of his Lord; he called his people to free themselves from the tribes' ethics and traditions and introduced a new approach to life. This interrelationship between faith and deeds is obvious in the Ten Commandments revealed to the Children of Israel in the Torah and confirmed in the Holy Qur'ān. The following verse mentions some of them:

> *And remember We took a Covenant from the Children of Israel (to this effect): worship none but Allāh; treat with kindness your parents and kindred, and orphans and those in need; speak kindly to the people; be steadfast in prayer; and practice regular charity. Then did you turn back, except a few among you, and you slid back. (Qur'ān 2:83)*

وَإِذْ أَخَذْنَا مِيثَاقَ بَنِي إِسْرَائِيلَ لَا تَعْبُدُونَ إِلَّا اللَّهَ وَبِالْوَالِدَيْنِ إِحْسَانًا وَذِي الْقُرْبَى وَالْيَتَامَى وَالْمَسَاكِينِ وَقُولُوا لِلنَّاسِ حُسْنًا وَأَقِيمُوا الصَّلَاةَ وَءَاتُوا الزَّكَاةَ ثُمَّ تَوَلَّيْتُمْ إِلَّا قَلِيلًا مِنْكُمْ وَأَنْتُمْ مُعْرِضُونَ

The teachings that the Divine conveyed through the Prophet Muḥammad came to clarify Moses' message:

Truly this the Holy Qur'ān does explain to the Children of Israel most of the matters in which they disagree. (Qur'ān 27:76)

إِنَّ هَذَا الْقُرْءَانَ يَقُصُّ عَلَى بَنِي إِسْرَائِيلَ أَكْثَرَ الَّذِي هُمْ فِيهِ يَخْتَلِفُونَ

Elsewhere the Prophet was asked by the Divine to remind the Children of Israel of their Commandments.

Say: "Come, I will convey what Allāh has (really) prohibited you from: join not anything as equal with Him; be good to your parents; kill not your children on a plea of want—We provide sustenance for you and for them; come not near to shameful deeds, whether open or secret; take not life, which Allāh has made sacred, except by way of justice and law. Thus does He command you, that you may learn wisdom. And come not near to the orphan's property, except to improve it, until he attains the age of full strength; give measure and weight with (full) justice." No burden do We place on any soul, but that which it can bear. Whenever you speak, speak justly, even if a near relative is concerned. And fulfill the Covenant of Allāh. Thus does He command you, that you may remember. Truly, this is My Way leading straight; follow it; follow not (other) paths; they will separate you from His (great) path. Thus does He command you, that you may remain conscious of Him. (Qur'ān 6:151-153)

قُلْ تَعَالَوْا أَتْلُ مَا حَرَّمَ رَبُّكُمْ عَلَيْكُمْ أَلَّا تُشْرِكُوا بِهِ شَيْئًا

وَبِالْوَالِدَيْنِ إِحْسَانًا وَلَا تَقْتُلُوا أَوْلَادَكُمْ مِنْ إِمْلَاقٍ نَحْنُ نَرْزُقُكُمْ
وَإِيَّاهُمْ وَلَا تَقْرَبُوا الْفَوَاحِشَ مَا ظَهَرَ مِنْهَا وَمَا بَطَنَ وَلَا تَقْتُلُوا
النَّفْسَ الَّتِي حَرَّمَ اللَّهُ إِلَّا بِالْحَقِّ ذَلِكُمْ وَصَّاكُمْ بِهِ لَعَلَّكُمْ
تَعْقِلُونَ. وَلَا تَقْرَبُوا مَالَ الْيَتِيمِ إِلَّا بِالَّتِي هِيَ أَحْسَنُ حَتَّى يَبْلُغَ
أَشُدَّهُ وَأَوْفُوا الْكَيْلَ وَالْمِيزَانَ بِالْقِسْطِ لَا نُكَلِّفُ نَفْسًا إِلَّا وُسْعَهَا
وَإِذَا قُلْتُمْ فَاعْدِلُوا وَلَوْ كَانَ ذَا قُرْبَى وَبِعَهْدِ اللَّهِ أَوْفُوا ذَلِكُمْ
وَصَّاكُمْ بِهِ لَعَلَّكُمْ تَذَكَّرُونَ. وَأَنَّ هَذَا صِرَاطِي مُسْتَقِيمًا فَاتَّبِعُوهُ
وَلَا تَتَّبِعُوا السُّبُلَ فَتَفَرَّقَ بِكُمْ عَنْ سَبِيلِهِ ذَلِكُمْ وَصَّاكُمْ بِهِ
لَعَلَّكُمْ تَتَّقُونَ

It is noteworthy that these commandments begin with the guidance to take no god with God; to Him alone should one surrender. Although the Ten Commandments in the Torah were worded differently, the main ideas are similar, with the first three commandments focusing on belief in God. When Jesus came, he called with yet different words:

> *Jesus said unto him, "You shall love the Lord your God with all your heart, and with all your soul, and with all your mind. This is the first and great commandment. And the second is like unto it: you shall love your neighbor as yourself. On these two commandments hang all the law and the Prophets." (Matt. 22:37-40)*

Loving the Lord is another way of expressing surrender to the One Divine Truth, and this love is reflected in one's love for one's fellow human beings. That is the core of the Islamic Call.

Liberation From Illusion

Without inner struggle, religious teachings turn into rigid, spiritless forms, and illusions replace true faith. Guiding the Children of Israel to the way of liberation from illusion is the core of the Prophets' message confirmed by the Holy Qur'ān and the Prophet Muḥammad's teachings.

Making Images of God

The Children of Israel did not follow the Straight Way, even in Moses' life. When he left them for a short period, they were confused between the real and the shadow. The following story from the Holy Qur'ān symbolizes this.

> *(Moses) said: "What then is your case, O Sāmirī?" He replied: "I saw what they saw not, so I took some of the dust left by the messenger and put it aside, thus did my ego suggest to me." (Moses) said: "Begone! But your punishment in this life will be that you will say, 'Touch me not'; and moreover (for a future penalty) you have a promise that will not fail. Now look at your god, of whom you have become a devoted worshipper: we will certainly melt it in a blazing fire and scatter it in the sea! But the God of you all is Allāh; there is no god but He; He comprehends all things in His knowledge." (Qur'ān 20:95-98)*
>
> قَالَ فَمَا خَطْبُكَ يَاسَامِرِي. قَالَ بَصُرْتُ بِمَا لَمْ يَبْصُرُوا بِهِ فَقَبَضْتُ قَبْضَةً مِنْ أَثَرِ الرَّسُولِ فَنَبَذْتُهَا وَكَذَلِكَ سَوَّلَتْ لِي نَفْسِي. قَالَ فَاذْهَبْ فَإِنَّ لَكَ فِي الْحَيَاةِ أَنْ تَقُولَ لَا مِسَاسَ وَإِنَّ لَكَ مَوْعِدًا لَنْ تُخْلَفَهُ وَانْظُرْ إِلَى إِلَهِكَ الَّذِي ظَلْتَ عَلَيْهِ عَاكِفًا لَنُحَرِّقَنَّهُ ثُمَّ لَنَنْسِفَنَّهُ فِي الْيَمِّ نَسْفًا. إِنَّمَا إِلَهُكُمُ اللَّهُ الَّذِي لَا إِلَهَ إِلَّا هُوَ وَسِعَ كُلَّ شَيْءٍ عِلْمًا

Sāmirī symbolizes anyone who mixes the real teachings with illusions. Shortly after Moses passed away, the Children of Israel fell in the same trap as Sāmirī, confusing forms and meanings. They became so wedded to the forms and literal instructions that they forgot why they were assigned in the first place.

The story in the Holy Qur'ān crystallizes what is mentioned sporadically in the Torah, in which Moses warned his people not to become victims of illusions. The Torah speaks of Moses' anger with his people when they failed to follow the way of God to which he had guided them, instead worshipping the calf.

> *"And I looked, and, behold, you had sinned against the Lord your God, and had made a molten calf. You had turned aside quickly out of the way which the Lord had commanded you." (Deut. 9:16)*

Moses reminded them to not make "images" of God, the greatest of illusions and one that triggers many others. He reminded them of the worst repercussion of worshipping "images," saying:

> *"Lest you corrupt yourselves." (Deut. 4:16)*

He guided them to consider the words of the Lord in their hearts, implying that they should do more than speak the words.

> *And he said unto them, "Set your hearts unto all the words which I testify among you this day." (Deut. 32:46)*

Moses reminded them that hearts need purification to be able to discern.

> *"Circumcise therefore the foreskin of your heart, and be no more stiffnecked." (Deut. 10:16)*

> *And the Lord your God will circumcise your heart, and the heart of your seed, to love the Lord your God with all your heart. (Deut. 30:6)*

Without reminding oneself who one's God is, man may fall into the hands of Satan. Jesus could distinguish very clearly between the deception of Satan and the true path. In the Gospel we read:

> *And say unto him, "All these things will I give you, if you will fall down and worship me." Then said Jesus unto him, "Get you hence, Satan: for it is written, "You shall worship the Lord your God, and him only shall you serve." (Matt. 4:9-10)*

In the Holy Qur'ān, we read:

> *When Jesus came with Clear Signs, he said: "Now have I come to you with Wisdom, and in order to make clear to you some of the points on which you dispute; therefore fear Allāh and obey me. For Allāh, He is my Lord and your Lord, so worship Him; this is a Straight Way." (Qur'ān 43:63-64)*

وَلَمَّا جَاءَ عِيسَى بِالْبَيِّنَاتِ قَالَ قَدْ جِئْتُكُمْ بِالْحِكْمَةِ وَلِأُبَيِّنَ لَكُمْ بَعْضَ الَّذِي تَخْتَلِفُونَ فِيهِ فَاتَّقُوا اللَّهَ وَأَطِيعُونِ. إِنَّ اللَّهَ هُوَ رَبِّي وَرَبُّكُمْ فَاعْبُدُوهُ هَذَا صِرَاطٌ مُسْتَقِيمٌ

Illusion Resides in a Defiled Heart and Dishonest Intention

The point that Jesus raised several times was quite crucial, for people can appear righteous even if evil resides in their hearts. Thus he admonished them to clean their hearts, because without purity of heart, confusion and illusion prevail.

> *Woe unto you, scribes and Pharisees, hypocrites! For you are like unto whitened sepulchers, which indeed appear beautiful outwardly, but are within full of dead men's bones, and of all uncleanness. Even so you also outwardly appear righteous unto men, but within you are full of hypocrisy and iniquity. (Matt. 23:27-28)*

How easily one can fall into illusion when one is strict in observing instructions, yet allowing one's deeds to contradict the common sense that motivates any benevolent person. Jesus argued with those who were blind at heart to clarify that point:

> *And, behold, there was a man who had his hand withered. And they asked him, saying, "Is it lawful to heal on the Sabbath days?" that they might accuse him. And he said unto them, "What man shall there be among you, that shall have one sheep, and if it fall into a pit on the Sabbath day, will he not lay hold on it, and lift it out? How much then is a man better than a sheep? Wherefore it is lawful to do well on the Sabbath days." (Matt. 12:10-12)*

The Holy Qur'ān describes this state of blindness:

> *. . . they inherited the Book, but they chose the vanities of this world, saying: "Everything will be forgiven us." (Even so), if similar vanities came their way, they would (again) seize them. Was not the Covenant of the Book made with them that they would not ascribe to Allāh anything but the truth? And they study what is in the Book. But best for the righteous is the Home in the Hereafter. Will you not understand? (Qur'ān 7:169)*

فَخَلَفَ مِنْ بَعْدِهِمْ خَلْفٌ وَرِثُوا الْكِتَابَ يَأْخُذُونَ عَرَضَ هَذَا
الْأَدْنَى وَيَقُولُونَ سَيُغْفَرُ لَنَا وَإِنْ يَأْتِهِمْ عَرَضٌ مِثْلُهُ يَأْخُذُوهُ أَلَمْ
يُؤْخَذْ عَلَيْهِمْ مِيثَاقُ الْكِتَابِ أَنْ لَا يَقُولُوا عَلَى اللَّهِ إِلَّا الْحَقَّ
وَدَرَسُوا مَا فِيهِ وَالدَّارُ الْآخِرَةُ خَيْرٌ لِلَّذِينَ يَتَّقُونَ أَفَلَا تَعْقِلُونَ

As the verse elucidates, those who believe in the Law of Life and in the continuation of life are capable of distinguishing between the illusory and the real. They can put aside the vanities of this world and focus on their ultimate goal in life.

Jesus criticized the hypocrisy of those Jews who did not relate to God, but pretended to be followers of His teaching and thereby acquired people's praise. They gave alms openly and prayed before others in order to display their piety. Jesus warned them and at the same time he founded a way that can protect man from vanity and pride, which may kill the soul and diminish spiritual endeavor.

> *"And when you pray, you shall not be as the hypocrites are: for they love to pray standing in the synagogues and in the corners of the streets, that they may be seen of men. Truly I say unto you, they have their reward. But you, when you pray, enter into your inner room, and when you have shut your door, pray to your Father in secret; and your Father which sees in secret shall reward you openly." (Matt. 6:5-6)*

Responding to the meticulous implementation of rites motivated by the belief that by performing those rites, purification would be mechanically achieved, Jesus commented:

> *"Not that which goes into the mouth defiles a man; but that which comes out of the mouth, this defiles a man."* (Matt. 15:11)

In the Holy Qur'ān, we read:

> *So woe to those who perform the prayers (but) whose hearts are remote from their prayers; Those who (want but) to be seen (of men), then they refuse (to supply even) neighborly needs. (Qur'ān 107:4-7)*[4]
>
> فَوَيْلٌ لِّلْمُصَلِّينَ. الَّذِينَ هُمْ عَنْ صَلَاتِهِمْ سَاهُونَ. الَّذِينَ هُمْ يُرَاءُونَ. وَيَمْنَعُونَ الْمَاعُونَ

The Prophet Muḥammad asserted that it is an illusion to think that performing religious rites is the ultimate goal, forgetting that those rites are meant to train us to experience ourselves as spirit. The fruit of those rites is demonstrated by the change in our ethics. To perform the rites without an inner focus is meaningless.

> *If a person's prayer does not take him far from evil, he gets further and further from God. (PH)*[5]
>
> من لم تنهه صلاته عن الفحشاء والمنكر لم يزدد بصلاته من الله إلا بعدا

> *It is very possible that a fasting person does not get anything from his fast but hunger and thirst. (PH)*[6]
>
> رب صائم ليس له من صيامه إلا الجوع والعطش

> *If reading the Qur'ān has not led you to quitting (evil), then you have not read it. (PH)*[7]

---

[4]Verses 4 and 5 are our translations.

[5]Narrated by Tabarānī, as quoted in *Al-Jāmi'Aṣ-Ṣaghīr Li's-Suyū textsub-dottī.*

الطبراني في الجامع الصغير للسيوطي

[6]Narrated by Aḥmad and Ibn Mājah

[7]Narrated by Tabarānī, as quoted in *Al-Jāmi'Aṣ-Ṣaghīr Li's-Suyū textsub-dottī.*

الطبراني في الجامع الصغير للسيوطي

اقرأ القرآن ما نهاك، فإن لم ينهك فلست تقرأه

Jesus says:

"Therefore when you do your alms, do not sound a trumpet before you, as the hypocrites do in the synagogues and in the streets, that they may have glory of men. Truly I say unto you, they have their reward. But when you do alms, let not your left hand know what your right hand does." (Matt. 6:2-3)

He also says:

Either make the tree good, and his fruit good, or else make the tree corrupt, and his fruit corrupt, for the tree is known by his fruit. O generation of vipers, how can you, being evil, speak good things? For out of the abundance of the heart the mouth speaks. A good man out of the good treasure of the heart brings forth good things; and an evil man out of the evil treasure brings forth evil things. (Matt. 12:33-35)

In the Holy Qur'ān:

Kind words and the covering of faults are better than charity followed by injury. Allāh is free of all wants, and He is Most Forbearing. O you who believe! Cancel not your charity by reminders of your generosity or by injury, like those who spend their substance to be seen of men, but believe neither in Allāh nor in the Last Day. They are as in the parable of a hard barren rock, on which is a little soil; on it falls heavy rain, which leaves it (just) a bare stone. They will be able to do nothing with what they have earned. And Allāh guides not those who deny the Truth. (Qur'ān 2:263-264)

قَوْلٌ مَعْرُوفٌ وَمَغْفِرَةٌ خَيْرٌ مِنْ صَدَقَةٍ يَتْبَعُهَا أَذًى وَاللَّهُ غَنِيٌّ حَلِيمٌ. يَاأَيُّهَا الَّذِينَ ءَامَنُوا لَا تُبْطِلُوا صَدَقَاتِكُمْ بِالْمَنِّ وَالْأَذَى كَالَّذِي يُنْفِقُ مَالَهُ رِئَاءَ النَّاسِ وَلَا يُؤْمِنُ بِاللَّهِ وَالْيَوْمِ الْآخِرِ فَمَثَلُهُ كَمَثَلِ صَفْوَانٍ عَلَيْهِ تُرَابٌ فَأَصَابَهُ وَابِلٌ فَتَرَكَهُ صَلْدًا لَا يَقْدِرُونَ عَلَى شَيْءٍ مِمَّا كَسَبُوا وَاللَّهُ لَا يَهْدِي الْقَوْمَ الْكَافِرِينَ

The preceding discussion of the confusion that occurred among the Children of Israel demonstrates that Jesus came to correct their way and that the Prophet Muḥammad confirmed Jesus' correction and clarified, through the Holy Qur'ān's guidance, what was missing. The Holy Qur'ān describes those who appear to be committed to divine teachings but are in truth attached to forms, overlooking the teachings' meanings, as victims of their own illusions, so that they gain nothing from divine wisdom.

> *The likeness of those who keep the Torah (as letters) but do not reflect it themselves (as meanings), is that of an ass which carries huge tomes (but understands them not). They are an example of the worst kind of people who falsify the Signs of Allāh. (Qur'ān 62:5)*[8]

مَثَلُ الَّذِينَ حُمِّلُوا التَّوْرَاةَ ثُمَّ لَمْ يَحْمِلُوهَا كَمَثَلِ الْحِمَارِ يَحْمِلُ
أَسْفَارًا بِئْسَ مَثَلُ الْقَوْمِ الَّذِينَ كَذَّبُوا بِآيَاتِ اللَّهِ

God Is Transcendent: His Messengers Represent His Light

The Holy Qur'ān and the Prophet Muḥammad's teachings clarify that God, as the Light of heaven and earth, manifests through those with pure hearts, in addition to whom come the Prophets and Messengers of God. They thus enlighten the way for seekers of Truth. Hence the Holy Qur'ān and the Prophet Muḥammad confirmed the teachings of Jesus, who said:

> *"I am the light of the world: he that follows me shall not walk in darkness, but shall have the light of life." (John 8:12)*

> *"I am the way, the truth, and the life: no man comes unto the Father, but by me. If you had known me, you should have known my Father also, and from henceforth you know him, and have seen him." (John 14:6-7)*

> *"He that loves father or mother more than me is not worthy of me, and he that loves son or daughter more than me is not*

[8] Our translation.

worthy of me. And he that takes not his cross, and follows after me, is not worthy of me." (Matt. 10:37-38)

The Holy Qur'ān states that the Prophet Muḥammad is

as a lamp spreading Light (Qur'ān 33:46)

سِرَاجًا مُنِيرًا

implying that Allāh's Light is followed through His Messenger.[9]

Believe, therefore, in Allāh and His Messenger, and in the Light which We have sent down. (Qur'ān 64:8)

فَآمِنُوا بِاللَّهِ وَرَسُولِهِ وَالنُّورِ الَّذِي أَنْزَلْنَا

God addresses the Prophet Muḥammad:

Say: "If you love Allāh, follow me; Allāh will love you and forgive you your sins, for Allāh is Oft-Forgiving, Most Merciful." (Qur'ān 3:31)

قُلْ إِنْ كُنْتُمْ تُحِبُّونَ اللَّهَ فَاتَّبِعُونِي يُحْبِبْكُمُ اللَّهُ وَيَغْفِرْ لَكُمْ ذُنُوبَكُمْ وَاللَّهُ غَفُورٌ رَحِيمٌ

Truly in the Messenger of Allāh you have a good example for him who looks unto Allāh and the Last Day, and remembers Allāh much. (Qur'ān 33:21)

لَقَدْ كَانَ لَكُمْ فِي رَسُولِ اللَّهِ أُسْوَةٌ حَسَنَةٌ لِمَنْ كَانَ يَرْجُو اللَّهَ وَالْيَوْمَ الْآخِرَ وَذَكَرَ اللَّهَ كَثِيرًا

You will not be truly a believer unless you love me more than your money, your offspring, and even yourself. (PH)[10]

لا يؤمن أحدكم حتى أكون أحب إليه من ماله وولده ونفسه التي بين جنبيه

[9]See the following chapter for more on this point.

[10]Narrated by Bukhārī, Muslim, and Aḥmad. The *ḥadīth*'s wording in Arabic is an amalgamation of the three sources.

The teachings of the Prophet Muḥammad confirm and clarify the teachings of Jesus. Both explained that messengers of Allāh represent His Love and Mercy to humanity and manifest His Grace. In his search, the seeker of truth is guided by Allāh's Light, which appears in His Messengers. The Holy Qur'ān stresses the oneness of the Messengers of Allāh, which stems from the fact that they are all manifestations of His Light. Accordingly the Holy Qur'ān criticizes

> *. . . those who deny Allāh and His Messengers, and (those who) wish to separate Allāh from His Messengers, saying, "We believe in some but reject others" and (those who) wish to take a course midway. (Qur'ān 4:150)*
>
> إِنَّ الَّذِينَ يَكْفُرُونَ بِاللَّهِ وَرُسُلِهِ وَيُرِيدُونَ أَنْ يُفَرِّقُوا بَيْنَ اللَّهِ وَرُسُلِهِ وَيَقُولُونَ نُؤْمِنُ بِبَعْضٍ وَنَكْفُرُ بِبَعْضٍ وَيُرِيدُونَ أَنْ يَتَّخِذُوا بَيْنَ ذَلِكَ سَبِيلًا

To say that the Prophets represent Allāh's Light is not to imprison the Divine in one of His Manifestations. The Holy Qur'ān makes it clear that the Prophets guide people to surrender to Allāh, but never claim that they are to be taken as gods with Him.

> *It is not (possible) that a man, to whom is given the Book, and Wisdom, and the Prophetic office, should say to people: "Be my worshippers rather than Allāh's." On the contrary (he would say): "Be worshippers of Him Who is truly the Cherisher of all, by teaching the Book and studying it earnestly." (Qur'ān 3:79)*
>
> مَا كَانَ لِبَشَرٍ أَنْ يُؤْتِيَهُ اللَّهُ الْكِتَابَ وَالْحُكْمَ وَالنُّبُوَّةَ ثُمَّ يَقُولَ لِلنَّاسِ كُونُوا عِبَادًا لِي مِنْ دُونِ اللَّهِ وَلَكِنْ كُونُوا رَبَّانِيِّينَ بِمَا كُنْتُمْ تُعَلِّمُونَ الْكِتَابَ وَبِمَا كُنْتُمْ تَدْرُسُونَ

From that perspective, the Holy Qur'ān and the Prophet Muḥammad highlight the very special place of Jesus and at the same time eliminate confusion concerning him. The Prophet Muḥammad says,

"I am the closest one to Jesus, the son of Mary, in this life and in the Afterlife."(PH)[11]

أنا أولى الناس بعيسى ابن مريم في الدنيا والآخرة

All the offspring of Adam are touched by the devil except Mary, the daughter of 'Imrān, and her son Jesus, peace be upon both of them. (PH)[12]

كل مولود من بني آدم يمسه الشيطان بأصبعه إلا مريم ابنة عمران وابنها عيسى عليهما السلام

First and foremost, the Holy Qur'ān confirms the Virgin Mary's miraculous birth of Jesus.

"O Mary! Allāh gives You glad tidings of a Word from Him: his name will be Jesus Christ." (Qur'ān 3:45)

إِذْ قَالَتِ الْمَلَائِكَةُ يَامَرْيَمُ إِنَّ اللَّهَ يُبَشِّرُكِ بِكَلِمَةٍ مِنْهُ اسْمُهُ الْمَسِيحُ عِيسَى ابْنُ مَرْيَمَ وَجِيهًا فِي الدُّنْيَا وَالْآخِرَةِ وَمِنَ الْمُقَرَّبِينَ

And Mary, the daughter of 'Imrān, who guarded her chastity; and We breathed into her of Our spirit; and she testified to the truth of the words of her Lord and of his Revelations, and was one of the devout (servants). (Qur'ān 66:12)

وَمَرْيَمَ ابْنَتَ عِمْرَانَ الَّتِي أَحْصَنَتْ فَرْجَهَا فَنَفَخْنَا فِيهِ مِنْ رُوحِنَا وَصَدَّقَتْ بِكَلِمَاتِ رَبِّهَا وَكُتُبِهِ وَكَانَتْ مِنَ الْقَانِتِينَ

And (remember) her who guarded her chastity: We breathed into her of Our Spirit, and We made her and her son a Sign for all peoples. (Qur'ān 21:91)

وَالَّتِي أَحْصَنَتْ فَرْجَهَا فَنَفَخْنَا فِيهَا مِنْ رُوحِنَا وَجَعَلْنَاهَا وَابْنَهَا ءَايَةً لِلْعَالَمِينَ

[11] Narrated by Bukhārī.

[12] This saying of the Prophet is mentioned in Aḥmad's *Musnad*. It is also mentioned in Bukhārī and Muslim's *Ṣaḥ=ıḥ* in similar wording.

The Holy Qur'ān clarified the confusion between the miraculous birth of Jesus and the so-called incarnation of God, or the "Son of God." When man loses his ability to attribute to God the transcendental, unseen aspects of life, man may materialize his God and as such may fail to harmonize with the Divine Eternal Law. He imprisons himself in a frame that he has created—a result contrary to any Prophetic teachings. The Holy Qur'ān terms that misconception an act of "exaggeration" or "excess" to which human beings are liable to fall victim.

> *O People of the Book! Commit no excesses in your religion, nor say of Allāh anything but the truth. Christ Jesus the son of Mary was a Messenger of Allāh, and His Word, which He bestowed on Mary, and a Spirit proceeding from Him. So believe in Allāh and His Messengers. Say not "Trinity," desist; it will be better for you, for Allāh is One God, glory be to Him. (High Exalted is He) above having a son. To Him belong all things in the heavens and on earth. And Allāh is sufficient as a Disposer of affairs. (Qur'ān 4:171)*

يَاأَهْلَ الْكِتَابِ لَا تَغْلُوا فِي دِينِكُمْ وَلَا تَقُولُوا عَلَى اللَّهِ إِلَّا الْحَقَّ
إِنَّمَا الْمَسِيحُ عِيسَى ابْنُ مَرْيَمَ رَسُولُ اللَّهِ وَكَلِمَتُهُ أَلْقَاهَا إِلَى مَرْيَمَ
وَرُوحٌ مِنْهُ فَآمِنُوا بِاللَّهِ وَرُسُلِهِ وَلَا تَقُولُوا ثَلَاثَةٌ انْتَهُوا خَيْرًا لَكُمْ
إِنَّمَا اللَّهُ إِلَهٌ وَاحِدٌ سُبْحَانَهُ أَنْ يَكُونَ لَهُ وَلَدٌ لَهُ مَا فِي السَّمَوَاتِ
وَمَا فِي الْأَرْضِ وَكَفَى بِاللَّهِ وَكِيلًا

Emphasizing that Jesus is a servant of Allāh, and that is how we should perceive our relation to him, the Holy Qur'ān provides an approach that gives earthly existence a dimension in which surrender to the Supreme elevates and purifies us so that the divinity within our hearts can enlighten our way.

> *Is one whose heart Allāh has opened so that he surrendered (to Allāh), and has received enlightenment from Allāh (no better than one hard-hearted)? (Qur'ān 39:22)*

أَفَمَنْ شَرَحَ اللَّهُ صَدْرَهُ لِلْإِسْلَامِ فَهُوَ عَلَى نُورٍ مِنْ رَبِّهِ فَوَيْلٌ

لِلْقَاسِيَةِ قُلُوبُهُمْ مِنْ ذِكْرِ اللَّهِ أُولَئِكَ فِي ضَلَالٍ مُبِينٍ

O you who believe! Fear Allāh, and believe in His Messenger, and He will bestow on you a double portion of His Mercy; He will provide for you a Light by which you shall walk, and He will forgive you; for Allāh is Oft-Forgiving, Most Merciful. (Qur'ān 57:28)

يَاأَيُّهَا الَّذِينَ ءَامَنُوا اتَّقُوا اللَّهَ وَءَامِنُوا بِرَسُولِهِ يُؤْتِكُمْ كِفْلَيْنِ مِنْ رَحْمَتِهِ وَيَجْعَل لَكُمْ نُورًا تَمْشُونَ بِهِ وَيَغْفِرْ لَكُمْ وَاللَّهُ غَفُورٌ رَحِيمٌ

Regardless of how high and sublime one may rise, the human being remains a servant of God. Indeed, to be a servant of God is not to be taken for granted, but is a goal. While all human beings are God's creatures, those who know how to be in harmony with the Divine Order can realize the aim of their existence and be servants of God[13]. Here again, the Holy Qur'ān reveals Jesus' special place and asserts his high rank as a servant of Allāh.

The nature of Jesus before Allāh is as that of Adam; He created him from dust, then said to him "Be": and he was. (Qur'ān 3:59)

إِنَّ مَثَلَ عِيسَى عِنْدَ اللَّهِ كَمَثَلِ ءَادَمَ خَلَقَهُ مِنْ تُرَابٍ ثُمَّ قَالَ لَهُ كُنْ فَيَكُونُ

This verse highlights a certain resemblance that made both Adam and Jesus very special, each in a certain way. The special status of Jesus, resembling Adam before whom God asked the angels to prostrate, was a sign of Allāh's power, but neither was to be worshipped in themselves. Speaking of Adam, the Holy Qur'ān says:

"When I have fashioned him (in due proportion) and breathed into him of My spirit, fall down before him in prostration." (Qur'ān 15:29)

فَإِذَا سَوَّيْتُهُ وَنَفَخْتُ فِيهِ مِنْ رُوحِي فَقَعُوا لَهُ سَاجِدِينَ

[13]Chapter Three elaborates more on the meaning of being a servant of God.

In these verses, the Holy Qur'ān emphasizes that Adam and Jesus acquired life through the direct word of God, "Be," *Kun*. The angels were asked to surrender to God, accepting Adam as His representative:

Behold, your Lord said to the angels: "I will create a representative on earth." (Qur'ān 2:30)

وَإِذْ قَالَ رَبُّكَ لِلْمَلَائِكَةِ إِنِّي جَاعِلٌ فِي الْأَرْضِ خَلِيفَةً

Therefore, when they fell down before Adam, they were not worshipping him; rather they were witnessing the manifestation of God in one of His creatures. In the teachings of the Holy Qur'ān, it is acceptable to attain the state of acknowledging the Unseen Power through His manifestations, but the Unseen remains always transcendental:

To Allāh belong the East and the West: wherever you turn, there is Allāh's countenance. For Allāh is All-Embracing, All-Knowing. (Qur'ān 2:115)

وَلِلَّهِ الْمَشْرِقُ وَالْمَغْرِبُ فَأَيْنَمَا تُوَلُّوا فَثَمَّ وَجْهُ اللَّهِ إِنَّ اللَّهَ وَاسِعٌ عَلِيمٌ

God manifested Himself in man in a special way:

We did indeed offer the Trust to the heavens and the earth and the mountains; but they refused to undertake it, because they were afraid of it, but man undertook it. (Qur'ān 33:72)

إِنَّا عَرَضْنَا الْأَمَانَةَ عَلَى السَّمَوَاتِ وَالْأَرْضِ وَالْجِبَالِ فَأَبَيْنَ أَنْ يَحْمِلْنَهَا وَأَشْفَقْنَ مِنْهَا وَحَمَلَهَا الْإِنْسَانُ إِنَّهُ كَانَ ظَلُومًا جَهُولًا

"God does not reveal Himself in anything like He did in the human being."[14]

ما ظهر الله في شيء مثل ظهوره في الإنسان

[14] A Sufi saying.

Hence genuine followers of Jesus acknowledge God's Might through the miraculous birth of His Word, Jesus. They worship God, the Supreme Transcendent, and know Him through His manifestation in His Word and Messenger. Hence they do not take the limited creature to be their God; rather they do as the angels did when they fell down before Adam.

Because man tends to deviate, confusion rises in the minds of those who hang onto words without delving into their meanings. The Holy Qur'ān soundly condemns such people, while at the same time introducing a method by which man may correct himself.

> *He may warn those (also) who say, "Allāh has begotten a son." No knowledge have they of such a thing, nor had their fathers. Dreadful is this saying that comes out of their mouths. What they say is nothing but falsehood! (Qur'ān 18:4-5)*
>
> وَيُنْذِرَ الَّذِينَ قَالُوا اتَّخَذَ اللَّهُ وَلَدًا مَا لَهُمْ بِهِ مِنْ عِلْمٍ وَلَا لِآبَائِهِمْ
> كَبُرَتْ كَلِمَةً تَخْرُجُ مِنْ أَفْوَاهِهِمْ إِنْ يَقُولُونَ إِلَّا كَذِبًا

Those who follow Jesus' teachings and guidance truthfully are those who acknowledge that he is a Messenger of God; through him God expresses His Might. In other words, they discern the two levels of divinity, the Transcendent and the Manifest, without confusing the one for the other. Therefore those who follow Jesus remain on the straight path.

> *Behold! Allāh said: "O Jesus! I will take you and raise you to myself and clear you (of the falsehood) of those who blaspheme; I will make those who follow you superior to those who deny the Truth, to the Day of Resurrection. Then shall you all return unto Me, and I will judge between you with regard to the matters wherein you dispute." (Qur'ān 3:55)*
>
> إِذْ قَالَ اللَّهُ يَاعِيسَى إِنِّي مُتَوَفِّيكَ وَرَافِعُكَ إِلَيَّ وَمُطَهِّرُكَ مِنَ الَّذِينَ
> كَفَرُوا وَجَاعِلُ الَّذِينَ اتَّبَعُوكَ فَوْقَ الَّذِينَ كَفَرُوا إِلَى يَوْمِ الْقِيَامَةِ
> ثُمَّ إِلَيَّ مَرْجِعُكُمْ فَأَحْكُمُ بَيْنَكُمْ فِيمَا كُنْتُمْ فِيهِ تَخْتَلِفُونَ

Summary

It is now clear that by confirming the message established in previous Revelations, the Revelation to the Prophet Muḥammad uncovered the core call of the One Primordial Religion revealed to the Prophets, from Adam to Jesus. Through this confirmation, the Revelation to the Prophet Muḥammad explained to the followers of Moses and Jesus their own teachings and clarified problematic issues that both had misconstrued.

The teachings to the Prophet Muḥammad renewed the Call for believing in One Origin, to whom everything will return. That knowledge has the potential to enlighten our way, so that we can find purpose in existence and focus in life. Faith in the oneness of God, the Supreme, is the way to support man to overcome fears and lead him to make his earthly life spiritually fruitful, despite all earthly challenges.

Literal commitment to commandments, without understanding and experiencing the divinity within, leads humans to hold onto dogmas and imprison themselves in frames of their own creation. By losing their way, they fall in the abyss of spiritual darkness and ignorance. Messengers of Allāh represent His Light by being living examples of their messages. They came to enlighten our way by their very existence. To follow them is to open one's heart to God's Light. Following their teachings enables us to liberate ourselves from illusions and thereby achieve salvation.

In confirming other Revelations' teachings through clarification, the Prophet Muḥammad provided the core concepts that continue to enlighten humanity's way. This is the main theme of the following chapter.

3
Main Concepts

Based on the meaning of "Islām" as broadly defined in Chapter One, this chapter aims to show how Islām as revealed to the Prophet Muḥammad (Peace be upon him) revived the primordial religion by establishing a conceptual frame of reference that can serve as a guideline for generations to come.

The Revelation to the Prophet clarifies in a unique way the main principles around which man's life can revolve. These principles spring from basic concepts that are connected to one another. We choose to call them "chain concepts" because they interlink. Each concept leads to the others and explains them. The concepts give orientation to man's life and motivate us to nurture our heart and soul. They clarify much of the confusion that has prevailed throughout human history. While it is true that some of the concepts were considered in other revelations, Islām as revealed to the Prophet Muḥammad focuses on certain dimensions of these concepts and develops them to enhance man's endeavor and to support us on our path. The four concepts examined in this chapter are: the Divine Order; man as a servant of Allāh; *"ash-Shahādah"* (witnessing that there is no god but God and Muḥammad is His Messenger); and *"al-Qiblah"* (to have a direction, with the *Ka'bah* as its symbol). These concepts were the basis on which the spiritual training system (also called "worship system") was constructed and practiced, and on which the guidance to encourage productive earthly activities is founded.[1]

Belief in the Divine Order, or Divine Law, is a prerequisite for any human being who seeks meaning in his or her life. This belief stimulates one's will to search for ways to develop spiritually according to that Law. Each person is endowed with the potentiality of living in harmony with the Divine Law. This is where the second

[1]These points are discussed in the following chapters.

concept emerges to enlighten our way. It will be made clear that the highest rank a person can achieve is to be a servant of Allāh, the ultimate goal of which is to be spiritually free. Witnessing that "There is no god but God" is the practical expression of that freedom, for the person will take no other power or authority as his or her ultimate goal. Everything he or she does is devoted to Allāh. In realizing our servanthood to Allāh, we are following in the footsteps of the great Teachers of humanity, among whom Muḥammad stands as a model. The *Shahādah*, the first pillar of Islām, establishes this relationship between faith in the Divine Order and a person's spiritual evolution. The *Qiblah*, the necessity to take a direction, is a concept of paramount importance in Islām. It is another way of expressing The *Shahādah*. It is to Allāh that one should direct all actions, and to Him that one should devote one's life. This cannot be accomplished without a clear way, for which one needs the Prophets. This explains why the *Qiblah* is symbolized by the *Ka'bah* as the "House of God," the *Baytullāh*. It is on earth, not in heaven, that one proceeds on the way to Allāh, and on earth the message of Allāh and His Messenger is realized through enlightened human beings and can be sought from within one's heart. The *Qiblah* is the direction that unifies not only the followers of Muḥammad, but also seekers of truth everywhere.

The Divine Order

Islām as broadly defined is the way "to surrender to the Divine Order." The Qur'ān uses different words for the Divine Order, such as *aṣ-Ṣirāṭ al-Mustaqīm* (the Straight Way), *al-Kitāb* (the Book), *al-Ḥaqq* (the Truth), *Fiṭratullāh* (the Divine Nature), and *Sunnatullāh* (the Way of Allāh).[2] Although all previous revelations' teachings implicitly guide man to earn the spiritual life through surrender to the Divine Order, Islām as revealed to the Prophet Muḥammad, with its intense focus on how to surrender, explains this thoroughly.

"Islām," "Muslim," and "*taslīm*" are words derived from the same root; *taslīm* (to be in surrender) is the core approach for a

[2]This point is discussed in Chapter One.

Muslim. *At-taslīm li'llāh* means, essentially, that a person should allow Allāh's grace to reach him. In other words, surrender to Allāh makes the Divine Order work for man's spiritual development.[3]

Surrender to the Divine Order is related to faith in the Unseen.[4] Belief in the divine nature of the Order implies, in part, that there is an Unseen and Supreme Power that has originated the Order. This Order is divine because its source is divine. To surrender (*taslīm*) does not imply a passive attitude towards life. Rather it is a positive, conscious attitude, as it requires awareness of the purpose of life. It postulates that everything is meaningful because there is an order, a lawfulness within the universe.

An analogy between the natural world and the spiritual one may further clarify this point. In the natural world, we need to know how to keep our environment clean, our bodies healthy, and our plants producing more crops. To do that, we study the nature of things. We believe that there are natural laws according to which everything in our natural world functions. The history of scientific knowledge is the history of attempting to discover these laws and make use of them. The more we know about the Law, the more we are capable of adjusting our methods and improving things. To surrender to the Order, or lawfulness, implies that we should not violate it or do anything to hinder its function.

To surrender to the Order does not signify surrendering our will or choices, but only to assume that everything will function without intervention. While it is true that everything in nature functions without our interference, we human beings have the privilege of being able to interact among ourselves and with nature. Out of this interaction, cultures emerged in which different value systems were created and civilizations developed. Throughout history, man has learned to coexist with nature, with his fellow man, and with the law of his own existence as a human being. He has made many discoveries when studying nature and these discoveries benefit his well-being. Man's knowledge and awareness of the natural world have been useful to him and he has continuously corrected his mis-

[3]This point is discussed in detail in Chapter One.

[4]Detailed discussion is included in the third section of Chapter One, "To Be a Muslim Is To Live According to the Divine Law." See also below in this chapter.

takes. It all began with man believing in the natural law and having the confidence to search for that law. The ability to know about the law is expanding and the more man knows, the more he realizes that he still does not know. Yet the search to know more continues.

Similarly, our spiritual well-being follows the Divine Law; all revelations have come to teach us about that Law. This teaching has not been theoretical but practical, in the sense that each individual is asked to experience its knowledge existentially. Accordingly, while we learn how to live from the knowledge given, we also know more when we live in harmony with what we believe. The development of knowledge and the enrichment of experience have no limitations; that is to say, our knowledge of the Divine Order is always expanding.

The basis on which we human beings establish our growing knowledge and experience is the faith in the ultimate Truth that transcends our senses. In the language of the Holy Qur'ān it is called *al-Ghayb*, translated as "the Unseen." This translation has its limitations in that it does not cover all implications inherent in *al-Ghayb*, which connotes, among other things, the existence of a Power that stands beyond our knowledge, not only beyond our sight. *Al-Ghayb* is a category of the Divine, because while the Divine becomes known to us or seen by us through manifestations, It remains Transcendent, (*Ghayb*). We know of the Divine Order through its manifestations in our spiritual experiences and through the guidance of Revelations. Yet to claim that we know everything about the Divine Order leads to stagnation and dogma. *Al-Ghayb* is the unattainable aspect of the Divine Order. In our limited capacity, we cannot have a proper image of the angels or of our life in the Hereafter. It is impossible for us to define the spirit, *ar-rūḥ*, or to know truly what life is. Our limited capacity should not prevent us from believing that there is a Divine Order, according to which all those unseen, unknown aspects of life work; while it is impossible to define what life is, we cannot argue as to whether we are alive or not.

Despite those limitations, we can learn about our spiritual development by living. Our insight enables us to learn and acquire experience. Our intellect may express acquired knowledge through ideas and symbols. This knowledge forms part of our spiritual development because it expresses part of our own experience. It can be communicated among those who are ready to open their hearts, but those who are blind at heart are incapable of receiving this knowledge.

> *Truly it is not their eyes that are blind, but their hearts which are in their breasts. (Qur'ān 22:46)*
>
> فَإِنَّهَا لَا تَعْمَى الْأَبْصَارُ وَلَكِن تَعْمَى الْقُلُوبُ الَّتِي فِي الصُّدُورِ

> *Do they not then earnestly seek to think of the Qur'ān, or are their hearts locked up? (Qur'ān 47:24)*
>
> أَفَلَا يَتَدَبَّرُونَ الْقُرْءَانَ أَمْ عَلَى قُلُوبٍ أَقْفَالُهَا

Man can open his heart by a continuous process of purification revealed through Revelations. Consequently man, as a unique creature, cannot exclude his given ability to choose. We either choose a way that leads to surrender to the Divine Order or deviate from that path of salvation by violating the Divine Order. By so doing we actually violate our inherently natural development and lose the potential of human life.

In the Prophet's teachings, the pure nature of things, the *fiṭrah*, is equivalent to the Eternal Divine Order.

> *So set your face towards the Primordial Religion, the Divine Order (Divine Nature) innate in human beings. There is no distorting (the nature of) Allāh's creation. This is the authentic religion: but most among mankind do not understand. (Qur'ān 30:30)*[5]
>
> فَأَقِمْ وَجْهَكَ لِلدِّينِ حَنِيفًا فِطْرَةَ اللَّهِ الَّتِي فَطَرَ النَّاسَ عَلَيْهَا لَا
> تَبْدِيلَ لِخَلْقِ اللَّهِ ذَلِكَ الدِّينُ الْقَيِّمُ وَلَكِنَّ أَكْثَرَ النَّاسِ لَا يَعْلَمُونَ

> *Every newborn is given the religion of fiṭrah, whether his parents give him the name of a creed, so he may become a Jew, a*

[5]Our translation.

Christian, or a Magian. (PH)[6]

ما من مولود إلا يولد على الفطرة فأبواه يهودانه أو ينصرانه أو يمجسانه

As such, *fiṭrah* is our innate nature as originally created by the Divine, containing the Law in its very texture. To live according to *fiṭrah* should not be confused with living according to one's instincts and giving oneself complete freedom in fulfilling one's desires. *Fiṭrah* is the hidden, sacred goal of all that was created. *Fiṭrah* reveals to the human heart the purpose of existence and guides one to live according to one's ultimate goal in life.

Islamic teachings guide us to search for the *fiṭrah* within. It is one of the Signs of Allāh that are everywhere, including in the very creation of man.

On the earth are Signs for those of inner certainty, as also in your own selves. Will you not then see? (Qur'ān 51:20-21)

وَفِي الْأَرْضِ ءَايَٰتٌ لِّلْمُوقِنِينَ وَفِي أَنْفُسِكُمْ أَفَلَا تُبْصِرُونَ

Teachings provide humanity with a method by which a person can make the most out of his life. The spiritual training system follows a process that responds to man's spiritual needs in a wonderful way[7]. The *Sharī'ah* (the series of Islamic divine principles organizing the life of the individual and the community) protects the less privileged and spreads justice and balance among members of a community.[8]

Deviation from the Divine Order leads people to go astray, to follow their own "illusory way," *hawāh*. In the language of the Holy Qur'ān, *hawāh* is explored semantically in various contexts.

Have you seen the kind of person who takes as his god his own vain desire (hawāh)? Allāh has, knowing (him as such), left

[6]Narrated by Bukhārī.
[7]This will be discussed in Chapter Four.
[8]This point is discussed in detail in Chapter Five.

him astray, and sealed his hearing and his heart and put a cover on his sight. (Qur'ān 45:23)[9]

أَفَرَأَيْتَ مَنِ اتَّخَذَ إِلَهَهُ هَوَاهُ وَأَضَلَّهُ اللَّهُ عَلَى عِلْمٍ وَخَتَمَ عَلَى سَمْعِهِ وَقَلْبِهِ وَجَعَلَ عَلَى بَصَرِهِ غِشَاوَةً فَمَنْ يَهْدِيهِ مِنْ بَعْدِ اللَّهِ أَفَلَا تَذَكَّرُونَ

Nay, those who are unjust follow their own lusts (ahwā'ahum), being devoid of knowledge, but who will guide those whom Allāh leaves astray? For them there will be no helpers. (Qur'ān 30:29)

بَلِ اتَّبَعَ الَّذِينَ ظَلَمُوا أَهْوَاءَهُمْ بِغَيْرِ عِلْمٍ فَمَنْ يَهْدِي مَنْ أَضَلَّ اللَّهُ وَمَا لَهُمْ مِنْ نَاصِرِينَ

And for such as had entertained the fear of the Majesty of his Lord and had restrained his soul from lower desires (hawāh), Paradise will be his home. (Qur'ān 79:40-41)

وَأَمَّا مَنْ خَافَ مَقَامَ رَبِّهِ وَنَهَى النَّفْسَ عَنِ الْهَوَى. فَإِنَّ الْجَنَّةَ هِيَ الْمَأْوَى

Hawāh in this context means a way opposite to the way of pure innate nature (*fiṭrah*), the Truth, or the Divine Order. It is anything originating in our desires that can divert us from the straight path to any attraction that causes confusion and hinders us from seeing or hearing the truth. A person that follows *hawāh* is unjust to himself and to others. If an individual is capable of removing *hawāh* from his way, he prepares himself to live in harmony with—to surrender to—the Divine Order.

---

[9]Transliterations in brackets in this and the following verses are added by the authors.

Representative of Allāh and Servant of Allāh

All revelations guide man to believe in the Supreme Power[10] and make this knowledge beneficial to our spiritual development. Islām as revealed to Muḥammad gave new dimensions to the relationship between man and the Supreme Power, God. According to the Divine teachings revealed to Muḥammad, to be "God's servant," *ʿabdullāh*, is the highest rank that can be achieved.

To elaborate: to surrender to the Divine Order is a choice. While man can destroy himself by violating the law of spiritual development, other creatures do not have that choice. They are in harmony with the order of the universe and follow the laws of their own existence.

> *The seven heavens and the earth, and all beings therein, declare His Glory. There is not a thing but celebrates His praise, and yet you understand not how they declare His glory! Truly He is Oft-Forbearing, Most Forgiving! (Qur'ān 17:44)*
>
> تُسَبِّحُ لَهُ السَّمَوَاتُ السَّبْعُ وَالْأَرْضُ وَمَنْ فِيهِنَّ وَإِنْ مِنْ شَيْءٍ إِلَّا
> يُسَبِّحُ بِحَمْدِهِ وَلَكِنْ لَا تَفْقَهُونَ تَسْبِيحَهُمْ إِنَّهُ كَانَ حَلِيمًا غَفُورًا

Because of man's ability to make mischief, continuous revelations came to correct man's way and to teach him how to live in harmony with himself, with his fellow humans, and with nature; that is, to be in harmony with the Divine Order. In other words, the revelations taught him how to follow the pure nature of Creation, *fiṭrah,* so that he can reach the rank of being a servant of Allāh.

The relationship between man, the angels, and Iblīs clarifies the status of man among creatures and his very special place as God's representative.

> *Behold, your Lord said to the angels: "I will create a representative on earth." They said, "Will You place therein one who will make mischief there and shed blood, while we celebrate*

[10]This is one of the main themes that reveal the oneness of Religion. The authors discuss this point in their book: *Beyond Diversities: Reflections on Revelations.*

> *Your praise and glorify Your holy (name)?" He said, "I know that which you do not know."* (Qur'ān 2:30)
>
> وَإِذْ قَالَ رَبُّكَ لِلْمَلَائِكَةِ إِنِّي جَاعِلٌ فِي الْأَرْضِ خَلِيفَةً قَالُوا أَتَجْعَلُ فِيهَا مَنْ يُفْسِدُ فِيهَا وَيَسْفِكُ الدِّمَاءَ وَنَحْنُ نُسَبِّحُ بِحَمْدِكَ وَنُقَدِّسُ لَكَ قَالَ إِنِّي أَعْلَمُ مَا لَا تَعْلَمُونَ

This verse contains a declaration of man's dual potential; he is a representative of God, but in practice he has the power to make mischief, as the angels perceive. The angels cannot disobey Allāh, but express their limitations when they say that they cannot see the wisdom of sending Adam to earth. They see one fact: that man has the ability to destroy and fight. The wisdom of creating "a representative on earth" lies in Allāh's Knowledge: *"I know that which you do not know."* Therefore, the angels fall down in obeisance.

> *And behold, We said to the angels, "Bow down to Adam." They bowed down. Not so Iblīs; he refused and was haughty. He became one of those who deny the Truth."* (Qur'ān 2:34)
>
> وإذ قلنا للملائكة اسجدوا لآدم فسجدوا إلا إبليس أبى واستكبر وكان من الكافرين

Iblīs (Satan) does not obey Allāh's commandment, as he denies that Adam is a representative of Allāh and asserts that Adam does not deserve to be of such high rank. By so doing, Iblīs, powerful and full of pride, refuses to accept his limitations. When Adam disobeys, out of ignorance, he is ready to repent. Herein lies the very unique character of Adam. Both Iblīs and Adam are given the power to obey or disobey the Divine Law. However, Adam may make mistakes out of ignorance or forget his mission and his way, while Iblīs disobeys God's directions out of arrogance and limited knowledge. He does not accept that he has made a mistake and is eager to prove that he is right. He challenges the Power of Truth, using illusions. His followers cling to illusions as real and reject the path to the Truth. Naturally, Iblīs and his followers will meet their destiny, one of great suffering.

(Allāh) said: "Go forth from here, disgraced and banished. If any of them follow you, I will fill Hell with all of you. (Qur'ān 7:18)

قَالَ اخْرُجْ مِنْهَا مَذْءُومًا مَدْحُورًا لَمَنْ تَبِعَكَ مِنْهُمْ لَأَمْلَأَنَّ جَهَنَّمَ مِنْكُمْ أَجْمَعِينَ

Iblīs succeeded in revealing Adam's inherent ability to violate his own nature, *fiṭrah*. Adam is compelled to start a journey in which he struggles against the power of illusions and to remember the Divine knowledge as revealed to him in Heaven.

And He taught Adam the names of all things. (Qur'ān 2:31)

وَعَلَّمَ آدَمَ الْأَسْمَاءَ كُلَّهَا

This verse points to what qualified Adam to be Allāh's representative on earth. Allāh has supported Adam and his children with continuous revelations and guidance, yet the ability to discern between Truth and illusion and to uncover the embedded knowledge requires much work on the part of Adam's children. Their ultimate achievement is to attain the rank of servant of Allāh so that they can be in complete serenity and security.

. . . there comes to you guidance from Me. Whoever follows My guidance, on them shall be no fear, nor shall they grieve. But those who deny the Truth and Our Signs, they shall be companions of the Fire; they shall abide therein. (Qur'ān 2:38-39)

فَإِمَّا يَأْتِيَنَّكُمْ مِنِّي هُدًى فَمَنْ تَبِعَ هُدَايَ فَلَا خَوْفٌ عَلَيْهِمْ وَلَا هُمْ يَحْزَنُونَ وَالَّذِينَ كَفَرُوا وَكَذَّبُوا بِآيَاتِنَا أُولَئِكَ أَصْحَابُ النَّارِ هُمْ فِيهَا خَالِدُونَ

The potential of being God's servants was given to the children of Adam; a great responsibility was thus bestowed upon man. If we follow the path of Allāh and surrender to His Divine Order, we prepare ourselves to be His servants. The root of *'abdullāh* is derived from the three letters *'a-b-d*, which if pronounced *'abbada* means "to prepare" or "to pave the way." An *'abdullāh* is a person who surrenders his or her self to Allāh, so that Allāh prepares him or her for Himself.

> *And I have prepared you for Myself. (Qur'ān 20:41)*[11]
>
> وَاصْطَنَعْتُكَ لِنَفْسِي
>
> *"Heavens and Earth contain Me not, but the heart of My believing servant contains Me." (HQ)*[12]
>
> ما وسعتني سمائي ولا أرضي ووسعني قلب عبدي المؤمن

We prepare ourselves for Allāh when we focus on how to become His servant. Our first step is to live up to the knowledge of the Oneness of Allāh, for which purification of the heart is a prerequisite.

> *O, man! Truly you are ever toiling on towards your Lord—painfully toiling—but you shall meet Him. (Qur'ān 84:6)*
>
> يَاأَيُّهَا الْإِنْسَانُ إِنَّكَ كَادِحٌ إِلَى رَبِّكَ كَدْحًا فَمُلَاقِيهِ

The Prophets are models of such struggle. When they prepared themselves, truth prevailed and Heavenly Guidance came to enlighten humanity's way. It all begins with man's sincere request and his working for it. It is that part of man, the secret of life with which God endowed him and which in the Holy Qur'ān is called "the Trust," *al-Amānah*, that can be awakened to support us in our struggle.

> *We did indeed offer the Trust to the heavens and the earth and the mountains, but they refused to undertake it, because they were afraid of it; but man undertook it; he was indeed unjust and foolish. (Qur'ān 33:72)*
>
> إِنَّا عَرَضْنَا الْأَمَانَةَ عَلَى السَّمَوَاتِ وَالْأَرْضِ وَالْجِبَالِ فَأَبَيْنَ أَنْ يَحْمِلْنَهَا وَأَشْفَقْنَ مِنْهَا وَحَمَلَهَا الْإِنْسَانُ إِنَّهُ كَانَ ظَلُومًا جَهُولًا

---

[11] Our translation.

[12] Used by Al-Ghazālī in *Iḥyā' 'Ulūm ad-Dīn*.

إحياء علوم الدين

The "Trust" is the hidden knowledge within man's heart. Without it, we would be "unjust and foolish." If we keep this Trust and follows its inspiration, we will achieve our goal. We can keep this Trust if we are aware of the Divine Reality. In other words, the Trust is the symbolic word for the potential to live in harmony with the Divine Reality. At that point we attain the status of Allāh's servant. If we follow the Truth embedded in our own nature, we will be guided to real life, but if we deviate from this path, we will go astray.

> *If it had been Our Will, We could have elevated him with Our Signs, but he inclined to the earth, and followed his own vain desires (hawāh). His similitude is that of a dog: if you attack him, he lolls out his tongue, or if you leave him alone, he (still) lolls out his tongue. That is the similitude of those who reject Our Signs. So relate this story, so that they may reflect. (Qur'ān 7:176)*
>
> وَلَوْ شِئْنَا لَرَفَعْنَاهُ بِهَا وَلَكِنَّهُ أَخْلَدَ إِلَى الْأَرْضِ وَاتَّبَعَ هَوَاهُ فَمَثَلُهُ كَمَثَلِ الْكَلْبِ إِنْ تَحْمِلْ عَلَيْهِ يَلْهَثْ أَوْ تَتْرُكْهُ يَلْهَثْ ذَلِكَ مَثَلُ الْقَوْمِ الَّذِينَ كَذَّبُوا بِآيَاتِنَا فَاقْصُصِ الْقَصَصَ لَعَلَّهُمْ يَتَفَكَّرُونَ

> *Therefore do not let anyone who does not believe in (the Last hour), but follows their own vain desires (hawāh), divert you from (belief in) it, lest you perish! (Qur'ān 20:16)*
>
> فَلَا يَصُدَّنَّكَ عَنْهَا مَنْ لَا يُؤْمِنُ بِهَا وَاتَّبَعَ هَوَاهُ فَتَرْدَى

> *But if they hearken not to you, know that they only follow their own desires, and who is more astray than one who follows his own desires, devoid of guidance from Allāh? For Allāh guides not people given to wrong-doing. (Qur'ān 28:50)*
>
> فَإِنْ لَمْ يَسْتَجِيبُوا لَكَ فَاعْلَمْ أَنَّمَا يَتَّبِعُونَ أَهْوَاءَهُمْ وَمَنْ أَضَلُّ مِمَّنِ اتَّبَعَ هَوَاهُ بِغَيْرِ هُدًى مِنَ اللَّهِ إِنَّ اللَّهَ لَا يَهْدِي الْقَوْمَ الظَّالِمِينَ

> *O you who keep the faith! Stand out firmly for justice, as witnesses to Allāh, even if it be against yourselves, or your parents, or your kin, and whether it be against rich or poor,*

> *for Allāh can best protect them. Don't follow mere desires (hawāh), lest you swerve, and if you distort justice or decline to do justice, truly Allāh is well-acquainted with all that you do. (Qur'ān 4:135)*
>
> يَاأَيُّهَا الَّذِينَ ءَامَنُوا كُونُوا قَوَّامِينَ بِالْقِسْطِ شُهَدَاءَ لِلَّهِ وَلَوْ عَلَى أَنْفُسِكُمْ أَوِ الْوَالِدَيْنِ وَالْأَقْرَبِينَ إِنْ يَكُنْ غَنِيًّا أَوْ فَقِيرًا فَاللَّهُ أَوْلَى بِهِمَا فَلَا تَتَّبِعُوا الْهَوَى أَنْ تَعْدِلُوا وَإِنْ تَلْوُوا أَوْ تُعْرِضُوا فَإِنَّ اللَّهَ كَانَ بِمَا تَعْمَلُونَ خَبِيرًا

For man to be a servant of Allāh he should vigorously resist the illusory tendency of *hawāh*. If he succeeds, he will be just to himself and to everything. Because he is a servant of God, the Qur'ān describes His Messenger thus:

> *He does not say a word out of hawāh; he is inspired, and he inspires. (Qur'ān 53:3-4)*[13]
>
> وَمَا يَنْطِقُ عَنِ الْهَوَى. إِنْ هُوَ إِلَّا وَحْيٌ يُوحَى

The teachings revealed to the Prophet Muḥammad clarify this relationship between humankind and God in a way that resolves the contradictions that prevailed among certain followers of other revelations regarding human nature and the nature of God. As God's representative and His servant, man carries divine nature within his soul; it is the "Trust" that God bestowed upon us and the spirit that He breathed into us.

> *"When I have fashioned him (in due proportion) and breathed into him of My spirit, fall down before him in prostration." (Qur'ān 15:29)*
>
> فَإِذَا سَوَّيْتُهُ وَنَفَخْتُ فِيهِ مِنْ رُوحِي فَقَعُوا لَهُ سَاجِدِينَ

> *But He fashioned him in due proportion, and breathed into him from His spirit. (Qur'ān 32:9)*
>
> ثُمَّ سَوَّاهُ وَنَفَخَ فِيهِ مِنْ رُوحِهِ

[13]Our translation.

Yet the human being is not God; nor is he an incarnation of God. The highest rank that one can achieve is the realization of the goal of existence, becoming God's servant and His representative. To represent Allāh on earth as representative (*khalifāh*) gives us the opportunity of being in complete harmony with the Divine.

> *"So My servant approaches Me by all means until I love him. If I love him I am the hearing with which he hears, the seeing with which he sees, the hands with which he works, and the legs with which he walks."(HQ)*[14]
>
> وما يزال عبدي يتقرب إلي بالنوافل حتى أحبه فإذا أحببته كنت سمعه الذي يسمع به وبصره الذي يبصر به ويده التي يبطش بها ورجله التي يمشي بها

Complete harmony or surrender to the Divine transforms a human being from an illusory, untrue existence to the realm of reality and truth. This inner transformation, which may not be apparent to an observer, empowers a servant of God with the capacity to foresee wisdom and truth beyond the common mind. Certain Prophets manifested supernatural power to show people that Almighty God can bestow that power upon those whom He chooses to be His servants. Jesus is an example.

> *Then will Allāh say: "O Jesus, the son of Mary! Recount My favor to you and to your mother. Behold! I strengthened you with the Holy Spirit, so that you spoke to the people in childhood and in maturity. Behold! I taught you the Book and Wisdom, the Law and the Gospel. And behold! You make out of clay, as it were, the figure of a bird, by My leave, and you breathe into it, and it becomes a bird by My leave; and you heal those born blind, and the lepers, by My leave. And behold! You bring forth the dead by My leave."* (*Qur'ān 5:110*)
>
> إِذْ قَالَ اللَّهُ يَاعِيسَى ابْنَ مَرْيَمَ اذْكُرْ نِعْمَتِي عَلَيْكَ وَعَلَى وَالِدَتِكَ إِذْ أَيَّدْتُكَ بِرُوحِ الْقُدُسِ تُكَلِّمُ النَّاسَ فِي الْمَهْدِ وَكَهْلًا وَإِذْ عَلَّمْتُكَ

[14]Narrated by Bukhārī and Aḥmad.

الْكِتَابَ وَالْحِكْمَةَ وَالتَّوْرَاةَ وَالْإِنْجِيلَ وَإِذْ تَخْلُقُ مِنَ الطِّينِ كَهَيْئَةِ الطَّيْرِ بِإِذْنِي فَتَنْفُخُ فِيهَا فَتَكُونُ طَيْرًا بِإِذْنِي وَتُبْرِئُ الْأَكْمَهَ وَالْأَبْرَصَ بِإِذْنِي وَإِذْ تُخْرِجُ الْمَوْتَى بِإِذْنِي

naïvely, we may think that those upon whom Allāh bestows His capability of the secret word "Be" will do for us what we cannot. We may also be tempted to increase our time of worship in order to gain this aptitude, thinking that we will develop great power with which to achieve our noble dreams. This is to misunderstand the teachings, because the will of the person who surrenders completely to Allāh reflects Allāh's will. He has no supernatural impact on the universe, but can have this shining light from Allāh and his presence may even transform his companions if they are ready to receive. The power of Truth in us can change the world. This occurred with all the Prophets—not abruptly, but gradually. Moses, for example, saved the Children of Israel, helping them escape the tyranny of the Pharaoh. That was a miracle. Jesus not only could heal the ill, bring the dead back to life, etc., but his call spread all over the world and caused the downfall of the most powerful empire of the time. Needless to say, Muḥammad's presence, and the message he conveyed, transformed Arabia and was a breakthrough in human history.

The opportunity to be a servant of God and His representative is given not only to the Prophets, but also to whomever surrenders fully and frees himself completely of illusions. A servant of God is not required to do miracles, as the most miraculous thing of all is to act and speak of the Truth embedded within one's heart, rather than out of *hawāh*—as did Zachariah, who emerged from solitude to inspire his people to remember God day and night.

> *So Zachariah came out to his people from his chamber; he told them through inspiration to celebrate Allāh's praises in the morning and in the evening. (Qur'ān 19:11)*

فَخَرَجَ عَلَى قَوْمِهِ مِنَ الْمِحْرَابِ فَأَوْحَى إِلَيْهِمْ أَنْ سَبِّحُوا بُكْرَةً وَعَشِيًّا

He aimed for nothing but the Truth and sought only God.

It has been the message of all revelations to teach us how to be linked to the Origin of life and to realize our potential. But the Islamic teachings stress the value of being a servant of God without reducing man to a mere ephemeral being and without magnifying him to the status of a god.

As simple as it may appear, this relationship between man and God was perplexing to the human mind. The Call to be a servant of God was misunderstood. For some, it meant that man should obey God's commandments blindly and fear God as the Supreme Power that will exercise His Might against those who disobey Him by burning them in Hell or exposing them to all kinds of torture. This personification of God is against the basic principle of believing in Him as beyond everything and within everything at the same time. He is not an entity and cannot be one. It is, therefore, a grave mistake to project a human image on Him, thinking of Him as a human lord who leads his slaves by force and violence. Hell and Paradise are symbolic images that explain the work of the Divine Law, demonstrating how man harvests the fruits of what he sows.

It is equally wrong to take good people as gods or as incarnations of God. While it is well understood that there is a sacred part within us that can carry us from the illusory world to the world of Truth, the Originator is above and beyond that; He is always Greater. *Allāhu Akbar* "Allāh is Greater" is a very significant phrase in Islām. No wonder, then, that the call to prayer begins with *Allāhu Akbar*. For this reason, in the Holy Qur'ān, Jesus is a Word of God, but that does not imply that he is a god. Jesus became a Sign of Almighty God who manifests His Divine Word in him. Jesus did not ask people to worship him:

> *"I never said anything to them except what You commanded me to say, that is, 'Worship Allāh, my Lord and your Lord.' And I was a witness over them while I dwelt among them; when You took me up You were the Watcher over them, and You are a witness to all things." (Qur'ān 5:117)*

مَا قُلْتُ لَهُمْ إِلَّا مَا أَمَرْتَنِي بِهِ أَنِ اعْبُدُوا اللَّهَ رَبِّي وَرَبَّكُمْ وَكُنْتُ
عَلَيْهِمْ شَهِيدًا مَا دُمْتُ فِيهِمْ فَلَمَّا تَوَفَّيْتَنِي كُنْتَ أَنْتَ الرَّقِيبَ

عَلَيْهِمْ وَأَنْتَ عَلَى كُلِّ شَيْءٍ شَهِيدٌ

Certain followers of Jesus portray Jesus as an incarnation of God. When Jesus said,

> *"Our Father Who art in Heaven, hallowed be Thy Name." (Matt. 6:9)*

he was emphasizing the greatness of God. This expression is the equivalent of *Allāhu Akbar*. Yet it was not understood as such by certain followers of Jesus.[15] The Prophet Muḥammad, in clarifying the position of Jesus as *ʿabdullāh*, introduced a concept and an approach that can protect human beings from making the same mistakes of those followers of Jesus. *Allāhu Akbar* added the dimension that can protect the human mind from perceiving any finite creature as a god.

There is no contradiction between Jesus saying,

> *"I am the way, the truth, and the life: no man comes unto the Father, but by me." (John 14:6)*

and being *ʿabdullāh*. Jesus came with the message of God that expressed the Truth and guided people to Life. To follow Jesus is to be one with him and to be truly alive. Yet God remains ever greater; "hallowed is His Name." Muḥammad explains that man is created to be man; that is, to be worthy of being a servant of God. To be a servant of God is a goal to be achieved. Discovering the divine knowledge within oneself is the first step towards that end.[16]

---

[15]Of course, certain followers of Jesus are well aware of the relation between the Son and the Father. When they perceive Jesus as their "lord," they express their belief in him as divine light and manifestation of the Father in Heaven. He is their higher source of guidance, the way, and the truth. They do not confuse him with the Lord, the Creator of heaven and earth, who is ever Transcendent and ever Greater. The above-mentioned clarification, then, focuses on the confusion of only some followers of Jesus.

[16]This concept is in full harmony with the teachings of Jesus, who was a living expression of what it is to be a servant of God. He did not follow the temptation of Satan, saying: *Get you hence, Satan: for it is written, You shall worship the Lord your God, and Him only shall you serve. (Matt. 4:10)* He also taught his disciples that serving God is a highly cherished goal: *No man can serve two masters: for either he will hate the one, and love the other; or else he will hold to the one, and despise the other. You cannot serve God and mammon. (Matt. 6:24)*

As human beings, we are capable of either realizing the sublime potential given to us or losing it; this is the challenge that human beings face in their lives.

Ash-Shahādah

Ash-Shahādah,[17] "the Testimony," "there is no god but God, Muḥammad is the Messenger of God," *Lā ilāha illā Allāh, Muḥammad rasūlu Allāh,* is related exclusively to the Islamic Call that Muḥammad conveyed. It is more than a statement or a declaration of the oneness of Allāh. The *Shahādah* is a reminder of the teachings of all revelations; namely, that the Origin of everything and of all creatures is One. The second part of the *Shahādah* introduces to humanity the path to the Truth that will always enlighten humanity's way.

Knowing that Muḥammad is the Messenger of Allāh prepares the individual to reflect upon Muḥammad's teachings and encourages him to follow his path. On another level, Muḥammad is a symbol of all the previous revelations and to follow him is to follow the teachings of Jesus, Moses, Abraham, and all other heavenly guidance that came to earth. In short, the *Shahādah* is a reminder of the primary call in all revelations and a summing up of them in the Islamic Call conveyed through Muḥammad.

Shahādah is derived from the root *sh-h-d* and the verb *shahāda,* which has various meanings, including "to see," "to declare," and "to testify" or "witness." *Shahādah* condenses all these meanings. When we begin by saying *ash-hadu,* we "declare" that we "witness" and as such emphasize to ourselves that this declaration transcends the field of knowledge; for we perceive the reality of the oneness of Allāh and the fact that Muḥammad is His Messenger.

A Reminder of the Eternal Covenant

The *Shahādah* is a reminder of the knowledge inherent in man's

---

[17] The statement symbolizing declaration of one's Islām: *Lā ilāha illā Allāh, Muḥammad rasūlu Allāh.* It is not said only once, but is uttered with every call to prayer.

soul which we tend to forget. The story of Adam in the Holy Qur'ān demonstrates the characteristics of his children and to what degree we are apt to forget the covenant taken since the creation of Adam.

> *When your Lord drew forth from the Children of Adam their descendants, and made them testify concerning themselves, (saying) "Am I not your Lord?" they said: "Yea! We do testify!" (This), lest you should say on the Day of Judgment: 'Of this we were never mindful.' (Qur'ān 7:172)*
>
> وَإِذْ أَخَذَ رَبُّكَ مِنْ بَنِي ءَادَمَ مِنْ ظُهُورِهِمْ ذُرِّيَّتَهُمْ وَأَشْهَدَهُمْ عَلَى أَنْفُسِهِمْ أَلَسْتُ بِرَبِّكُمْ قَالُوا بَلَى شَهِدْنَا أَنْ تَقُولُوا يَوْمَ الْقِيَامَةِ إِنَّا كُنَّا عَنْ هَذَا غَافِلِينَ

> *We had already, beforehand, taken the covenant of Adam, but he forgot and We found on his part no firm resolve. (Qur'ān 20:115)*
>
> وَلَقَدْ عَهِدْنَا إِلَى ءَادَمَ مِنْ قَبْلُ فَنَسِيَ وَلَمْ نَجِدْ لَهُ عَزْمًا

Revelations came to remind people of their commitment. Muḥammad, as did the Prophets who preceded him, came to remind people of the commitment that they had made. Accordingly, people can set their priorities, define their goals and forgo any trivial attractions. The *Shahādah,* the first pillar of Islām, is meant to remind people of how to live according to the knowledge and experience of the Oneness of God.

To witness that "there is no god but God" reminds us that we should not be deceived by any illusory, impermanent powers that cannot represent the absolute Truth.[18] Nothing, then, is the Truth but God. To God alone should one direct one's deeds and Him alone should one seek.

> *High above all is Allāh, the Sovereign, the Truth! (Qur'ān 20:114)*
>
> فَتَعَالَى اللَّهُ الْمَلِكُ الْحَقُّ

[18]Chapter Five examines this point in detail, demonstrating how man's relationship with himself, with nature, and with his fellow human beings harmonizes around the *Shahādah.*

This is so, because Allāh is the Truth; it is He Who gives life to the dead, and it is He Who is capable of everything. (Qur'ān 22:6)

ذَلِكَ بِأَنَّ اللَّهَ هُوَ الْحَقُّ وَأَنَّهُ يُحْيِي الْمَوْتَى وَأَنَّهُ عَلَى كُلِّ شَيْءٍ قَدِيرٌ

Thus it is because Allāh is the Truth, and those besides Him whom they invoke, they are but vain falsehood; truly Allāh is He, Most High, Most Great. (Qur'ān 22:62)

ذَلِكَ بِأَنَّ اللَّهَ هُوَ الْحَقُّ وَأَنَّ مَا يَدْعُونَ مِنْ دُونِهِ هُوَ الْبَاطِلُ وَأَنَّ اللَّهَ هُوَ الْعَلِيُّ الْكَبِيرُ

What It Means To Witness that Muḥammad Is the Messenger of God

The second part of the *Shahādah,* "Muḥammad is the Messenger of God," *Muḥammad rasūlu Allāh,* can be interpreted on two levels. The first is that in which Muḥammad is a Prophet who came during a certain period of time, conveying a precise, learned Call, and who had a great, even historical, impact on the world. For no one can deny the impact that the Call of the Prophet had in changing the nature of Arabia and setting the groundwork for the Islamic civilization that later flourished. Those changes were the natural outcome of the great inner spiritual transformation of people who believed in Muḥammad and the Islamic Call.

On a second level, Muḥammad's greatness transcends the great impact that he made on history. Muḥammad is a symbol of the Message of God, the Primordial Religion, *ad-Dīn al-Ḥanīf*— that Religion to which all the Prophets called.[19] "Muḥammad is the Messenger of God" is a call to believe that the Call he conveyed is the one that came with all previous Prophets. The *Shahādah* is a continuous Call to other people from all walks of life to believe in their

[19]See Chapter One for discussion of this point.

religion as introduced by the Divine through Muḥammad, regardless of whether they convert to Muḥammad's creed or not.

> *Invite (all) to the Way of your Sustainer with wisdom and kind counsel; and if you argue with them choose the best way (to make them see what is better for them) for your Sustainer knows best who have strayed from His path, and who receive guidance. (Qur'ān 16:125)*
>
> ادْعُ إِلَى سَبِيلِ رَبِّكَ بِالْحِكْمَةِ وَالْمَوْعِظَةِ الْحَسَنَةِ وَجَادِلْهُمْ بِالَّتِي هِيَ أَحْسَنُ إِنَّ رَبَّكَ هُوَ أَعْلَمُ بِمَنْ ضَلَّ عَنْ سَبِيلِهِ وَهُوَ أَعْلَمُ بِالْمُهْتَدِينَ

On the level of spiritual experience, to witness that "Muḥammad is the Messenger of God" means more than acknowledging the Prophethood of Muḥammad. "To witness" is not merely to admit or testify, but also to see the reality of Muḥammad as a Messenger of God. The act of seeing is possible because Muḥammad is not only part of history but exists also in the present and can be seen in the hearts of his followers. The teachings of the Prophet are not words to be uttered, theological theories to be learnt, or logical statements to be comprehended. Those teachings were alive in the life of the Prophet and have expanded in those who have revived them in their hearts. They have continued his Call. Muḥammad as a Messenger of God symbolizes the continuous guidance that exists and will remain on earth. In that respect, Muḥammad is a symbol of heavenly guidance.

Following in the Prophet's footsteps is not done in blind imitation, nor by adhering to his teachings as a mere label, but by following the methodology that he represented throughout his earthly life. His way is the way of all the Prophets, that of a continuous search for the Truth, with honesty and sincerity, at all times and in any place.

The *Shahādah* Is the Cornerstone of All Revelations

While it is true that the *Shahādah*, the first pillar of Islām, distinguishes between those who follow the Primordial Religion as conveyed by Muḥammad and those who follow other Prophets, this distinction is not arbitrary. The "unifying principle" that gathers the followers of Muḥammad and the "People of the Book"[20] is the belief in the oneness of God.

> *Say: "O People of the Book! Let us acknowledge the unifying principle, between you and us: that we worship none but Allāh; that we associate no partners with Him; that we erect not, from among ourselves, Lords and patrons other than Allāh." If then they turn back, say: "Bear witness that we are Muslims (bowing to Allāh's Will)." (Qur'ān 3:64)*[21]
>
> قُلْ يَاأَهْلَ الْكِتَابِ تَعَالَوْا إِلَى كَلِمَةٍ سَوَاءٍ بَيْنَنَا وَبَيْنَكُمْ أَلَّا نَعْبُدَ إِلَّا اللَّهَ وَلَا نُشْرِكَ بِهِ شَيْئًا وَلَا يَتَّخِذَ بَعْضُنَا بَعْضًا أَرْبَابًا مِنْ دُونِ اللَّهِ فَإِنْ تَوَلَّوْا فَقُولُوا اشْهَدُوا بِأَنَّا مُسْلِمُونَ

The very belief in the oneness of Allāh leads a person, regardless of creed, to "bow to Allāh's will" and to be a Muslim at heart.

Those who follow the Primordial Religion under any name are, in fact, following the Prophets' path. The core of the *Shahādah* is the surrender to the Divine Law. What matters is not the labels given to people, but the quality o their relationship to God.

> *And there are, certainly, among the People of the Book, those who believe in Allāh, in the revelation to you, and in the revelation to them, bowing in humility to Allāh. They will not sell the Signs of Allāh for a miserable gain! For them is a reward with their Sustainer, and Allāh is swift in account. (Qur'ān 3:199)*
>
> وَإِنَّ مِنْ أَهْلِ الْكِتَابِ لَمَنْ يُؤْمِنُ بِاللَّهِ وَمَا أُنْزِلَ إِلَيْكُمْ وَمَا أُنْزِلَ إِلَيْهِمْ خَاشِعِينَ لِلَّهِ لَا يَشْتَرُونَ بِآيَاتِ اللَّهِ ثَمَنًا قَلِيلًا أُولَئِكَ لَهُمْ أَجْرُهُمْ عِنْدَ رَبِّهِمْ إِنَّ اللَّهَ سَرِيعُ الْحِسَابِ

---

[20] "People of the Book" is a term frequently used in the Holy Qur'ān to refer to Christians and Jews, in particular, and to any believers in the Divine, in general.

[21] This point is discussed in detail in Chapter Six.

The People of the Book were asked not to make a distinction between God's messengers. The Qur'ān reveals to them that Allāh took the covenant of the Prophets, in which they all agreed to believe in the message to Muḥammad and to support him.

> *Behold! Allāh took the Covenant of the Prophets, saying: "I give you a Book and Wisdom; then comes to you a Messenger, confirming what is with you; believe him and render him help." Allāh said: "Do you agree, and take this My Covenant as binding on you?" They said: "We agree." He said: "Then bear witness, and I am with you among the witnesses." (Qur'ān 3:81)*[22]
>
> وَإِذْ أَخَذَ اللَّهُ مِيثَاقَ النَّبِيِّينَ لَمَا ءَاتَيْتُكُمْ مِنْ كِتَابٍ وَحِكْمَةٍ ثُمَّ
> جَاءَكُمْ رَسُولٌ مُصَدِّقٌ لِمَا مَعَكُمْ لَتُؤْمِنُنَّ بِهِ وَلَتَنْصُرُنَّهُ قَالَ
> ءَأَقْرَرْتُمْ وَأَخَذْتُمْ عَلَى ذَلِكُمْ إِصْرِي قَالُوا أَقْرَرْنَا قَالَ فَاشْهَدُوا وَأَنَا
> مَعَكُمْ مِنَ الشَّاهِدِينَ

The implication of this verse is very helpful in enlightening our understanding of the meaning of "Muḥammad is the Messenger of God." It implies that the Prophets in Heaven were asked to follow Muḥammad, for he would confirm and perfect their Call on earth. While it is true that there is one Primordial Religion, each Prophet came to clarify part of that Religion. All revelations before Muḥammad were part of the very Revelation he carried. The followers of those Revelations share his path and, whether they declare it or not, are linked to his message.

Ash'hadu an lā ilāha illā Allāh, wa ash'hadu anna Muḥammad rasūlu Allāh. "I bear witness that there is no god but God and that Muḥammad is the Messenger of God" points to the necessity of following a direction. It is the direction of all the Prophets. Hence to witness that Muḥammad is the Messenger of God is to follow his light within the hearts enlightened by his wisdom. Those hearts are the

---

[22] In the traditional interpretation of this verse, Ibn Kathīr, Ṭabarī, and others find it difficult to understand that that covenant was held between Allāh and the Prophets, as for them those Prophets preceded the Prophet Muḥammad. They concluded that the verses refer to the followers of those Prophets.

master guides that have existed throughout the ages and throughout the world.

Thus, despite the fact that the *Shahādah* is an outward sign of the followers of Muḥammad, the *Shahādah* also represents a Way that can be followed by people from different creeds; that is, they should follow a guide. By sincerely following the way to the Truth, they follow the same journey taken by all the spiritual masters; they are, in truth, following the path of Muḥammad.

Each Part of the *Shahādah* Expresses the Same Meaning

Lā ilāha illā Allāh, Muḥammad rasūlu Allāh, "There is no god but God and Muḥammad is the Messenger of God," cannot be taken apart, as each part of this statement expresses the same meaning from a different perspective and relates to the other part. The *Shahādah* reveals a law: the oneness of God cannot be lived and experienced fully if a person does not know his direction. Muḥammad is that direction. In other words, the Originator of life and death, the Omnipresent and Unseen, the Hidden and Revealed is Allāh, while Muḥammad is the teacher of humankind, the exemplar for all, and the guide who will lead the way. Without direction, we lose our way. And without determining our goal, we cannot choose a direction. Human beings are guided to live truly by following the Prophet Muḥammad's example. Within this context, Muḥammad is not only a figure, but a symbol.

Spiritual freedom, which is achieved by experiencing the oneness of God, implies that the deeds and the orientation of a faithful one describe his inner attachment to the One God. In so doing, he is actually following the Prophet Muḥammad, who came as an exemplar of living that experience. On the other hand, to follow the Prophet Muḥammad's example is to experience the oneness of God. Following Muḥammad's Way, his *sunnah,* is to be connected to him spiritually through living the experience of the oneness of God. To witness that the Prophet is the Messenger of God is for one to revive this inner voice as he did, so that one can be linked to him.

One's inner voice is the messenger of the Sublime Source. It is the sign that Life is present within.

Those that are living and those that are dead are not equal. Allāh can make any that He wills to hear; but you cannot make those hear who are in graves. (Qur'ān 35:22)

وَمَا يَسْتَوِي الْأَحْيَاءُ وَلَا الْأَمْوَاتُ إِنَّ اللَّهَ يُسْمِعُ مَنْ يَشَاءُ وَمَا أَنْتَ بِمُسْمِعٍ مَنْ فِي الْقُبُورِ

The heavens and the earth contain Me not, but the heart of My believing servant contains Me. (HQ)[23]

ما وسعتني سمائي ولا أرضي ووسعني قلب عبدي المؤمن

The heart is the house of the Lord. (PH)[24]

القلب بيت الرب

He who knows his Self knows his Lord.[25]

من عرف نفسه عرف ربه

Without a direction, a person tends to go astray. By directing oneself to the path of the spiritual guides, taking them as exemplars and discerning their teachings, it is possible to achieve the goal and realize the aim of one's own existence; that is, one will be in harmony with the law of life, by becoming a servant of God, a Muslim, and a witness that there is no god but God and Muḥammad is His Messenger.

---

[23]Used by Al-Ghazālī in *Iḥyā' 'Ulūm ad-Dīn*.

إحياء علوم الدين

[24]This saying is commonly considered a Prophetic *Ḥadīth*. The phrasing is not exactly as above, but there are *ḥadīths* that say, *"Allāh exists in the hearts of His faithful servants" and "Allāh loves most the compassionate and tender hearts for therein He exists."* (Narrated by Ibn Mājah and Tabarānī, respectively.)

رواه ابن ماجة بلفظ: «إن لله آنية من أهل الأرض، وآنية ربكم قلوب عباده الصالحين، وأحبها إليه ألينها وأرقها.» وأخرجه الطبراني بإسناد حسن بلفظ: «إن لله أواني في أرضه وهي القلوب، فأحب الأواني إلى الله ألينها وأرقها»

[25]A wise saying documented in ancient tradition.

Al-Qiblah

Al-Qiblah[26] simply means "the direction," "the end station," or "the way." To know the *Qiblah* is to know your way, your goal, and your direction. The *Ka'bah*[27] was chosen to symbolize that direction, that way. This choice conveys a message that reveals itself, in part and with time, to people who take it as their direction.

Unified Direction

In the Holy Qur'ān, the guidance to the Prophet came as follows:

> *We see the turning of your face (for guidance) to the heavens; now shall We turn you to a Qiblah that shall please you. Turn then your face in the direction of the Sacred Mosque; wherever you are, turn your faces in that direction. The people of the Book know well that that is the truth from their Lord, nor is Allāh unmindful of what they do. (Qur'ān 2:144)*
>
> قَدْ نَرَى تَقَلُّبَ وَجْهِكَ فِي السَّمَاءِ فَلَنُوَلِّيَنَّكَ قِبْلَةً تَرْضَاهَا فَوَلِّ وَجْهَكَ شَطْرَ الْمَسْجِدِ الْحَرَامِ وَحَيْثُ مَا كُنْتُمْ فَوَلُّوا وُجُوهَكُمْ شَطْرَهُ وَإِنَّ الَّذِينَ أُوتُوا الْكِتَابَ لَيَعْلَمُونَ أَنَّهُ الْحَقُّ مِنْ رَبِّهِمْ وَمَا اللَّهُ بِغَافِلٍ عَمَّا يَعْمَلُونَ

Reflecting upon this verse, it seems that the *Qiblah* was "the direction" that provided security and serenity to the Prophet, who was turning his face to Heaven, trying to find a basis for attachment to Allāh. The Divine guidance came to support the Prophet in his search. The Sacred Mosque[28] was the chosen symbol that points to that direction.

---

[26] *Al-Qiblah* means the point to which one turns one's face. It refers to the Holy Shrine of the *Ka'bah,* to which Muslims turn their faces when performing ritual prayers.

[27] The *Ka'bah* is the holy shrine in Mecca that symbolizes the House of God on Earth.

[28] The Sacred Mosque refers to the holy shrine of the *Ka'bah.*

That choice must have been one of wisdom; it conveyed several messages to the Prophet and to his followers. Certain messages can be seen and observed directly; for example, having a common direction stresses the idea of unity among the Prophet's followers. The *Qiblah* also symbolically points to the one direction for which seekers of Truth search. There is, then, an underlying message sent to the followers of Muḥammad as well as to the whole world; that is, **regardless of their diverse affiliations, those who seek the Truth have one goal and one direction.**

The *Qiblah* is the Symbol of the One Primordial Religion

The choice of the *Ka'bah* is significant.

> *The first Home appointed for humankind was that at Bakka (Mecca); full of blessing and of guidance for all kinds of beings. In it are Signs manifest; the Station of Abraham; whoever enters it attains security; pilgrimage to it is a duty people owe to Allāh, those who can afford the journey; but if any deny faith, Allāh stands not in need of any of His creatures. (Qur'ān 3:96-97)*
>
> إِنَّ أَوَّلَ بَيْتٍ وُضِعَ لِلنَّاسِ لَلَّذِي بِبَكَّةَ مُبَارَكًا وَهُدًى لِلْعَالَمِينَ. فِيهِ ءَايَاتٌ بَيِّنَاتٌ مَقَامُ إِبْرَاهِيمَ وَمَنْ دَخَلَهُ كَانَ ءَامِنًا وَلِلَّهِ عَلَى النَّاسِ حِجُّ الْبَيْتِ مَنِ اسْتَطَاعَ إِلَيْهِ سَبِيلًا وَمَنْ كَفَرَ فَإِنَّ اللَّهَ غَنِيٌّ عَنِ الْعَالَمِينَ

> *Remember We made the House a place of assembly for men and a place of safety; and take the Station of Abraham as a place of prayer; and We made a covenant with Abraham and Ismā'īl, that they should sanctify My House for those who circle around it, or use it as a retreat, or bow, or prostrate themselves. (Qur'ān 2:125)*
>
> وَإِذْ جَعَلْنَا الْبَيْتَ مَثَابَةً لِلنَّاسِ وَأَمْنًا وَاتَّخِذُوا مِنْ مَقَامِ إِبْرَاهِيمَ مُصَلًّى وَعَهِدْنَا إِلَى إِبْرَاهِيمَ وَإِسْمَاعِيلَ أَنْ طَهِّرَا بَيْتِيَ لِلطَّائِفِينَ

وَالْعَاكِفِينَ وَالرُّكَّعِ السُّجُودِ

And remember Abraham and Ismā'īl raised the foundations of the House (with this prayer): "Our Lord! Accept this service from us: for You are the All-Hearing, the All-Knowing." (Qur'ān 2:127)

وَإِذْ يَرْفَعُ إِبْرَاهِيمُ الْقَوَاعِدَ مِنَ الْبَيْتِ وَإِسْمَاعِيلُ رَبَّنَا تَقَبَّلْ مِنَّا إِنَّكَ أَنْتَ السَّمِيعُ الْعَلِيمُ

From these verses, we know that this House is related to Abraham, who was commanded by the Divine to lay its foundations and purify it. Because Muḥammad's Call is the revival of Abraham's, to take this House as the *Qiblah* is a symbolic way of linking the one Call of the Primordial Religion that Muḥammad conveyed and that which was brought by Abraham, which itself revived the path of Adam and Noah. Certainly "the House" does not refer to a building; rather, it was used metaphorically to point to the message of Abraham, to the Primordial Religion. Abraham represents the authentic Call as part of which Moses and Jesus came with their messages. Reviving the path of Abraham through the Revelation to the Prophet Muḥammad was meant to remind people of the authenticity of this path.[29] The *Qiblah* is a symbol that represents a constant reminder of that path.[30]

The *Baytullāh,* the house of God, is a concept that suggests impersonalized Divine guidance. For Muḥammad's followers, *Baytullāh* is a symbol of Muḥammad's message. Yet that message did

[29]That oneness of the authentic path is expressed symbolically in the teachings of Jesus, in his conversation with those who claimed to be believers in Abraham, but could not discern that Jesus revealed the same truth that Abraham did: *"Your father Abraham rejoiced to see my day: and he saw it, and was glad." Then said the Jews unto him, "You are not yet fifty years old, and have you seen Abraham?" Jesus said unto them, "Truly, truly, I say unto you, before Abraham was, I am." (John 8:56-58)* The Prophet Muḥammad asserted that truth when saying, *"I was a Prophet at the time that Adam was in a middle stage between spirit and matter."* (A *ḥadīth* documented by Tirmidhī.)

كنت نبيا وآدم بين الروح والجسد

[30]The relationship between the call of Abraham and that of Muḥammad is examined in Chapter Two.

not come exclusively to those who follow the rites as they were revealed to Muḥammad; this message is a universal one, in the sense that it reveals the authentic unity among the messengers of Allāh. As mentioned in the discussion of the *Shahādah*, "the Messenger of God" is an abstract concept connected to the Divine message on earth, which was carried out by all spiritual teachers. The emphasis on directing oneself to the *Qiblah*, the *Baytullāh*, is a constant assurance that the Divine message is on earth and that there are master guides to convey that message.

The *Qiblah*, then, is an abstract concept expressed symbolically by *Baytullāh*; it is the common orientation that can gather the whole world together, transforming it into a big family. Expressing the Divine Call through the *Baytullāh* provides the seekers of Truth worldwide with a sense of intimacy and connection. The *Qiblah*, as revealed to Muḥammad, addresses not only those who follow his creed, but calls on the whole world to unify their direction by making the Truth their goal. At the same time, the choice of a certain place to represent that direction does not give that place, that concrete building, a sacred dimension; it is the underlying message which is sacred. That is, seekers of Truth should search for a Divine source of light by following master guides who appear in various places on earth and in diverse cultures to serve the same primordial message. Even if a person does not meet one of the teachers of humanity, he is assured that the source of light on earth will reach him. Having a metaphorical place for this spiritual force conveys that message permanently.

In short, followers of Muḥammad unify their direction by making the *Ka'bah* their focus—that is, their *Qiblah*. Believers also can interact with this symbol by taking the Prophet as their master guide and observing him as manifest within those spiritual teachers who represent his continuous existence. By allowing oneself the opportunity to attain the knowledge of the heart, one revives one's very inner being and knows that within one's small existence lies the ultimate reality. As such, believers have one direction, the *Qiblah*, as a symbol of the Divine Truth. Metaphorically, this is a central point on earth that identifies the permanent existence of the Divine Light. By introducing the concept of the *Qiblah*, the teachings of the Prophet demonstrate that all revelations have one goal.

Summary

Islām as revealed to the Prophet Muḥammad introduced key concepts that elucidate the basis of the one Primordial Religion that was expressed gradually through all revelations. Those concepts constitute the guidance that can help humanity for generations to come. In reading the teachings of Islām, certain concepts are revealed, some of which were included in this chapter.

First, surrender to the Divine Order is a goal that is sought by people who have faith in the Unseen Transcendental Invisible Power, *al-Ghayb*. Faith in the Unseen directly affects our approach to ourself and the ultimate goal of our life. It is a faith that liberates us from the prison of whatever is transient or limited, from stagnation and dogma. Faith in *al-Ghayb* leads us to experience ourself as spirit, to discern the divinity within. That is what, in Islām, the word *"fiṭrah"* refers to. *Fiṭrah* is the Divine Law as manifested in the very existence of man. The Revelation to Muḥammad clarifies that our ability to know the Law is expanding and the more we know, the more we realize that we still do not know. Yet our search to know more will continue. It is because of *fiṭrah* that man deserves to be God's representative.

Second, Islām defines man as God's representative, referring to the fact that the divinity within allows one to make of the earthly journey a means of spiritual growth. It is that divinity that makes one reach the rank of a servant of God. Because man is endowed with a working will, he can either go the way of spiritual growth, achieving the potential for which man was created, or he can deviate from that path and go to the abyss of annihilation.

Third, the way of spiritual growth and salvation may be achieved through two interrelated and interdependent processes; that is, there must be a continuous struggle to keep the faith in the One Supreme God and one should follow the guidance of those who have realized that goal. The *Shahādah* expresses those processes. "There is no god but God, and Muḥammad is the Messenger of God" is not a statement to be uttered by the tongue alone; it is a way of life which all revelations guide man to fulfill. The first part of the *Shahādah*, "there is no god but God," implies a Call to man to liberate himself from any illusions. For us to do that, we need to go through the journey of liberation from the limitations of matter, with all its repercussions. Along that journey, we need the support of a higher source; herein lies the significance of the second part of the *Shahādah*, "Muḥammad is the Messenger of God." It does not refer to Muḥammad as a mere person, but as a symbol of the truth manifested in all the Prophets. It is because of that truth that the Revelation to Muḥammad mandated, as part of the belief in Muḥammad, that his followers should express faith in all the preceding Prophets. It is implicit that one who really wants to surrender to God would not refrain from receiving His Light as manifested in enlightened and enlightening people.

That oneness of Light is expressed in the **fourth** concept, the *Qiblah*. When directing Muslims to turn their faces towards the *Ka'bah*, the holy shrine that symbolizes the *Baytullāh*, "the House of God" that the Prophet Abraham founded, the Revelation to the Prophet Muḥammad pointed to the oneness of the Prophets as manifestations of Light. Among other things, the *Qiblah* points to that oneness. Everyone needs to learn how to have a direction and a focus. That process is essential to live a well-balanced life and to be saved. By guiding people to turn their faces in the one direction, revelations support us in achieving our ultimate goal. If we succeed in focusing, we will be attached to Light as manifested in a higher source of guidance. The *Qiblah* as such is not a place and is not confined to rites. It is a concept that reminds man of his direction on earth. Hence even followers of other revelations, who do not direct their prayers in the direction of the *Ka'bah* because of their own rites, are still following the same *Qiblah* if they face the Light of God that has always been there and will always exist. They would thus be surrendering to the Law, and be Muslims at heart, regardless of their religious affiliation.

These concepts form the basis on which the spiritual training system is founded. They also form the main principles that guide us to live on earth, where we are compelled to interact with nature and with our fellow human beings, as the following chapters will explain.

4
The Spiritual Training System

The basic "chain concepts," discussed in the previous chapter, form the basis on which the system of spiritual training (commonly known as rituals) was founded. Prayers (*Ṣalāt*), Fasting (*Ṣawm*), Alms-giving (*Zakāt*), and Pilgrimage (*Ḥajj*), together with the Testimony (*Shahādah*) of *Lā ilāha illā Allāh, Muḥammad rasūlu Allāh,* are called the five pillars of Islām. They share the fact that they train us to experience ourselves as spirit and not to over-indulge in earthly desires. They are rich in symbols, which unveil themselves continuously to those who practice the system with dedication and work to enlighten their hearts.

While the concepts underlying these rituals exist in all revelations,[1] Islam as revealed to the Prophet Muḥammad (Peace be upon him) revives these primordial concepts through a comprehensive system that echoes in human life in a wonderful way. This system continuously nurtures the human spirit and can make our whole life spiritually fruitful. They follow the natural order, *fiṭrah,* because they are arranged according to the cosmological order, and because they respond to our spiritual needs in a practical way.

While the *Shahādah*[2] is first among these pillars, the other four pillars actively represent the *Shahādah,* which, in essence, is both a point of departure and the ultimate goal for any person who seeks the truth and wants to be on the straight path.

A seeker of truth is not satisfied with uttering the words, nor even with believing in them, but looks forward to "living" them. The worship system that the Divine taught the Prophet Muḥammad

---

[1]This point is researched in the authors' book: *Beyond Diversities: Reflection on Revelations.*

[2]This concept is explained in detail in Chapter Three.

and commanded him to teach to his followers supports man in that endeavor. Each pillar has a place in the structure as a whole and the structure is not complete without the four other pillars.

In examining the pillars, we must distinguish between the main concepts (namely, how to surrender to Allāh, to live the *Shahādah,* to be on the straight path, oriented toward the *Qiblah,* and to be the servant of Allāh and His representative, His *khalifāh,* and artificially imposed, goals, and quests for meanings. People mistakenly think that the ultimate goal is the achievement of the pillars. Hence they focus on the form rather than the meaning. The meanings can only be grasped if the previously discussed key concepts are the basis on which these pillars are practiced. The Islamic pillars are also taken as a framework for distinguishing cultural identities. That was not the reason for which they were established. They were not meant to serve any political goals; nor did they set up a framework to isolate the Muslim from his fellow human beings in different cultures.

The pillars of Islam are symbolically performed according to Muḥammad's guidance. He taught them to Muslims upon receiving the Divine's guidance through Revelation. In essence, the pillars were introduced as symbolic reminders that reawaken our consciousness when we risk forgetting our ancient covenant with Allāh. Each symbol explains the others and each of them says the same thing in a different way. They all confirm that there is one Truth, one God, one Goal, and one Religion.

The Messenger of Allāh has come to guide humanity to achieve the intended goal; that is, to surrender to the Divine Order. Harmony is another word that explains how to surrender; it is in the nature of things because everything is in complete surrender to Allāh's Will.

> *Do you not see that to Allāh bow down in worship all things that are in the heavens and on earth, the sun, the moon, the stars, the hills, the trees, the animals? (Qur'ān 22:18)*
>
> أَلَمْ تَرَ أَنَّ اللَّهَ يَسْجُدُ لَهُ مَنْ فِي السَّمَوَاتِ وَمَنْ فِي الْأَرْضِ
> وَالشَّمْسُ وَالْقَمَرُ وَالنُّجُومُ وَالْجِبَالُ وَالشَّجَرُ وَالدَّوَابُّ
>
> *Whatever is in the heavens and on earth declares the praises*

and glory of Allāh: to Him belongs dominion, and to Him belongs praise. (Qur'ān 64:1)

يُسَبِّحُ لِلَّهِ مَا فِي السَّمَوَاتِ وَمَا فِي الْأَرْضِ لَهُ الْمُلْكُ وَلَهُ الْحَمْدُ

Because man is given a will and a choice, he needs to struggle within himself in order not to hurt himself through ignorance of the Law of Life. He needs to know how to link himself to his origin in order to be in harmony with the Divine Law. The *Shahādah,* which is expressed by various tools through the remaining four pillars, is meant to attune man to be in harmony with the Divine Law. That is the only way that he can be spiritually alive and gradually achieve being *'abdullāh* (the servant of God).

Without awareness of the limitations of living on earth, we risk indulging ourselves indefinitely in fulfilling our earthly requirements and succumbing to our growing desires. Consequently, we may forget our real mission on earth, why we are here, and where we are going. We thus risk throwing ourselves in the abyss of spiritual death.

Each of the pillars has its parallels in other revelations. The beauty of the pillars lies in the fact that they echo in our lives in a purposeful order and interrupt the flow of temporal life according to a certain system. In the Revelation to Muḥammad, that interruption is meant to remind people of the core reason of their existence and to make their lives a continuous communication with Allāh. In fact, every aspect of worship is a means of exposing us to God's grace and blessings, which nurture us and lead to spiritual growth. They also purify our souls and help us manage our daily life with proper perspective.

Your Lord makes His Graces available during certain times. So, let yourselves be exposed to them. (PH)[3]

إن لربكم في أيام دهركم لنفحات ألا فتعرضوا لها.

[3]Narrated by]Ṭabarānī.

Aṣ-Ṣalāt (Ritual Prayers)

Prayers are known in all revelations as the means of purification and an expression of man's longing for his Originator. The symbolic significance of the timing and movements of prayers as assigned in Islām, as well as the impact of prayer on man's life, are discussed in this section.

Intention

Expressing "intention" is an essential part of the Prayers and the starting point of the ritual. The intention points to a degree of inner will and to the understanding that a person needs spiritual power from a higher source and asks for it. This intention is emphasized by the preparatory ablution. In this process, we are not only washing the body to become physically clean; we are washing away the dirt that directly or indirectly defiles our souls through our interaction with the world. In this way, we prepare to be in the presence of the Holy in a clean-hearted and open-minded way.

Once we stand, directing ourselves to the *Qiblah*, we declare our intention with words. "God is Greater," *Allāhu Akbar*, is the phrase that announces that we have started our Prayers. *Allāhu Akbar* is also the first statement in the call to Prayer that is traditionally pronounced by the *mu'ādhdhin*, the person who calls to Prayer. *Allāhu Akbar* is a reminder that Allāh is beyond and above, transcendental and unseen. Thus, regardless of the extent to which we achieve being one with the Divine, Allāh is always greater.

The Significance of the Timing of Ritual Prayers

Worship is known in all revelations as a means of purification and as an appeal from the human being to his Originator.[4] The specific times of worship in Islam were part of the Divine Revelation. The teachings to Muḥammad recommended that people should per-

[4]Jesus told his disciples to pray all the time, but did not specify a certain time for ritual prayer. However, his followers were inspired to specify certain times for their regular prayers.

form Prayers at certain times during the day. Those times are defined by the earth's daily revolution around its axis and its path around the sun. The human being was assigned to worship five times a day. The first Prayer is to be performed between dawn and sunrise, the second one between noon and mid-afternoon, the third between mid-afternoon and sunset, the fourth between sunset and the complete absence of the light of the sun from the sky and the last Prayer is to take place between the moment the sky becomes completely dark and dawn. It is recommended to pray at those times and not to postpone a Prayer deliberately. However, if one fails to pray at the assigned time for one reason or another, one can pray as soon as it is possible. Therefore, there is a continuous reminder throughout the day that prompts man's attention to make Allāh his direction, to be close to Him, remember Him, and call for Him.

The Prayers also harmonize man's earthly activities with his relationship with Allāh. One of the messages seen in the order designed for the believer to follow is the fact that the interruption of the flow of life throughout the day is meant to transform one's whole life into a way of becoming closer to Allāh. When we finish our assigned Prayers, we return to our ordinary life with a fresh spirit, now that we have reminded ourselves of our attachment to Allāh. If we were angry before the Prayers, our anger has faded. If we intended to take revenge on someone, we now reconsider this plan. In the long run, Prayers develop within us an approach to life on earth that is continuously drawing us closer to our Lord. During a person's lifetime, one may notice changes in the way one sets priorities, copes with problems, treats others, etc. As a matter of fact, these changes are the criteria by which one can discern between those who simply act as if they are praying and those who truly seek Divine support through Prayer.

> *. . . and establish Prayer, for Prayer restrains from shameful and unjust deeds, and remembrance of Allāh is the greatest without doubt.* (*Qur'ān 29:45*)
>
> وَأَقِمِ الصَّلَاةَ إِنَّ الصَّلَاةَ تَنْهَى عَنِ الْفَحْشَاءِ وَالْمُنْكَرِ وَلَذِكْرُ اللَّهِ أَكْبَرُ

If a person's Prayer does not take him far from atrocity, he gets further and further from God. (PH)[5]

من لم تنهه صلاته عن الفحشاء والمنكر لم يزدد بصلاته من الله إلا بعدا

Prayers, then, link man's worldly activities and his innate desire to be attached to his Lord. There is no contradiction between the two realms; harmony prevails. In this way, we will learn the meaning of surrender to Allāh existentially, for we are never remote from our Lord. Our calls for our Lord are not limited to the time of prayer, as we come to consider all our deeds as means to bring us closer to the Divine. We will also listen to Him as events occur. When we are trained to be with our Lord at times scattered throughout the day, our inner hearing improves and our inner sight becomes stronger. Once we return to ordinary life, we listen to the messages and read the Signs of the Lord. We can then learn not only scientific knowledge, but also knowledge of the heart.

Arranged according to cosmological order, Prayers draw our attention to the magnificent creation of the universe. We tend to forget that our own existence is a miracle; observing the coming of day and night and the passing of time can create a sense of reverence and open the heart to praise the Almighty. Praying at different times of the day can also unveil some of the symbols revealed to us during the day. With the beginning of the day, when the sun is just on the horizon, man remembers Allāh. The sun symbolizes the Truth that is hidden and then reveals itself to the hearts of believers. Out of mercy, the revelation is accomplished gradually over time, and throughout this unfolding, man should not stop calling his Lord. When the world is full of light and the sun is in the middle of the sky, our eyes cannot look directly at it, but the presence of the light guides our steps. Allāh is the Light of heaven and earth; we should remember His presence as Light as we pray. That the light later fades and then disappears altogether should not stop us

[5]Narrated by Ṭabarānī, as quoted in *Al-Jāmi'Aṣ-Ṣaghīr Li's-Suyū textsubdottī.*

الطبراني في الجامع الصغير للسيوطي

from praying. Even in darkness, we have to remember Allāh whose Light should fill our hearts. In this way, we look for His Light to fill our souls and be reflected in our hearts; thus the sun will never disappear. By God's Grace, we escape darkness to the Light.

The Significance of What Should Be Said and Done

In the Islamic teachings, prayers include hidden spiritual treasures that are revealed by practicing them with dedication. The general meaning of the gestures and movements in Islamic prayer also provides teachings that can be studied and communicated with those who do not follow the same spiritual training system. Each movement has its parallel in man's life.

A *Rak'āh* is a set of movements and a unit that defines the duration of a prayer. For example, the morning prayer consists of two *Rak'āhs*, the Noon prayer consists of four *Rak'āhs*, etc.

Reciting the Fātiḥah

The followers of the Prophet Muḥammad are guided as to what to say and do when performing ritual prayers. Reciting the *Fātiḥah*, the opening *sūrah* of the Holy Qur'ān, is an essential part of the ritual prayers. In this *sūrah* we learn how to address Allāh in His own words. We praise Him as the Lord of all the Worlds, the overpowering Truth on the Day of Judgment. From Him we obtain support and to Him we surrender. We ask Him for guidance so that we can be on the straight path. This is the only *sūrah* in which the initial phrase "In the Name of Allāh, the Most Merciful and the Most Compassionate" is counted as part of the *sūrah*.[6] Addressing Allāh

[6]In the Holy Qur'ān, every *sūrah* (except *Sūrah* 9, *At-Tawbah*) begins with the verse "In the Name of Allāh, the Most Merciful and the Most Compassionate," but this verse is not numbered. *Fātiḥah* contains seven verses, and "In the Name of Allāh, the Most Merciful and the Most Compassionate" is the first and is numbered (here and only here). The Holy Qur'ān refers to *Fātiḥah* with these words to the Prophet:

> *And We have bestowed upon you the seven oft-repeated (verses) and the Exalted Qur'ān. (Qur'ān 15:87)*
>
> وَلَقَدْ ءَاتَيْنَاكَ سَبْعًا مِنَ الْمَثَانِي وَالْقُرْءَانَ الْعَظِيمَ

in His own words helps to remove the false barriers that stand in the way to Allāh. It is the Divine within us that addresses Allāh the Greatest. By feeling this attachment to the Almighty Allāh, the process of inner transformation can take place.

Reciting *Fātiḥah* is an essential part of prayer. A Muslim recites this *sūrah* while standing upright, the first posture in the prayer. One can extend this posture by reciting more verses from the Holy Qur'ān after *Fātiḥah*, following the Prophet's way of praying.[7]

The *Fātiḥah*, which means "the opening," allows the heart to recite God's words. We recite *Fātiḥah* and other verses of the Holy Qur'ān in a standing position, directing ourselves to the *Qiblah*. We visualize the *Qiblah* in the symbolic form of the *Ka'bah*. This visualization helps us create the condition whereby we know that we are following the path of Abraham and Muḥammad; in other words, the path of Divine Guidance.[8] Interacting with the Almighty by reciting *Fātiḥah* is another way to witness that there is no god but God. The presence of the Divine makes our limited existence vanish.

The Significance of the Rak'āh

The first posture in which we recite *Fātiḥah* is that of standing straight. This posture resembles the number one. It is where we begin; all our existence is directed toward Allāh.

Having finished reciting *Fātiḥah*, we may continue with another verse(s) or *sūrah*, following the Prophet's *Sunnah*, and then bowing. In this second position in the *Rak'āh*, the upper part of the body forms a ninety-degree angle with the lower part of the body. The head as symbol of the mind and the chest as symbol of the heart become points on the same line parallel to the ground. The mind and heart both express their subordination to Allāh the Greatest. The *Sunnah* of the Prophet expresses that meaning clearly, for during this posture he said, "O my Lord, the Greatest" *Subhāna Rabbiya al-*

---

[7]The Prophet would recite further holy verses after *Fātiḥah*; Muslims follow his way (*Sunnah*) voluntarily. However, if a Muslim recites *Fātiḥah* only, he is still in full accordance with the Divine teaching.

[8]See the meaning of *Qiblah* in Chapter Three.

'Azīm. We stand once more to prepare ourselves for the last posture in the *Rak'āh*. The Prophet used to say, during this brief interval, "Allāh listens to those who praise Him," and then, "Our Lord, You we praise and You we thank," before prostrating.

The last posture, *Sujūd*, "prostration," is a way to express immense gratefulness to Allāh and complete surrender to Him. Now the head is on the floor and the heart above. Here the heart takes the lead. Following the Prophet's *Sunnah* we say, "O my Lord, the Highest," *Subhāna Rabbiya al-'Alā*. Having reached that zenith, man stands up to perform another set of movements, *Rak'āh*. It is common practice after every two *Rak'āhs* to sit on the floor in a special posture and recite what is called the *Tahiyyāt*. A person who prays visualizes that he is in the presence of the Prophet; he salutes him and prays for him. This particular action emphasizes the meaning of "Muḥammad is the Messenger of God": he is the leader of the way; he is the human *Qiblah*. The Prayer ends when one turns one's head to the right and then to the left, saying: *as-salāmu 'alaykum wa raḥmatullāhi wa barakatuhu*, "Peace be upon you as well as the mercy and blessings of Allāh." In ending his prayer a worshiper gives salutations to the heavenly presence in whose company he was and returns to practical life.

The dawn prayer consists of two *Rak'āhs*, while the noon, mid-afternoon, and night prayers are four *Rak'āhs*. The sunset prayer consists of three *Rak'āhs*.

The Significance of Prayer in Our Lives

Each movement we make and each word we utter during prayer corresponds to certain meanings that we cherish in our life. They express several positions and attitudes of which we should be aware.

Directing ourselves to the House of Allāh represents our attitude in life, whereby we are clear about where we are going. One should sail through the earthly journey, knowing one's way, not drifting astray.[9]

Bowing during prayer and declaring that "Allāh is Greater" can be made into an overall attitude towards life. This awareness pro-

[9]This is the core meaning of *Qiblah* as examined in detail in Chapter Three.

tects one from giving an absolute value to the ephemeral life. Happiness or misery, strength or weakness, wealth or poverty are not to be sought or avoided for their own sake. What we pass through in our lives should be evaluated in relation to the deep faith that Allāh is beyond all that merely happens. In other words, any worldly goals should be considered in relation to spiritual goals. That can be accomplished only when we are profoundly confident that Allāh is Greater. This training system is a means of preparing us for complete surrender to Allāh. This preparation is also apparent when we remind ourselves to praise Allāh, for "He listens to those who praise Him." Those who praise Him can see beyond pain or pleasure; they are grateful to Allāh for their very being. The culmination of a *Rak'āh* is when we prostrate; in our life this means complete surrender to Allāh and complete freedom. If we succeed in surrendering fully, we will be tools in the hands of the Supreme, continuously trying to act out of the wisdom of the heart, not the illusions of the lower self. The Prophet guided people to consult the heart as a primary source of guidance; it is a symbol of the divine guidance within. Once we surrender truly to Allāh, the divine guidance, the inner messenger, will awaken. It is a culmination in the sense that it shows complete surrender to Allāh, whereby one's heart rules over one's entire existence.

Az-Zakāt (Alms-giving)

Zakāt is the third pillar of Islām. It is difficult to translate the word or to find a synonym in English. The word is derived from the root *z-k-a*; the verbal form is *zakka*, which means "to purify" and also "to make something grow and develop." *Zakāt* is traditionally rendered as "alms giving." This translation is inaccurate, however, if we consider the philosophy behind this pillar. There is a difference between alms-giving, *ṣadaqa*, and *Zakāt*. *Ṣadaqa* is a "voluntary service" of any kind, given from one person to another. The Prophet Muḥammad encourages everyone to give *ṣadaqa*. A smile, words of sympathy, half of a date can be *ṣadaqa*. *Zakāt*, on the other hand, is an assigned amount of money or crops to be paid to the community.[10] *Zakāt* is not a tax system whereby everyone pays in return for public services provided by the government. Nor is it a system of social insurance whereby the rich guarantee services in case of an emergency.

The community has the right to take this percentage of money or crops from all its members; it is then used to support the less privileged among them. In this sense, the person who pays *Zakāt* gives the needy "their rights":

> *And in their wealth and possessions (was remembered) the right of him who asks (the needy), and him who is deprived. (Qur'ān 51:19)*[11]
>
> وَفِي أَمْوَالِهِمْ حَقٌّ لِلسَّائِلِ وَالْمَحْرُومِ

The philosophy behind this act has multiple dimensions. *Zakāt* considers that rich people's properties are not absolutely theirs. Unless they pay the rights of the poor, they are considered transgressors. *Zakāt* is also a yearly reminder of the fact that what we earn and what we have are not really ours, but are a gift from God. With this gift come certain responsibilities. Because what we have is ours legally and socially, we are prone to become attached to what we have and thus to forget that we are merely passing through this temporal life. *Zakāt* emphasizes that fact indirectly. Awareness of that dimension protects an individual from feeling superior, and raises his feelings of responsibility towards others. Furthermore, it makes him acutely conscious of how he uses, in the interest of all, what is seemingly his own property.

To witness that there is no God but God through *Zakāt* has a specific sense. *Zakāt* makes us aware of the Origin of All. To awaken our souls to that reality, we remove false barriers and feel how much we belong to one another, because we belong to Allāh. In this process, our ego melts and diminishes. We realize that it is God who gives through us and that every one of us is a medium, a messenger

---

[10] *Zakāt* amounts to 2.5% of savings, 1/10 of crops watered by rains or natural wells and 1/20 of those irrigated by using water wheels or any other machine. The owner of the crops should deduct all expenses before calculating the sum of money to be paid as *Zakāt*.

[11] Our translation.

from Allāh. We are one with Muḥammad, the Messenger of Allāh; he is the symbolic expression of our oneness.

Zakāt removes our social identity and highlights the spirit as the core of our existence. It is no coincidence that *Zakāt* is derived from the verb "to purify." Elevating ourselves to a higher, abstract level means that we are abandoning our egoism. This is an act of purification. What defiles us is our lower self, with its power to pull us down and drag us into the abyss of pride and arrogance.

Zakāt is the way that a person becomes a channel through which Allāh reaches the needy; it is accomplished, therefore, if one is connected to the higher source. It is not merely an act of giving, but a kind of prayer. No wonder, then, that in most verses that mention Prayers, *Ṣalāt*, *Zakāt* follows. The message to the entire world is to open ourselves to be channels for love. That is only possible when the individual is truly aware that he belongs to Allāh alone. Consequently, what he owns here in this world is but a mirage.

While *Zakāt* is mainly a purifying ritual, it has social and economic impact. The feelings of belonging to one another and to the Supreme in a community creates an attitude of self-observation whereby the interest of the whole takes precedence over mere individual interests. This can lead to economic prosperity and the alleviation of poverty, without government interference to limit the growth of individual property. People whose thoughts are directed to what is best for the whole community are likely to invest rather than to set their money aside. The more they earn, the more they think of how to support and invest.[12]

Ṣawm Ramaḍān (Fasting during the Holy Month)

Fasting during the month of *Ramaḍān* is the fourth pillar. Traditionally, during *Ramaḍān* a Muslim refrains from all his worldly desires (eating, drinking, etc.) from dawn until sunset. He is advised to increase, as much as possible, his prayers, meditation time, and reading of the Holy Qur'ān.

[12] In the time of the Caliph 'Umar ibn 'Abd al-'Azīz, the Muslim population was prosperous, to the extent that there were no citizens who were in need of receiving *Zakāt*. As a result, the caliph proposed to support poor people in other countries.

As it is a lunar month, the beginning of *Ramaḍān* is set according to the appearance of the crescent moon. The wording of the Holy Qur'ān states this requirement in an inspiring way:

> *Those of you who witness the month (ash-shahr) should spend it in fasting. (Qur'ān 2:185)*[13]
>
> فَمَنْ شَهِدَ مِنْكُمُ الشَّهْرَ فَلْيَصُمْهُ

Reflecting upon this verse, one can say that those who "witness" the beginning of the month truly know their goal.

Fasting Is a Tool of Purification

The goal of fasting is not to torture the body, nor to scorn physical desire, but to provide the opportunity to experience oneself as spirit. Clearly, fasting is not merely the deprivation of bodily pleasures, as one can enjoy these pleasures after breaking the fast. The "intention" of renouncing these pleasures for a fixed amount of time, which is also part of the ritual, implies that one seeks purification and preparation for God's graces. When the body enters the state of hunger, the spirit takes over and begins to ask for nourishment through the means of God's remembrance, *Dhikrullāh*. Fasting is a condensed form of spiritual training.

This spiritual experience is granted to man once every year. During certain hours of the day, when we forgo all earthly desires, we opens channels for heavenly connection. We have the opportunity of an immense spiritual transformation that cannot be counted or measured.

Fasting is a type of training, the basis of which is to give man will, power, and control over desires, and the culmination of which is to witness the oneness of God through the awakening of the divinity within. It provides an interlude during which the mind can reflect, the will can become stronger, and the heart can flourish. If we achieve the required purification and provide the opportunity for the spirit to take over, we experience the divine link that ties us to our Origin and ties all human beings in a sacred bond. With that

[13] Transliteration, between brackets, is added by the authors.

awakening, we open ourselves to the Grace of Allāh, which cannot be counted or expected. In one of the *Ḥadīth Qudsī* we read,

> *Every work of a child of Adam is counted for him, except fasting. It is for Me and I reward for it. (HQ)*[14]
>
> «كل عمل ابن آدم له إلا الصوم فإنه لي وأنا أجزي به»
>
> *Whoever fasts during Ramaḍān, devoting himself to Allāh, his sins will be forgiven and he will become as pure as a newborn. (PH)*[15]
>
> «من صام رمضان إيمانا واحتسابا غفر له ما تقدم من ذنبه»

Ramaḍān is called the Gracious and Blessed Month, *ash-Shahr al-Karīm al-Mubārak*. The spiritual gains to be achieved far exceed the struggle through which we go. The Night of God's Grace, *Laylat al-Qadr,* is the metaphoric expression describing the rewards which cannot be measured or counted.[16]

> *We have indeed revealed this (Message) in the Night of God's Grace. And what will explain to you what the Night of God's Grace is? The Night of God's Grace is better than a thousand months. Therein come down the angels and the Spirit by Allāh's permission, on every errand. Peace! This until the rise of Morn! (Qur'ān 97:1-5)*[17]
>
> إِنَّا أَنْزَلْنَاهُ فِي لَيْلَةِ الْقَدْرِ، وَمَا أَدْرَاكَ مَا لَيْلَةُ الْقَدْرِ، لَيْلَةُ الْقَدْرِ خَيْرٌ مِنْ أَلْفِ شَهْرٍ، تَنَزَّلُ الْمَلَائِكَةُ وَالرُّوحُ فِيهَا بِإِذْنِ رَبِّهِمْ مِنْ كُلِّ أَمْرٍ، سَلَامٌ هِيَ حَتَّى مَطْلَعِ الْفَجْرِ

[14]Narrated by Bukhārī, Muslim, Ibn Majāh and Aḥmad.

[15]Narrated by Bukhārī and Muslim.

[16]We translate *Laylat al-Qadr* as "the Night of God's Grace," not "the Night of Power" as most translations do. That is because *al-Qadr* means, among other things, the "rank" or "value" of something. On that night, God rewarded the Prophet with the Revelation which had unlimited blessing. The "measure" according to which Allāh gives is beyond our understanding. God's Mercy is unlimited. "The value," *Qadr,* of His blessing is beyond reckoning. Hence the night when He gives according to His bounty and His gift cannot be known or speculated. His gift is a grace and a blessing.

[17]Our translation.

Muḥammad as an Exemplar opened the door of Mercy for his followers; Allāh's blessing awaits them if they devote themselves to Allāh under his guidance. This blessing is expressed metaphorically by "the Night of God's Grace." Those who struggle within their soul to experience the closeness to God will reap the fruit of this struggle, not according to their calculation, but according to God's generosity. The very word "night" shows that man is incubated in darkness, waiting for blessing. Out of this darkness, the eternal Light of Allāh shines from within one's heart. This is not an unanticipated event; man prepares for this moment throughout the month. It is no coincidence that one is advised to expect the Night of God's Grace, *Laylat al-Qadr*, in the last ten days of the month, as the first twenty days constitute the incubation period for the immature being to nourish his very core of existence, his heart.

Sympathizing with the needy as a result of experiencing their pain does not stop with the end of the fast, but remains, due to the discovery of man's inner link as spirit enclosed in matter. The spiritual gains may exceed all one's expectations.

Revelations came from heaven to the Prophets while they were fasting. Moses, Jesus, and Muḥammad all went through this experience. None fasted in anticipation of a specific outcome. They fasted in order to meditate properly, think clearly, and purify themselves from worldly defilement. They may have chosen to fast because they were passing through a spiritual stage in which they rejected things that bound them to earth, but regardless of their motivations, of which we cannot be certain, they prepared themselves spiritually through purification and received God's Grace in a way that they did not expect. It is God's Mercy to show us human beings how to prepare for His Grace.

The Significance of Fasting According to a Specific Pattern

Other revelations guide man to purification through fasting in different ways, all of which support man in feeling himself as spirit. The Revelation to Muḥammad organizes the method of fasting in a way that is within man's capabilities. By disciplining the body with hunger, the maximum benefit of fasting may be achieved. The goal is to get closer to Allāh. The intention of using this tool to achieve such a sublime goal is what makes man experience spiritual elevation, which can be heightened in meditation and prayers.

In other fasting systems, the hours of fasting are counted and they may lead to a similar kind of spiritual elevation. However, the system of fasting revealed to the Prophet Muḥammad expresses the beautiful relationship between man and the natural order directly and clearly. Fasting is related to the movement of the earth around its axis and around the sun. During periods of light, our body is elevated by its deprivation from desire. We return to our normal, earthly desires during periods of dark, after sunset. Like the relation between the earth and the sun, our spiritual training is meant to allow us to absorb the light when the truth (symbolized by the sun) is shining, while the opaque nature of the earth (our own opaque nature) reflects that light during darkness. We should be aware of the source of light, awaiting its return, when it will feed us once more.

Because *Ramaḍān* is a lunar month, its time changes according to the solar years, so that it may take place during hot, cold, or mild seasons. We thus experience fasting at different periods of time. At times one gets more thirsty than hungry, while at others one gets more hungry than thirsty, etc. Regardless of the body's complaints, we are asked to awaken the divine within through prayer and meditation. Out of the pain of hunger and thirst, the quest for transcendence increases.

The Significance of Increasing Night Prayers during *Ramaḍān*

Because *Ramaḍān* is a month that maximizes our spiritual potential, we must devote ourselves to Allāh at all times. In the midst of darkness, prayers are extended, following the tradition of the Prophet's *Sunnah*. During *Ramaḍān*, it is recommended that a special prayer be performed following the regular night Prayer. This signifies that even though food, drink, and other desires of the body are allowed, we should not be completely indulgent. In other words, being guided to perform more prayers at night during *Ramaḍān* is a symbol of man's awareness of the need for spiritual support in the heart of darkness. Without that support, physical desires could be overwhelming.

Control of our desires continues even after we are permitted to break the fast. By the end of the month, we acquire the capacity to be in control of our lives. However, the spiritual strength we gain during this month may weaken and fade with time, as a result of the factors in our earthly lives that pull us downwards; the recurrence of *Ramaḍān* saves us from falling too deeply into the layers of darkness.

Fasting during *Ramaḍān* with the intention of getting closer to Allāh can change our lives completely; we open ourselves to a great transformation from earthly mud to the realm of light.

Ḥajj (Pilgrimage)

Pilgrimage, *Ḥajj*, is a journey, as is our life on earth. Where are we heading in life? We may go astray, lose focus, or forget our mission. Pilgrimage is a reminder. To Allāh we return after this journey on earth and to Allāh we should return during this life. Without a continuous awareness of the Divine, we are lost.

When we intend to return (repent) to the Originator of life, we must leave behind all worldly affairs. The first rite of Pilgrimage conveys this meaning within it.

Al-Iḥrām (A State of Sanctity)

The first step in *Ḥajj* is to wash, with the intention of being wholly purified and prepared for the holy journey, and to don special clothes. In addition, a pilgrim is forbidden from doing certain ordinary things. This rite is called *iḥrām*, "a state of sanctity." By appearing in this state, the pilgrim declares his intention to begin the sacred journey. While in this state, as a symbol of being transferred wholly to a spiritual realm, the pilgrim is not allowed to kill or attack any animal or insect; he should not cut his nails or hair.

Men wrap themselves in an unstitched piece of white cloth,[18] which somewhat resembles the material covering a dead person.

Aṭ-Ṭawāf (Circumambulation)

The journey of the pilgrim proceeds to the *Baytullāh*, symbolized by the *Ka'bah*. In the presence of the *Ka'bah*, one should offer one's appreciation and respect in the form of circumambulation.

". . . circumambulate the Ancient House." (*Qur'ān* 22:29)

وَلْيَطَّوَّفُوا بِالْبَيْتِ الْعَتِيقِ

This action has a parallel in our life: when we recognize where we are heading in our journey on earth, we must make our ultimate goal our focus and make our rounds with an eye open to the House of God, the *Baytullāh*, as the center point around which our life revolves. This ritual is but the first step. During *Ḥajj*, this circumambulation is called *Ṭawāf al-Qudūm*, the circumambulation that one performs once one sees the Holy Shrine.

The rich symbolism of the *Ḥajj* requires reflection and meditation. It is an assertion that we now know our way and make our life revolve around our main goal. We seek nothing but Allāh and His messenger. The *ṭawāf* around the *Baytullāh* is another way of witnessing that "Muḥammad is His messenger," as the *Baytullāh* is a symbol of the eternal Light on earth.[19]

Standing on Mount ʿArafāt

"O Allāh, here we are responding to your call. Oh God, (we witness that) You have no partners. To You belongs all praise, grace, and dominion." *Labayk, Allāhuma, labayk. Labayk, lā sharīka laka, labayk. Innal-ḥamda wan-niʿmata laka wal-mulk.* All pilgrims chant

---

[18] Choosing white for the pieces of cloth is not a requirement; it is merely a symbolic tradition.

[19] As was illustrated in Chapter Three, in which the *Baytullāh* is described as a symbol of Light that is manifest on earth through Teachers of humanity—the Prophets and spiritual guides.

these prayers together on Mount ʿArafāt. This rite of *Ḥajj* must be done in a group, on a certain day—the ninth day of *Dhu'l-Ḥijjah*—and at a specific time, between the dawn Prayer and sunset. All pilgrims gather together, standing on and around Mount ʿArafāt, saying the same words in response to Allāh's call. At that awesome moment, they are united as one soul. This is a reminder of their origin. Are they not, after all, created from one soul?

> *O mankind! Revere your Lord, who created you from one soul, created of like nature its mate, and from the two scattered (like seeds) countless men and women. (Qur'ān 4:1)*
>
> يَاأَيُّهَا النَّاسُ اتَّقُوا رَبَّكُمُ الَّذِي خَلَقَكُمْ مِنْ نَفْسٍ وَاحِدَةٍ وَخَلَقَ مِنْهَا زَوْجَهَا وَبَثَّ مِنْهُمَا رِجَالًا كَثِيرًا وَنِسَاءً

Standing on Mount ʿArafāt is so significant that the Prophet Muḥammad said,

> *Pilgrimage is ʿArafā (ʿArafāt). (PH)*[20]
>
> الحج عرفة

The name of the holy mount is derived from the root *ʿa-r-f*. The pronunciation is the same as that of the verb that means "to know." The "knowledge" that is revealed at this sacred moment to the purified heart is that of our belonging to one another and to Allāh. On Mount ʿArafāt, the fact that there is nothing but Allāh is experienced in the depths of the heart. This divine experience is the prerequisite for complete purification, achieved by the following rites of Pilgrimage.

Sacrifice

On the day of the sacrifice, which is that of the Great Feast, *ʿEīd al-Aḍḥā'*, complete purification is realized and the pilgrim's rebirth is celebrated. The slaughter of an animal, required of every head of family, is done immediately after the prayer of the feast. Sacrificing an animal is a symbol of eradicating our animal-like side. Its timing,

[20]Narrated by Nasā'ī.

after the prayer, conveys a message; it is only when we surrender to Allāh (through prayer) that we are capable of being purified and liberated from our egos, represented by the animals.

> *Therefore turn to your Lord in prayer and sacrifice. (Qur'ān 108:2)*
>
> فَصَلِّ لِرَبِّكَ وَانْحَرْ

The sacrifice is also a reminder of Prophet Abraham and his son, whom he was ready to sacrifice for the sake of Allāh. However, Allāh sent Abraham a sheep to be sacrificed in his place. The message is complete; Allāh saved the son when the father surrendered completely to the will of Allāh. To be ready to sacrifice one's son for the sake of Allāh is to give of oneself in response to Allāh's call. When Abraham was prepared to do that, there was no longer the need to carry through with the sacrifice of his son. The symbol of slaughtering an animal, however, remains to convey the message over and over again. Ideally, one who is ready to give oneself and one's dearest to Allāh receives Allāh's Mercy by being given a new birth, the birth of the spirit. The Prophet asserted that spiritual birth[21] when he said,

> *"He who performs Pilgrimage without committing any act of corruption during it returns as a newborn baby." (PH)*[22]
>
> من حج فلم يرفث ولم يفسق رجع كهيئته يوم ولدته أمه.

Stoning Iblīs (*Rajm Iblīs*)

Being a member of the *Baytullāh* requires further struggles. The other Pilgrimage rites express what man should do during his life in order to deserve being accepted in the *Baytullāh*. One cannot be part of the *Baytullāh* unless one is completely free of the stains of the lower self, i.e., the devilish nature within. Hence the ritual of

[21]Spiritual birth is not alien to the teachings of Jesus, who told his disciples: *Truly, truly, I say unto you, except a man be born again, he cannot see the kingdom of God. (John 3:3). Marvel not that I said unto you, you must be born again. (John 3:7)*

[22]Narrated by Aḥmad.

stoning Iblīs. Throwing pebbles at a rock, imagining that it is Iblīs, seems a naïve act, but it is intended to make the person reflect on whether he has such enthusiasm, in real life, to struggle against bad thoughts or evil deeds. Once he has done it, he has come closer to Allāh. The main circumambulation, *Ṭawāf al-Ifāḍa*, a symbol of this truth, should be accomplished as soon as one finishes stoning Iblīs. *Ifāḍa* means "radiance." Now that man has rid himself of his devilish side, he is ready to receive Allāh's Light. He circumambulates His House once again, expressing a new journey of life in which he is enlightened and enlightening by Allāh's awesome benediction.

Running between Mounts Ṣafā and Marwa

Another ritual involves shuttling seven times from Mount Ṣafā (*Ṣafā* is derived from the verb "to purify") to Mount Marwa (*Marwa* is derived from the verb "to quench one's thirst"). The place names are highly symbolic. The act of shuttling between Ṣafā and Marwa seven times symbolizes the continuous search for a source of spiritual satisfaction. The purer one becomes, the more one is capable of receiving spiritual support: once one's spiritual thirst is quenched, one is purer, forever. In this movement between the two holy mounts, the pilgrim accomplishes the same act done by Ismā'īl's mother, Hagar, some centuries ago, when she sought water for her son. Added to the places' spiritual symbolism, there is the reminder of the struggle of a mother who surrendered to Allāh's will and was guided to save herself and her son. The underlying meaning is that regardless of any difficulties, one should take hope in Allāh's Mercy.

Visiting the Prophet

A saying of the Prophet encourages pilgrims to remember his message through remembering his life.

> *Whoever comes for Pilgrimage and does not pay a visit to me is as though he is turning his back on me. (PH)*[23]

---

[23]This *ḥadīth* is narrated by]Tabarānī and Ibn Ḥabbān. However, there are other *ḥadīths* in which the Prophet guides people to come and remember him by visit-

من حج ولم يزرني فقد جفاني

Certainly the Prophet does not reside in his tomb. His saying, however, signifies that remembering him is a way to follow his message. It is also a reminder that he, the Messenger of God, was and is not a mere transient being, but rather an eternal meaning that transcends limitations of any sort.

A pilgrim is considered a newborn in the sense that all his sins are forgiven. The Prophet says:

> *He who accomplishes Pilgrimage without committing any act of corruption during it, all his previous sins are forgiven. (PH)*[24]

من حج فلم يرفث ولم يفسق غفر له ما تقدم من ذنبه

People often mistake the symbolic for the real, but it is a grave mistake to assume that performing a rite will guarantee forgiveness. The true pilgrim, then, does not perform rituals only physically, but realizes the goal and remembers who he is and what he is doing in this life. Through ritual, he may experience the meaning of the oneness of God. Within this context, we can reflect upon the saying of the Prophet:

> *A person who declares that there is no god but God out of his deep heart is destined to enter Heaven. (PH)*[25]

---

ing his mosque, where he was buried. The following one is narrated by the five great scholars (Bukhārī, Muslim, Abū Dā'ūd, Tirmidhī, and Nasā'ī): *One should be destined for three mosques only: this mosque of mine, the Holy Mosque, and al-Aqṣā Mosque.*

لا تشد الرحال إلا إلى ثلاثة مساجد مسجدي هذا والمسجد الحرام والمسجد الأقصى

The following two are narrated by Al-Qāḍī Al-Ghayyād (*At-Tāj al-Jamī'lil-Uṣūl*)

التاج الجامع للأصول

He who visits me even after my death is as if he visited me when I was alive.

من زارني بعد موتي فكأنما زارني في حياتي

When someone visits me in my grave, it becomes my duty to grant them my intercession.

من زارني في قبري وجبت له شفاعتي

[24] Narrated by Tirmidhī.
[25] Narrated by Aḥmad.

من قال لا إله إلا الله صادقا بها قلبه دخل الجنة

Pilgrimage is intended to lead man to achieve that goal. Pilgrimage, with its rich symbolism, confirms that "there is no god but God and Muḥammad is His messenger" in the broad sense of the *Shahādah*.[26]

Summary

The five pillars of Islām, here termed "the system of spiritual training," are meant to emphasize the basic belief on which the Revelation to the Prophet Muḥammad and other Revelations were founded; they aim to nurture the heart and mind with Light and thus to prepare man to receive God's Grace.

The "system of spiritual training" or worship system, as revealed to the Prophet Muḥammad is very special in the sense that it uncovers man's deep link with the universal order. Each "ritual" points to that bond in some way. Prayers are performed according to the movement of the earth around its axis and around the sun. *Ramaḍān*, the holy month of fasting, is a lunar month, the ninth in the Arab Calendar. Fasting itself follows the cycle of day and night. Pilgrimage is performed on the last lunar month, *Dhu'l-Ḥijjah*. It is a reminder that the ultimate goal of man's earthly journey is to relate to Allāh. *Zakāt* is due at the beginning of every new lunar year, as an annual reminder of purifying oneself on different levels.

The spiritual training system intersects man's daily life and cuts across the running stream of worldly activities. It therefore supports each of us during our journey on earth and provides us with insight, through which we can set priorities and fix goals.

In the teaching to the Prophet Muḥammad, the pillars point to the essential "means" necessary to nourish the soul and fulfill the spiritual needs of a human being. This is why they are considered "duties," *furūḍ*, but not in the sense that they are imposed or that one should be forced to practice them. They are "duties" in the sense that the concepts and meanings embedded in that spiritual training system constitute a way to attune oneself with the law of

[26] As was discussed in detail in Chapter Three.

spiritual growth. This is why the Prophet Muḥammad advised his followers to make themselves available to Allāh's Grace.

While it is true that the pillars express certain abstract concepts, that can be practiced in various ways, they are divinely tailored to maximize man's gains through his earthly existence. The pillars represent God's Mercy and Love of mankind. If they are to be performed, it is because one should express gratitude and appreciation to the Divine.

Following this spiritual training system provides us with a wonderful experience. In introducing to the world certain underlying meanings of this spiritual training system, we hope to show the message of all revelations in the language and method revealed to the Prophet Muḥammad. People from different creeds may learn from this spiritual training system without necessarily converting to Islām. The ultimate goal of all spiritual systems in all revelations is to bring spiritual consciousness to man's awareness throughout his earthly journey. Understanding the underlying meanings of the Islamic worship system and practicing them may also encourage the faithful of other religious affiliations to make the most out of their own rites.

5
Balance and Justice on Earth

In our earthly life, one cannot live alone; instead, we live together in groups called societies. The history of humankind is how we develop to live together in peace and harmony within ourselves, with our fellow human beings, and with nature.

Throughout history, mankind has learned how to see beyond the immediate goals of survival. When individuals, , or societies are limited to fulfilling their needs to survive, they are apt to think that their survival and prosperity cannot be realized unless they conquer or make use of others. The earth has witnessed wars, bloodshed, oppression, and exploitation. Revelations came to provide man with the basic principles according to which we can live in peace within ourselves and with all creatures in the natural world. These principles guide us to live a spiritually fruitful life by experiencing and respecting the unity of life in all its manifestations. Following these principles leads to the establishment of a balanced and just life on earth.

Like other Revelations, the teaching to the Prophet Muḥammad (Peace be upon him) guides man to see earthly life from the perspective of the spiritual eternal life.

> *"Do for this world as if you are living forever and do for the Hereafter as if you are dying tomorrow."*[1]
>
> «اعمل لدنياك كأنك تعيش أبدا واعمل لآخرتك كأنك تموت غدا.»

By following this wisdom, one can enjoy a balanced life. The Prophet's life was an example of that balance. His devotion to the spiritual message that the Divine commanded him to convey did

[1]This saying goes back to Imām ʿAlī ibn Abī Ṭālib. It is commonly offered as sound wisdom.

not contradict his role as a leader. He taught humankind how to bring their earthly activities into harmony with their ultimate goal in life. That lesson was not learned from his sayings alone, but also through his behavior and his organization of the Islamic community using the well-defined principles of a legal system, the *Sharīʿah*. Allāh's love for man is represented by the guidance evident in the general rules revealed in the Holy Qur'ān. The *Sharīʿah* was and is followed as a divine path according to these rules. Moreover, the life of the Prophet, including his sayings and deeds, *Sunnah*, has been and always will be a source of inspiration and thus the *Sunnah* is part of the *Sharīʿah*.

If the *Sharīʿah* was considered primarily as, or reduced to, a mere legal system or literal rules and orders, it would betray its principal aim: to help man manage his earthly problems. Therefore the *Sharīʿah* is not a set of laws to be implemented mechanically or rules to be simply followed. It is a "method" rather than a series of explicit orders. To follow the *Sharīʿah* correctly requires the conceptual base discussed earlier. Those concepts emphasize the necessity of believing in the Divine Order, knowing the purpose of life, directing oneself to that purpose, and affirming that there are Teachers of humanity who preceded us along the way, and whose guidance we are naturally inclined to follow.

Thus there is no rigidity in the implementation of the *Sharīʿah*. It is the task of legislators to probe into the underlying messages of the legal system and to develop it; that is what is called *Ijtihād*. *Ijtihād* is part of the wider discipline of jurisprudence, *fiqh*. *Ijtihād* is the creative mental and spiritual effort that should be exerted to reach a new understanding or a new implementation of the general principles of the *Sharīʿah* when confronting a new problem. In order to encourage people to exert such efforts, the Prophet said that those who try to find a solution by concentrating their minds on certain problems by reflecting on the *Sharīʿah* will be rewarded for their effort even if they make mistakes. For those who make accurate conclusions, God will double their rewards.[2]

[2]According to a Prophetic *ḥadīth* narrated by Aḥmad ibn Ḥanbal: *If a judge applied his creative thinking, and reached a proper judgment, he is rewarded (by the Divine) tenfold. If he tried hard but made a mistake, he is still rewarded once or twice-fold.*

To discuss the entire legal system in the *Sharī'ah* is beyond the scope of this book; it is a subject of research in its own right. Here we are primarily interested in the role of the guidance embedded in the *Sharī'ah* in establishing an order of justice based on Islām's principal beliefs. *Ijtihād*, the human effort to be in harmony with divine guidance, is accomplished through understanding the holy text as well as deriving conclusions from the explicit rules in the Holy Qur'ān and Prophetic *Sunnah*. *Ijtihād* and *fiqh* are continuous endeavors that will continue as long as man lives.

Although this chapter examines certain problematic issues in the *Sharī'ah*, this is not done from a legal perspective. Our interest here is to show certain underlying principles of the *Sharī'ah*. Our principal aim, however, is to discover how the guidance of the Islamic *Sharī'ah* helps one live a balanced life.

This discovery process will take place on four levels. The first is that of the relationship between man and himself: how we perceive the meaning of life and develop our understanding into a workable plan and how our faith places us on the right path so that we are fully aware that our life ties earth and heaven together in perfect harmony.

The second level, that of balance and harmony, relates man to the natural world. Perceiving his body as part of that world, man should respect its needs and care for it, as it is his tool to fulfill his mission on earth. In that process he interacts with nature. On this level, unity of life prevails, as the natural world is considered as much a part of ourselves as we are a part of it. Science and art emerge as a result of man's interaction with the world. Science develops as an attempt to understand the natural order and art is the offspring of approaching nature as a source of inspiration.

On the third level, experiencing the oneness of humankind while at the same time accepting diversity creates balance in human relationships. Each individual is a part of all humanity and reflects that whole. With growing awareness of this unity, a person is more likely to achieve balance and seek justice; men and women are more apt to understand that they complement one another, rather than compete

---

إذا قضى القاضي فاجتهد فأصاب فله عشرة أجور وإذا اجتهد فأخطأ كان له أجر أو أجران

with each other. Within the community, that realization can support each individual in overcoming egoistic tendencies.

On the fourth level, seeking justice is the expression of balance in society and in the whole world. Injustice is an outcome of hidden idolatry. Within each human being there is an inclination to assign value to that which is perishable and false. People exploit, control, cheat, and even kill in order to achieve their goals, their perishable deities. Guiding man to resist this tendency is the focus of the discussion on this level. Economic and political systems based on the principle of the oneness of Allāh would protect the weak and punish those who transgress.

Basic Principles of Living in Balance as an Individual

Human beings are asked to protect their lives as gifts from Allāh and to live in inner peace so that they can spread peace in the world. With a sense of inner balance, they know their way and create balance around them. In other words, their relationships with the wider world are defined and shaped by their inner state. Man should be able to go through a process of inner transformation to reach inner peace and balance. He should express his gratitude by realizing the purpose of his existence and moving toward being a servant of God.[3]

> *Truly never will Allāh change the condition of a people until they change it themselves. (Qur'ān 13:11)*
>
> إِنَّ اللَّهَ لَا يُغَيِّرُ مَا بِقَوْمٍ حَتَّى يُغَيِّرُوا مَا بِأَنْفُسِهِمْ
>
> *It is loathsome in the sight of Allāh that you say that which you do not do. (Qur'ān 61:3)*
>
> كَبُرَ مَقْتًا عِنْدَ اللَّهِ أَنْ تَقُولُوا مَا لَا تَفْعَلُونَ

Living on earth, veiled from his Divine Origin, man tends to deviate from the straight path—that which leads him to make earthly

[3]The implications of what it is to be a "servant of God" are examined in detail in Chapter Three.

life fruitful. Conflict between outer attractions and the inner guidance of the pure primordial nature, *fiṭrah,* is unavoidable. Yet harmony between the two is attainable if one corrects one's approach to life and approaches earthly activities from a spiritual perspective. The Revelation to the Prophet explains that conflicts arise when we fail to link our deeds to the ultimate goal of living—being a servant of God—or when we lose the focus and direction, our *Qiblah,* when we are not in harmony with the Law of Life or when we worship some transient objective. We need to remind ourselves that we are a representative of God, that we are given the opportunity to attain to being His servant. With this in mind, we may take on responsibility for ourselves, our fellow human beings, and nature. The way and the method of taking on that responsibility are revealed to us gradually through our life journey.

The following points represent the processes of how this inner interaction can affect our self-image and our approach to life. The ultimate goal is to be in harmony with the purpose of our own creation, which will allow us to be balanced and live in peace within and without.

Faith Develops into a Workable Blueprint

Without faith, man is like a feather that moves according to the direction of the winds, i.e., nowhere in particular.

> *. . . their works are as ashes, on which the wind blows furiously on a tempestuous day; no power have they over what they have earned; that is the straying far, far (from the goal). (Qur'ān 14:18)*
>
> أَعْمَالُهُمْ كَرَمَادٍ اشْتَدَّتْ بِهِ الرِّيحُ فِي يَوْمٍ عَاصِفٍ لَا يَقْدِرُونَ مِمَّا كَسَبُوا عَلَى شَيْءٍ ذَٰلِكَ هُوَ الضَّلَالُ الْبَعِيدُ

> *. . . their deeds are like a mirage in sandy deserts, which the man parched with thirst mistakes for water; until when he comes up to it, he finds it to be nothing. (Qur'ān 24:39)*
>
> أَعْمَالُهُمْ كَسَرَابٍ بِقِيعَةٍ يَحْسَبُهُ الظَّمْآنُ مَاءً حَتَّىٰ إِذَا جَاءَهُ لَمْ يَجِدْهُ

شَيْئًا

Hence the basic chain concepts that the Islamic teachings[4] introduce are not merely a philosophical outlook; their validity lies in the fact that they can be experienced existentially. Once they become part of life, they enlighten our way and transform our faith into a workable blueprint. One begins by believing in a Just Divine Law. This kind of faith assures us that our good deeds will never be in vain and that our bad deeds will affect us, as well. Throughout, we are never certain that what we are doing is completely pure and truly devoted to Allāh. We therefore ask for Allāh's forgiveness. Such a feeling protects us from being overly proud of our deeds and is a constant reminder that we are not perfect. To awaken to this reality reduces our vanity and increases our readiness to move forward along the path of spiritual development. Within that struggle, we accept our limitations. By so doing, new realms of harmony with the Divine Order open.

Heaven and Earth Meet within Man's Existence

We are always alternating between earthly desires and the inner spiritual call. Creating unnecessary conflicts between the secular and the spiritual results in an unbalanced life. The spiritual training system[5] supports us in leading a meaningful spiritual life in which there is harmony between the secular and the spiritual. When we purify ourselves through spiritual training, we prepare ourselves to bear our responsibilities on earth from a spiritual perspective; that is, our motives depend on spiritual attainment as opposed to earthly gains. Consequently, we learn to peel off the layers of illusion that cause us to go astray. We focus on the ultimate goal of life, rather than on the limited aspirations of the world. Our sight sees through the limited earthly existence to what is beyond, and our deeds are devoted to improving living conditions for ourselves and for others. Our deeds, then, become another form of worship linking us to the Supreme. We may realize that our secular activities become

[4]Explored in Chapter Three.
[5]Discussed in detail in Chapter Four.

channels to support us in our spiritual journey on earth. In other words, obstacles can be facilitators. Conflicts gradually disappear, to be replaced with harmony and peace.

We can thus live in two worlds at the same time; earth and heaven can meet within our existence. In such a way we maintain balance in our life; this is what is called in the Holy Qur'ān *aṣ-ṣirāṭ al-mustaqīm*, the straight path, as in the Prophet's saying that what is best is to maintain balance, *al-amr al-wasaṭ*.

> *Once the Prayers are performed, you may spread through the land and seek the Bounty of Allāh, and remember Allāh often, that you might prosper. (Qur'ān 62:10)*[6]
>
> فَإِذَا قُضِيَتِ الصَّلَاةُ فَانْتَشِرُوا فِي الْأَرْضِ وَابْتَغُوا مِنْ فَضْلِ اللَّهِ
> وَاذْكُرُوا اللَّهَ كَثِيرًا لَعَلَّكُمْ تُفْلِحُونَ

Every act is a way to remember Allāh.

> *When you finish your prayer, remember Allāh while standing, sitting, or lying on your sides. (Qur'ān 4:103)*
>
> فَإِذَا قَضَيْتُمُ الصَّلَاةَ فَاذْكُرُوا اللَّهَ قِيَامًا وَقُعُودًا وَعَلَى جُنُوبِكُمْ

To lose balance is to lose a spiritual opportunity. Those in balance are continuously working to serve, but do their work out of devotion to their Lord and are fully aware that they are not in complete control; the Unseen Power is ever present in their consciousness. They do not fear authorities or power; they only weigh their action against spiritual criteria. Spiritual training cuts across the stream of secular life, supporting them in continuously cleaning their soul of egoistic motivations.

To retain balance requires continuous spiritual training, sought throughout a person's journey on earth. Once one loses that balance, one is in danger and must become aware of where he is going and why he is here. Such an individual will not stop searching for a better spiritual outlook to maintain balance. The dynamism of

[6]Our translation.

man's movement to maintain balance cannot be measured by a stagnant frame of reference, as it is built on inner experiences and motivated by spiritual aspects. There will be no end to man's struggle to maintain balance; a struggle that transforms earthly deeds into ways of being attached to Allāh and converts his spiritual training into energy for good deeds. It is no wonder, then, that the Holy Qur'ān frequently speaks of those who *"keep faith and work righteousness."*

الذين آمنوا وعملوا الصالحات

Our life can be a chain of good deeds leading to spiritual elevation if we never stop searching for what is better for ourselves and for others. We move forward according to our own judgment and to the way that we interact with events. One prescription, then, does *not* fit all. Each individual should lead his own experience and correct himself in his own way.

Intention as a Measure of Good Deeds

Almost any activity that we undertake can be used to build a spiritual life. What matters is what lies behind the action.

> *". . . Whoever expects to meet his Lord, let him do righteous deeds and, in the worship of his Lord, admit no one as partner." (Qur'ān 18:110)*
>
> فَمَنْ كَانَ يَرْجُوا لِقَاءَ رَبِّهِ فَلْيَعْمَلْ عَمَلًا صَالِحًا وَلَا يُشْرِكْ بِعِبَادَةِ رَبِّهِ أَحَدًا

Because faith is an energy that can be expressed through deeds, righteous work is not judged outwardly, but according to the intention, which is subjective and proportionate to one's outlook and approach to life. Therefore, regardless of how little or how much one does, the value of that work is measured by the intention behind it. The Prophet says,

> *The value of one's work lies in the intention of the doer, who will be rewarded according to his intention. (PH)*[7]

[7]Narrated by Bukhārī, Abū Dā'ūd, and Ibn Mājah.

إنما الأعمال بالنيات ولكل إمريء ما نوى

According to the Prophet's sayings, to offer water to a thirsty dog, remove a harmful object out of a person's way, or simply say soothing words to a depressed person may lead to Heaven and Paradise. On the other hand, if one accomplishes a great task motivated by ego alone, there is no spiritual reward. The Prophet narrated a parable about the Day of Judgment, when a group of people thinking that they deserve to enter Paradise are told by the angels that they do not deserve to, because they had acted seeking superiority—a scholar seeking fame, a wealthy man using charity work to gain distinction, a soldier wanting to be known for his courage. Angels term such people "liars" and hypocrites destined for Hell.[8] The Prophet said,

> *Allāh does not consider the outward appearances of people but the intentions that lie deep in their hearts, and the deeds that follow. (PH)*[9]
>
> إن الله لا ينظر لصوركم وأموالكم ولكن ينظر إلى قلوبكم وأعمالكم

The emphasis on the spiritual implications of the intention embedded in man's heart awakens the conscience, which takes the lead when he initiates or accomplishes any action. Thus he observes his own behavior continuously, using the spiritual frame of reference rather than social evaluations. Self-observation is a process undertaken by those who search for balance and truth.

Righteousness, then, is not a "form" of action or a quantity of any sort, but a "quality" defined by our intention.

The Relationship between Man and the Natural World

While the starting point of any reformative transformation stems from the will of the individual, this reform is reflected in the way

[8]In a *ḥadīth qudsī* narrated by Bukhārī and Muslim.

[9]Narrated by Muslim and Ibn Mājah.

that man approaches himself as part of nature and approaches the natural world as part of himself. In reaching this state of awareness, the oneness of Allāh is seen as the oneness of life.

The unity of life is a concept frequently found in the Islamic teachings.

> *Glory to Allāh, Who created in pairs all things that the earth produces, as well as their own (human) kind and (other) things of which they have no knowledge. (Qur'ān 36:36)*
>
> سُبْحَانَ الَّذِي خَلَقَ الْأَزْوَاجَ كُلَّهَا مِمَّا تُنْبِتُ الْأَرْضُ وَمِنْ أَنْفُسِهِمْ وَمِمَّا لَا يَعْلَمُونَ

> *There is not an animal on the earth, nor a being that flies on its wings, but (forms part of) communities like you. Nothing have We omitted from the Book, and they shall be gathered to their Lord in the end. (Qur'ān 6:38)*
>
> وَمَا مِنْ دَابَّةٍ فِي الْأَرْضِ وَلَا طَائِرٍ يَطِيرُ بِجَنَاحَيْهِ إِلَّا أُمَمٌ أَمْثَالُكُمْ مَا فَرَّطْنَا فِي الْكِتَابِ مِنْ شَيْءٍ ثُمَّ إِلَىٰ رَبِّهِمْ يُحْشَرُونَ

That is, all creatures come from one origin and return to that origin. To Allāh everything returns. Therefore, all creatures belong to one another.

Man should always be aware of the unity of life, as it represents an aspect of experiencing the oneness of Allāh. Man can build his relationship with nature and with his fellow man according to this principle. On his way to fulfill his earthly needs, he should not violate that principle.

Fulfilling a person's human needs is not the simple response that it is in the animal kingdom. It is related to complex sets of relationships, between man and nature, within himself (is he greedy or moderate?), between him and his fellow human beings (with whom he shares and for whom he provides) and between him and society (in which he should respect others' ownership and privacy).

While one's ultimate goal is to be a servant of Allāh, one should begin one's earthly journey using the gifts that make achieving that goal possible. As representatives of Allāh, we should behave according to the ideal of servanthood and strive to be worthy of that rank. Accordingly, we should be just to ourselves by being just to everything in the world—refraining from destroying plants, shooting birds for pleasure, hurting animals. We should respect life in all its forms. The Prophet's respect for life was so great that he advised believers to continue planting even if they foresee the coming of the Final Hour.[10]

This respect for the unity of life serves two purposes. It emphasizes man's awareness of the Divine Law and its manifestations and, as such, encourages man to seek understanding of the Divine Law within the natural world. Out of this understanding, science develops. Secondly, to observe the Creator in His creatures provokes an awesome feeling within one's heart, whence comes art.

> *. . . wherever you turn, there is Allāh's countenance. (Qur'ān 2:115)*
>
> فَأَيْنَمَا تُوَلُّوا فَثَمَّ وَجْهُ اللَّهِ

As representative of Allāh, man is asked to build and invest, not to destroy or cause mischief.

> *Allāh loves not mischief. (Qur'ān 2:205)*
>
> وَاللَّهُ لَا يُحِبُّ الْفَسَادَ

Out of respect for Allāh's creations, we should reflect on the relationship among natural phenomena and take care not to misuse natural gifts.

The Physical Body as Part of the Natural World

Our responsibility for our physical body is related to our responsibility to nature. To take care of our own health and well-being can be accomplished without damaging the natural world.

---

[10]The *ḥadīth* narrated by Aḥmad ibn Ḥanbal is: *If the Final Hour arrives and any of you has a seed in his hand, he should not refrain from planting it, if he can.*

إن قامت الساعة وبيد أحدكم فسيلة فإن استطاع أن لا يقوم حتى يغرسها فليفعل

So eat and drink of the sustenance provided by Allāh. And do no evil nor mischief on the earth. (Qur'ān 2:60)

كُلُوا وَاشْرَبُوا مِنْ رِزْقِ اللَّهِ وَلَا تَعْثَوْا فِي الْأَرْضِ مُفْسِدِينَ

One should treat one's body as part of the natural world. One should therefore take care of it, fulfilling its requirements without over-indulging in desires. The Prophet said:

It is enough for the child of Adam to feed himself with an amount of food that keeps him going. (PH)[11]

بحسب ابن آدم لقيمات يقمن بها صلبه

In order to achieve the necessary balance, we need to remove the contradictions that exist between earthly requirements and spiritual longing. We should therefore be aware that our physical existence is a gift from Allāh to be thankful for and that taking care of the body is a sacred task, an expression of gratitude to our Creator. In other words, the body acquires its importance as a tool through which the spirit expresses itself. It is understood that Allāh provides us with instincts to ensure our survival on earth. Assured that we are here for a purpose and that each of us has a mission, we should then try to fulfill our mission through this physical existence and take care of this tool.

In order to fulfill our physical needs we encounter the natural world; in order to survive, for example, we need to eat. The teachings of Islam came to include a divine dimension in the way that man fulfills his needs. Man is advised to say "in the name of Allāh," *bismillāh,* before any action he intends to do. That statement serves as a continuous reminder that we aspire to live up to the meaning of the divine words that we utter. The implication is that we become tools in the hands of the Divine, doing what we do in His name. Out of respect for Allāh, who made man his representative, we should not exceed our limits and should always maintain a balance between satisfying our needs and protecting natural resources.

Because all revelations, including the teachings of Islām, respect Life in all its manifestations, it is understandable that the killing

[11] Narrated by Aḥmad and Tirmidhī.

of animals for consumption is questioned by certain non-Prophetic revelations. However, the apparent paradox between respecting life in all its manifestations and using animals for food is resolved in Islām. Belief in the oneness of life and the unity of all its aspects implies that, in eating animal meat, the life of the animal nourishes the life of man; as such, the animal's soul is blessed by moving to a higher level of existence. Thus the slaughter of animals for food consumption is allowed, but must obey certain values and regulations that reflect the oneness of all.[12]

During the act of slaughtering, one must pray for the animal's soul by saying, "In the name of Allāh. Allāh is Greater." Man is addressing the soul, asking it to surrender to Allāh's will. The act of slaughtering should be done with a very sharp knife and directed to the neck nerve quickly, without hesitation, in order to minimize the creature's pain. This act should never be done in the presence of another animal, so as not to frighten it. There is a clear injunction that the meat of animals slaughtered without following these procedures is forbidden; neglecting these rules is considered a sinful action.

---

[12]Within the spiritual dimension, much wisdom is derived from reading the message prohibiting certain food according to the Islamic *Sharīʿah*:

> *He has only forbidden you carrion, and blood, and the flesh of swine, and that on which any other name has been invoked besides that of Allāh. (Qur'ān 2:173)*
>
> إِنَّمَا حَرَّمَ عَلَيْكُمُ الْمَيْتَةَ وَالدَّمَ وَلَحْمَ الْخِنْزِيرِ وَمَا أُهِلَّ بِهِ لِغَيْرِ اللَّهِ

Because of the spiritual relationship among all creatures, human beings as rational beings should be aware of what risks polluting their system. Although it may add to the spiritual elevation of the consumed, the consumption of food can also lead to the spiritual pollution of the consumer if he does not choose carefully. Heavenly guidance came to shed light in that sense. Aside from the unknown divine wisdom, which can be revealed, in part, to those who contemplate, one can notice how each item in the above verse is impure in itself and a metaphor for impurity. For example, "carrion" is, by definition, that which has previously died, and thus cannot be considered a source of nourishment. "Blood" is the liquid of life within living creatures; if it is used for drink, it implies drawing away the life given to another creature. The "flesh of swine" is impure, because it is the only animal that can eat its own excrement. This is not an exhaustive explanation of the reasons those items are forbidden, but they point to the approach adopted in this book, in which unity of life is believed to be the basis of human behavior.

Thus we must take care not to indulge ourselves in any destructive action. We become more and more aware of the inner connection that ties us human beings to the whole. With a growing awareness of that connection, we become more balanced. To be in balance requires continuous self-observation and openness to the inspiration of Revelations, without being fanatical or too literal-minded.

In other words, while man's quest to satisfy his physical needs is considered "naturally legitimate," fulfilling those needs should be done in harmony with the objective of creation. In fulfilling those needs, one humanizes them by elevating them from the instinctive, animalistic level to meaningful responses that are purely human. By so doing, one does not cause harm to other life forms, but helps them conform to the purpose of their existence.

The teachings of Islam are intended to facilitate life, not to complicate it. For example, it would be impossible for people who live in deserts to live without the products of sheep. This is one of the reasons that the consumption of meat is allowed. In modern times, we have come to realize that meat and animal products provide the human body with essential amino acids that cannot readily be substituted by other food sources.

In certain circumstances, the principle of facilitating man's life also allows what is otherwise forbidden. If man is obliged to eat forbidden food to survive, he is allowed to do so.

> *But if one is forced by necessity, without willful disobedience, nor transgressing due limits, then he is guiltless. For Allāh is Oft-Forgiving, Most Merciful. (Qur'ān 2:173)*
>
> فَمَنِ اضْطُرَّ غَيْرَ بَاغٍ وَلَا عَادٍ فَلَا إِثْمَ عَلَيْهِ إِنَّ اللَّهَ غَفُورٌ رَحِيمٌ

Rediscovering the Oneness of Life through Science and Art

Man is linked to the natural world not just to satisfy his basic needs, but also in order to appreciate the order according to which the natural world was created. This appreciation is reflected in man's ability to comprehend the relations among the natural phenomena and to seek the rules that regulate those phenomena. It is also reflected in the deep contemplation which resulted in learning about the Divine through artistic works as they appear in great civilizations.

The unity of life was revealed to us through our developing knowledge of the world and through contemplation and meditation. Many verses in the Holy Qur'ān encourage us to exercise our mind and heart and criticize those *"without understanding."*

لا يعقلون ؛ لا يفقهون ؛ جاهلون

Islam responded to the human quest to make earthly life spiritually fruitful by directing our way. We are asked to make use of our potential; because we were created with the ability to think, we should use our minds to search constantly for what is better for us. Our senses should be purified so that we may listen to the hidden messages embedded in the natural world. Our worldly activities should then describe our appreciation for Allāh's gifts within ourselves and in the world. Islam encourages science, in which our mental power is used, and art, where the hidden insight of the heart takes over. The cohesion between mind and heart, reason and passion, highly recommended in Islamic teachings, is another expression of the balance referred to in the Prophet's teaching by the term *al-amr al-wasaṭ*.

Science

When we observe the order of the natural world, we become eager to understand the relationships among natural phenomena. Responding to this curiosity, the Holy Qur'ān and the Prophet's teachings encouraged man to seek and reflect on everything. The Prophet encouraged people to acquire knowledge even if the end of the world were near. He said,

> *He who chooses a way of life in which seeking knowledge is his primary goal, God paves his way to Heaven. (PH)*[13]
>
> من سلك طريقا يبتغي فيه علما سلك الله به طريقا إلى الجنة
>
> *Seeking Knowledge is a religious commandment for all Muslims. (PH)*[14]

[13]Narrated by Tirmidhī and Aḥmad

[14]Narrated by Ibn Mājah.

طلب العلم فريضة على كل مسلم

The Holy Qur'ān consistently advises us to roam the earth and discover the secrets of creation.

> *Do they not look at the camels, how they are created? And at the sky, how it is raised high? And at the mountains, how they are fixed firm? And at the earth, how it is spread out? (Qur'ān 88:17-20)*
>
> أَفَلَا يَنْظُرُونَ إِلَى الْإِبِلِ كَيْفَ خُلِقَتْ وَإِلَى السَّمَاءِ كَيْفَ رُفِعَتْ وَإِلَى الْجِبَالِ كَيْفَ نُصِبَتْ وَإِلَى الْأَرْضِ كَيْفَ سُطِحَتْ

> *Now let man consider how he came into an earthly existence. He is created from a gushing fluid, proceeding from between the backbone and the ribs. (Qur'ān 86:5-7)*
>
> فَلْيَنْظُرِ الْإِنْسَانُ مِمَّ خُلِقَ خُلِقَ مِنْ مَاءٍ دَافِقٍ يَخْرُجُ مِنْ بَيْنِ الصُّلْبِ وَالتَّرَائِبِ

Science is based on the fact that there is order in the universe. For believers, that order is a manifestation of the Divine Law. Science explains the oneness of life in a magnificent way.

> *. . . You can see no fault in the Beneficent One's creation; then look again: Can you see any rifts? (Qur'ān 67:3)*
>
> مَا تَرَى فِي خَلْقِ الرَّحْمَنِ مِنْ تَفَاوُتٍ فَارْجِعِ الْبَصَرَ هَلْ تَرَى مِنْ فُطُورٍ

It is now commonly known that there are striking similarities between the living cell, the smallest order man can observe, and the vast order of the solar system. Those similarities demonstrate that there is one Order that points to the One Creator Who is Omnipresent within His creatures, connecting them in a way that will remain always beyond our limited abilities to discover. Thus, regardless of man's growing knowledge, he remains in a state of wonder, as the more he knows, the more he realizes that he does not know.

It is well understood that the holy text is not a source of scientific knowledge. However, it is amazing that what we now know as scientific fact does not contradict what appears in the verses of the Holy Qur'ān. Moreover, there are certain verses that were not completely clear at the time of the Revelation, which are now clarified owing to scientific discoveries—the examples are numerous; many books explore this subject. Our intention here is not to speculate upon the relationship between the Holy Qur'ān and scientific knowledge; rather, we are interested in the fact that the Holy Qur'ān and the teachings of the Prophet guide human beings to think, contemplate, and interact with the natural world.

The Prophet himself was ready to learn from his companions about the natural world. When he discovered that palm trees no longer produced dates due to his advice not to germinate them, he told his companions to do as they did before. He told them,

> *"You know better in the affairs of this life."* (PH)[15]
>
> أنتم أعلم بأمر دنياكم

Thus there should be no confusion between spiritual and scientific knowledge. Spiritual guides are not necessarily knowledgeable about the latest scientific findings, but they believe in the Divine Order that is revealed in the natural one; while scientists pursuing objective observations must be highly disciplined to achieve that goal.

In short, to know the world better is in harmony with believing in the one order and the oneness of life. Because of this, Islamic culture was open to all other cultures and civilizations and contributed a great deal to scientific knowledge.

Art

In the Islamic teachings man was and is asked to contemplate nature so that he can awaken to the spiritual experience of existentially recognizing Allāh's Face all around and within. That experience directly opens the heart to see what the eyes cannot see. An artist experiences the oneness of God within his heart. Such a deep

---

[15]Muslim mentions the event.

interaction cannot be expressed directly, so the artist living that experience uses metaphors when writing poetry or in any other artistic expression, such as painting, sculpture, or architecture.

Islam opens the hearts of believers to interact intensely with the natural world; that interaction brought to the world a civilization distinguished by its artistry of various sorts. No matter the art form, an artist considers his work to be a tool of remembering Allāh.

Artists are inspired by the hidden music in the Qur'ān and by the perfect model of beauty that addresses the heart. Reading the Qur'ān with devotion and openness nourishes our artistic talent. We can then experience a very specific kind of balance, whereby our heart is attuned to our senses.

Human Relationships

Man is supported to lead a spiritually fruitful life through the direct teachings of Prophets, who were living models of those teachings. The ultimate goal of following those teachings is to enhance the spiritual transformation of the individual. Yet not only the individual is addressed; so is the entire community. Spiritually awakened individuals can enhance progress and development in all spheres of society, thus helping it to become one in which all citizens compete to serve and to work out of devotion to God, rather than one in which individuals compete to advance their egos. In such a world, each individual's achievements would be measured against their satisfaction in fulfilling noble goals, such as supporting the needy, providing jobs for the poor, removing bitterness from the hearts of the deprived, keeping the environment clean, and so on.

In short, educating people to live according to spiritual values creates a society that abides by those values—not due to the force of laws, but owing to the aspiration of the spirit. This experience was realized during the Prophet Muḥammad's life.

The following themes represent the main principles according to which we can continuously transform our social world into a better one. These principles form the frame of reference according to which we can observe our relationships on both the familial and societal levels.

The Oneness of Humanity

The oneness of humanity is another expression of the oneness of life; here the focus is on the relationships among human beings. The oneness of life on the level of humankind means that deep within, man does not see himself as an individual being separated from his fellow human beings; rather he recognizes himself in his fellows. From this perspective, a person's misery is shared collectively and everyone tries to solve his problems. It is everyone's responsibility to support one's fellow human beings, irrespective of national, ideological, cultural, racial, social, or any other affiliation. Out of respect, an individual should not be cruel to his fellows for any reason. Because of this the Prophet, for instance, advised his followers not to hurry to buy something that they knew another person intended to buy, or propose marriage to a woman if they knew that another person intended to propose to her. They should respect their fellows' desires, imagining themselves in their position. It is a way to guide people to realize another dimension of balance, to be just to oneself and to others. These teachings guide every person to control his selfish side and his individual ego.

The Prophet expressed this meaning by saying,

> *No one can be truly faithful unless he loves for his brother what he loves for himself. (PH)*[16]
>
> لا يؤمن أحدكم حتى يحب لأخيه ما يحب لنفسه

This kind of human attachment reflects the belief in the oneness of God. Indeed, that kind of love is a living experience of the oneness of God. It is the basis on which human relationships should be built.

When the Prophet Muḥammad told his followers,

> *All of you are guardians, and each guardian is responsible for taking good care of those who are under his care. (PH)*[17]
>
> كلكم راع وكلكم مسئول عن رعيته

[16]Narrated by Bukhārī and most scholars of *ḥadīth*.

[17]Narrated by Bukhārī and most scholars of *ḥadīth*.

he was referring to the responsibility of every human individual in caring for all. He also referred to the responsibilities shared among all individuals and emphasized their belonging to one another. This is a principle that can be observed on the family level, the group level, and the society level.

That kind of belonging and caring is in accordance with the pure nature of man, *fiṭrah*. Conflicts arise from being deceived by the illusory attractions that result from egoistic perspectives. When individuals build their relationships with others from an individualistic perspective, they look for individual success and compete with their fellows in realizing their individual goals, even using unfair means to achieve them. Selfishness opens wide the door to mischief and corruption.

The Islamic teachings do not address the symptoms of corruption superficially, but focus on the very roots of corruption. Departure from *fiṭrah* is the primary reason for being attracted to illusions, which nourish the propensity for mischief. Returning to *fiṭrah* is a discovery of that inner connection that binds all creatures together; one should experience this connection existentially rather than theoretically.

In a world guided by the process of discovering this human connection, each individual would be a part of a marvelous symphony. Each person would be given the chance to realize their potential and use it to serve. No contradictions would develop between caring for one's family, community, or society and one's interests to reach out and contribute to the wider circle of the global community.

> *The best of you are those who do the best for their families.* (PH)[18]
>
> خيركم خيركم لأهله

When this experience of love and connection is shared among the world's inhabitants, economic and political systems will orient themselves toward achieving the prosperity of all people on earth and spreading peace among nations.

---

[18]Narrated by Tirmidhī and Ibn Mājah.

Oneness of Humanity within Diversity

The oneness of life and the oneness of humanity do not negate the reality of heterogeneity. We are created with varied potentialities, talents, and personalities; every person is unique. Within that context, equality means providing each human being with the chance to develop their potential. According to Islamic guidance, each person should be respected and valued as a human being regardless of how modest their profession is or how limited their income. While the belief in the oneness of life directs man's orientation and guides his step in interacting with the natural world and with his fellow human beings, the process of improving the conditions of earth's inhabitants should take into account existing diversity. Such consideration reminds us to support individuals according to their needs.

Diversity is in the nature of things. The world was created to incorporate varied creatures. In this respect, we learn a great lesson from the world's ecosystems. The order of the natural world expresses relations among different beings.

> *And the sun runs its course for a period determined for it; that is the decree of (Him), the Exalted in Might, the All-Knowing. And the moon, We have measured for it phases (to traverse) until it returns like the old (and withered) lower part of a date-stalk. It is not permitted for the sun to catch up to the moon, nor can the night outstrip the day: each (just) travels in (its own) orbit (according to law). (Qur'ān 36:38-40)*
>
> وَالشَّمْسُ تَجْرِي لِمُسْتَقَرٍّ لَهَا ذَٰلِكَ تَقْدِيرُ الْعَزِيزِ الْعَلِيمِ وَالْقَمَرَ قَدَّرْنَاهُ مَنَازِلَ حَتَّىٰ عَادَ كَالْعُرْجُونِ الْقَدِيمِ ۝ لَا الشَّمْسُ يَنْبَغِي لَهَا أَنْ تُدْرِكَ الْقَمَرَ وَلَا اللَّيْلُ سَابِقُ النَّهَارِ وَكُلٌّ فِي فَلَكٍ يَسْبَحُونَ

> *Behold! In the creation of the heavens and the earth; in the alternation of the night and the day; in the sailing of the ships through the ocean for the profit of mankind; in the rain which Allāh sends down from the skies, and the life which He gives therewith to an earth that is dead; in the beasts of all kinds that He scatters through the earth; in the change of the winds and the clouds which they trail like their slaves between the*

> *sky and the earth, (here) indeed are Signs for a people that are wise. (Qur'ān 2:164)*

> إِنَّ فِي خَلْقِ السَّمَوَاتِ وَالْأَرْضِ وَاخْتِلَافِ اللَّيْلِ وَالنَّهَارِ وَالْفُلْكِ الَّتِي تَجْرِي فِي الْبَحْرِ بِمَا يَنْفَعُ النَّاسَ وَمَا أَنْزَلَ اللَّهُ مِنَ السَّمَاءِ مِنْ مَاءٍ فَأَحْيَا بِهِ الْأَرْضَ بَعْدَ مَوْتِهَا وَبَثَّ فِيهَا مِنْ كُلِّ دَابَّةٍ وَتَصْرِيفِ الرِّيَاحِ وَالسَّحَابِ الْمُسَخَّرِ بَيْنَ السَّمَاءِ وَالْأَرْضِ لَآيَاتٍ لِقَوْمٍ يَعْقِلُونَ

There is a remarkable degree of natural integration among creatures in the natural world. When conflict occurs, it is to solve particular problems and then nature reverts to its harmony.

Diversity exists for a purpose. We are not created differently so as to kill one another, but to support each other.

> *O mankind! We created you from a male and a female, and made you into nations and tribes, that you might know each other. (Qur'ān 49:13)*[19]

> يَا أَيُّهَا النَّاسُ إِنَّا خَلَقْنَاكُمْ مِنْ ذَكَرٍ وَأُنْثَى وَجَعَلْنَاكُمْ شُعُوبًا وَقَبَائِلَ لِتَعَارَفُوا

In human societies, when we respect nature, accepting that we are created with different biological and mental capabilities, creeds, and cultures, we then seek to integrate the contributions of all to create a better world. As much as people differ in color and language, they also differ in degrees of intelligence, talent, health, knowledge, capital, and creativity. Yet they are equal, in the sense that each can use their capabilities to maximize their contribution to humanity. In such a world, a person would be respected not for the prestigious position they enjoy, but for the sincerity and love conveyed through their work.

In such a society, each would be given equal opportunity to develop their potential. Equal opportunity, however, does not imply

[19] Our translation.

uniformity; it allows the diverse to be integrated in a higher system. Regardless of social rank, one's primary goal would be to progress spiritually. Even a ruler would be considered a failure if he did not use his position as a means to serve his people.

Determining which task is better and which is worse is related, for the most part, to *how* a person performs their task, not *which* task they are performing. The position of a dust collector can be more appreciated than that of a minister, if the latter does not do his work properly. The more one serves, the more one "earns" spiritually—that is the criteria by which an individual should evaluate their role in society. The criterion for judging an occupation is the degree of perfection and honesty.

Injustice arises from a system that does not give individuals equal opportunity to develop their potential. If equal chances were given to all, some would choose mechanical or domestic labor, while others would be more qualified for intellectual or administrative work. There is no injustice in that dissimilarity, as long as it is not imposed or a result of the lack of equal chances for all.

Reasons for Imbalance

When false values are given to certain positions, and people compete to attain those positions even if they are not capable of doing them or of enjoying them, a social imbalance is created. This imbalance can also be created when people use power, in the form of wealth or authority, to control and dominate others or impose beliefs on them.

On a global level, differences in language, culture, and lifestyle do not necessarily lead to confrontation or conflict. On the contrary, different cultures and diverse belief systems can enrich all. Unfortunately, when those differences are emphasized, enmity is created among cultures, which can lead to clashes.

Diversity should not be used to serve the interests of the powerful over the weak or to allow one person, thinking that he is better than others, to impose his attitudes on them. Diversity should always be managed through equal opportunity and the just distribution of wealth and power. This can be achieved not only by a particular economic system, but also by common awareness of the importance of spiritual gains through worldly activities.

Acknowledging diversity from the perspective of the oneness of humanity means creating a system that allows each individual to contribute to the community from their position as a unique person with special talents and the right to be respected.

Family: Oneness of Man and Woman

Man and woman are created from one soul, as written in the Holy Qur'ān. In marriage they experience their original oneness; the Holy Qur'ān therefore calls marriage a "solemn covenant."

> *. . . they have taken from you a solemn covenant. (Qur'ān 4:21)*
>
> وَأَخَذْنَ مِنْكُمْ مِيثَاقًا غَلِيظًا۔

Marriage is deemed "a relation of mercy and love" and "one of Allāh's Signs."

> *And among His Signs is this, that He created for you mates from among yourselves, that you may dwell in tranquility with them, and He has put love and mercy between your hearts; truly in that are Signs for those who reflect. (Qur'ān 30:21)*
>
> ومن ءاياته أن خلق لكم من أنفسكم أزواجا لتسكنوا إليها
> وجعل بينكم مودة ورحمة إن في ذلك لآيات لقوم يتفكرون

Man and woman are created biologically different in order to reproduce and thereby populate the earth with their descendants. That biological difference does not make one of them better than the other, for they both belong to one Origin.

The family is the unit in which they realize their belonging to one another. Their relationship is sacred because it is a means by which the process of creation takes place. It is also a reminder that they both belong to Allāh. For Him, their differences are irrelevant; what matters is how they make their relationship a way to become closer to Allāh. Ideally, love and compassion should pervade the relationship among members of the family. The family is a unit in which each can experience being part of the whole. Children learn from this relationship how each member devotes himself to serve the whole family.

The Balance in the Relationship between Man and Woman

The Islamic *Sharī'ah* considers the oneness of man and woman in broad terms of how each can take care of the other and enjoy being cared for by the other in turn, in a way that values each person's role. The *Sharī'ah* does not impose rigid roles to be literally or strictly followed, failing which one is considered deviant from the *Sharī'ah*. The husband, for instance, is given the responsibility to provide for the family in order to allow his wife to rest during the rigors of pregnancy and, later, of nursing and caring for infants. As mothers, women enjoy the ability to give without limit and to love unconditionally. This division of labor between husband and wife in the Qur'ān encourages both man and woman to respond to their natural roles, defined for biological differences, but is not to imprison them in those roles or to humiliate either of them.

> *Men are the protectors and maintainers of women, because Allāh has given the one more (strength) than the other, and because they support them from their means. Therefore the righteous women are devoutly obedient, and guard in (the husband's) absence what Allāh would have them guard. (Qur'ān 4:34)*
>
> الرِّجَالُ قَوَّامُونَ عَلَى النِّسَاءِ بِمَا فَضَّلَ اللَّهُ بَعْضَهُمْ عَلَى بَعْضٍ وَبِمَا أَنْفَقُوا مِنْ أَمْوَالِهِمْ فَالصَّالِحَاتُ قَانِتَاتٌ حَافِظَاتٌ لِلْغَيْبِ بِمَا حَفِظَ اللَّهُ

Allāh chooses women to be mothers, who deserve respect and appreciation. That is the meaning of the Prophet's oft-repeated saying: *Paradise is under the feet of mothers.*

الجنة تحت أقدام الأمهات

It is out of respect that a man should take on complete economic responsibility for the family. Husbands are asked to take complete care of their wives, to treat them well and respect them. Even when a husband is not—or no longer—in love with his wife, he should stay on good terms with her and sustain the marriage for as long as she does not want to divorce. The Holy Qur'ān and the Prophet repeatedly advise men to care for their wives.

> *O you who believe! You are forbidden to inherit women against their will. Nor should you treat them with harshness, that you may take away part of the dowry you have given them, except where they have been guilty of open lewdness; on the contrary, live with them on a footing of kindness and equity. If you take a dislike to them, it may be that you dislike something which Allāh might yet make a source of abundant good. (Qur'ān 4:19)*
>
> يَاأَيُّهَا الَّذِينَ ءَامَنُوا لَا يَحِلُّ لَكُمْ أَنْ تَرِثُوا النِّسَاءَ كَرْهًا وَلَا تَعْضُلُوهُنَّ لِتَذْهَبُوا بِبَعْضِ مَا ءَاتَيْتُمُوهُنَّ إِلَّا أَنْ يَأْتِينَ بِفَاحِشَةٍ مُبَيِّنَةٍ وَعَاشِرُوهُنَّ بِالْمَعْرُوفِ فَإِنْ كَرِهْتُمُوهُنَّ فَعَسَى أَنْ تَكْرَهُوا شَيْئًا وَيَجْعَلَ اللَّهُ فِيهِ خَيْرًا كَثِيرًا

In various ways and expressions, the Prophet asked his followers to take care of women.

> *The best of you are the best to their wives. (PH)*[20]
>
> خياركم خياركم لنسائهم

> *Attain righteousness through being good to women. (PH)*[21]
>
> «««اتقوا الله في النساء»»»

For her part, a woman has the right to ask for divorce due to any pain she suffers, even if it is "only" emotional. Whether a man divorces his wife or it was she who asked for divorce, he should not take that which he gave to his wife, be it dowry or gifts. The Holy Qur'ān stipulates the minimum that a husband should give

[20] Narrated by Tirmidhī and Ibn Mājah.
[21] Narrated by Muslim, Ibn Mājah, Abū Dā'ūd, and Dārimī.

his wife in case of divorce. These principles should inspire legislators to elaborate laws that support women who devote their lives to their husbands and have no financial resources to live on following their divorce.

A man can divorce his wife and come back to her twice if they agree to resume their marriage. After the third divorce, they are forbidden to resume their marital life again unless the divorced woman marries another man and then divorces him. The logic is simple: a couple should take the bond of marriage seriously and know that there are limits that both should respect.

> *A divorce is only permissible twice; after that, the parties should either hold together on equitable terms, or separate with kindness. It is not lawful for you (men) to take back any of your gifts (from your wives), except when both parties fear that they would be unable to honor the limits ordained by Allāh. If you (judges) do indeed fear that they would be unable to honor the limits ordained by Allāh, there is not blame on either of them if she give something for her freedom. These are the limits ordained by Allāh, so do not transgress them. If any do transgress the limits ordained by Allāh, such persons wrong themselves (as well as others). (Qur'ān 2:229)*
>
> الطَّلَاقُ مَرَّتَانِ فَإِمْسَاكٌ بِمَعْرُوفٍ أَوْ تَسْرِيحٌ بِإِحْسَانٍ وَلَا يَحِلُّ لَكُمْ أَنْ تَأْخُذُوا مِمَّا ءَاتَيْتُمُوهُنَّ شَيْئًا إِلَّا أَنْ يَخَافَا أَلَّا يُقِيمَا حُدُودَ اللَّهِ فَإِنْ خِفْتُمْ أَلَّا يُقِيمَا حُدُودَ اللَّهِ فَلَا جُنَاحَ عَلَيْهِمَا فِيمَا افْتَدَتْ بِهِ تِلْكَ حُدُودُ اللَّهِ فَلَا تَعْتَدُوهَا وَمَنْ يَتَعَدَّ حُدُودَ اللَّهِ فَأُولَئِكَ هُمُ الظَّالِمُونَ

Because men take on complete financial responsibility, they are entitled to inherit from their parents twice what their sisters inherit. In other situations, inheritance law is much more complicated and in specific cases, a woman might inherit twice as much as a man. Since our primary concern in this chapter is not the legal side of the issue, there is no need to discuss the inheritance law further. It must be understood, however, that a daughter is allotted half the share of a son not because she is a woman, but because this division is a fair one.

Doubling the share of the son is not just a right, but a message to the whole community that men should take on financial responsibility and that women should be looked after so that they can fulfill their sacred duties. That is not to say that women are created just to be child-bearers and housekeepers. Even in the Prophet Muḥammad's time, women had certain other responsibilities. His wife Khadījah, for example, was involved in commerce and his wife ʿĀ'ishah was a source of the Prophet's sayings. In other words, when the Islamic *Sharīʿah* made it men's duty to take care of women and to be responsible for supporting the family, it does not imply any restraints whatsoever on the freedom of women to play any role they choose in life. It merely recognized their privileged role as mothers.

The difference in the inheritance shares between sons and daughters, hence, does not imply preference of males over females; nor does it imply depriving girls of any rights that boys might enjoy. The Prophet continuously insisted that parents should treat their daughters and sons equally.

> *He who has a daughter and keeps her alive, never insults her or prefers his son to her, is destined for Heaven. (PH)*[22]
>
> من كانت له أنثى فلم يئدها ولم يهنها ولم يؤثر ولده عليها أدخله الله الجنة.
>
> *He who has three or two daughters or sisters, and is good to them, following a righteous relation with Allāh, is destined for Heaven. (PH)*[23]
>
> من كان له ثلاث بنات أو ثلاث أخوات أو ابنتان أو أختان فأحسن صحبتهن واتقى الله فيهن فله الجنة

It is obvious that women, according to Islamic teachings, should be treated as individual human beings enjoying full rights in ev-

[22]Narrated by Abū Dā'ūd. That guidance was revealed at a time when burying girls alive was quite common among Arabs.

[23]Narrated by Tirmidhī and Abū Dā'ūd.

ery respect. Their gender should not limit them from opportunities to develop their potential and contribute to their societies. This does not in any way make them identical to men; women should be proud of their femininity, ready to take on the responsibility of motherhood, and should not feel guilty if they depend on men financially. In other words, a woman's contribution to society should not be done out of economic need. That is the message of the *Sharīʿah* as it relates to inheritance law.

In practice, situations vary from one family to another and, in many cases, households require the financial contribution of the wife and mother. And in the case of a single parent—a widow or a divorced woman—she must take care of herself fully.

The *Sharīʿah* is flexible, too, in giving an individual full responsibility in dividing his fortune, during his lifetime, among his children as long as one does so in a reflective spirit. Parents can divide their fortunes among their male and female children equally, if they feel that this would be more just. Indeed, they can do anything that they consider fit as long as it is done during their lifetime. Their only and constant criterion should be their freedom from any illusions.

Considering Allāh within the Family

Because human relations can be so deceiving, parents and children should always remind themselves that their destiny is to Allāh. Human beings tend to love their children out of love for themselves and see in them their own image, to be introduced to the world.

> *Wealth and sons are allurements of the life of this world. (Qur'ān 18:46)*
>
> الْمَالُ وَالْبَنُونَ زِينَةُ الْحَيَاةِ الدُّنْيَا

This tendency limits human freedom, imprisoning us in the realm of the ego. It is similar to the "tribal pride," *ʿaṣabīyyah,* that prevailed before the Revelation to the Prophet Muḥammad. The teachings of the Prophet warned against this tendency.

The general principle, to be remembered always, is that we own nothing, not even ourselves, let alone other human beings. Children are independent human beings given to parents in order to have the opportunity to seek just as their parents seek. Parents are bestowed with special feelings for their children so that they take care of them. Yet they should be careful not to indulge in the feeling that they "own" their children. Nor should parents try to "shape" children according to their will, ignoring the child's individuality and independent soul.

Parents should safeguard their children with love and care, and not consider them a burden.

> *Kill not your children for fear of want; We shall provide sustenance for them as well as for you. Truly the killing of them is a great sin.* (Qur'ān 17:31)
>
> وَلَا تَقْتُلُوا أَوْلَادَكُمْ خَشْيَةَ إِمْلَاقٍ نَحْنُ نَرْزُقُهُمْ وَإِيَّاكُمْ إِنَّ قَتْلَهُمْ كَانَ خِطْئًا كَبِيرًا

In tribal life, parents dreaded having baby girls, going so far as burying them alive. The Qur'ān criticized fathers' attitudes towards baby girls and banned this kind of killing.

> *When news is brought to one of them, of (the birth of) a female, his face darkens, and he is filled with inward grief! With shame does he hide himself from his people, because of the bad news he has had! Shall he retain it on (sufferance and) contempt, or bury it in the dust? Ah, how evil are the choices they consider¡* (Qur'ān 16:58-59)
>
> وَإِذَا بُشِّرَ أَحَدُهُمْ بِالْأُنْثَى ظَلَّ وَجْهُهُ مُسْوَدًّا وَهُوَ كَظِيمٌ يَتَوَارَى مِنَ الْقَوْمِ مِنْ سُوءِ مَا بُشِّرَ بِهِ أَيُمْسِكُهُ عَلَى هُونٍ أَمْ يَدُسُّهُ فِي التُّرَابِ أَلَا سَاءَ مَا يَحْكُمُونَ

Caring for children from the stage where they are helpless until they grow older and become adults who can take care of themselves, is a great responsibility that is honored and rewarded. Children, for their part, should thank Allāh by being grateful to their parents.

Taking care of children may be the natural tendency of parents, but taking care of parents requires awareness and inner balance. It is easy for children to justify neglect of their parents—they are too busy with their own individual concerns such as their career, their family life, their future, etc. The Prophet and the Qur'ān, therefore, frequently admonish children to take care of their parents. When the Prophet asked one of his companions to stay with his elderly parents, to take care of them instead of leaving with the Muslim army to defend the Islamic call, he gave the message that looking after one's elderly parents is no less important than the sacred task of *jihād*. The Qur'ān links belief in the oneness of Allāh to taking care of one's parents.

> *Your Lord has decreed that you worship none but Him, and that you be kind to your parents. Whether one or both of them attain old age in your life, say not to them a word of contempt, nor repel them, but address them in terms of honor. (Qur'ān 17:23)*
>
> وَقَضَى رَبُّكَ أَلَّا تَعْبُدُوا إِلَّا إِيَّاهُ وَبِالْوَالِدَيْنِ إِحْسَانًا إِمَّا يَبْلُغَنَّ عِنْدَكَ الْكِبَرَ أَحَدُهُمَا أَوْ كِلَاهُمَا فَلَا تَقُلْ لَهُمَا أُفٍّ وَلَا تَنْهَرْهُمَا وَقُلْ لَهُمَا قَوْلًا كَرِيمًا

Taking care of one's parents is a sacred duty, regardless of differences as to ideas or beliefs. Certainly children are not required to follow their parents' beliefs blindly; using their minds, they should choose their own way with their free will.

> *No bearer of burdens can bear the burden of another. (Qur'ān 17:15)*
>
> وَلَا تَزِرُ وَازِرَةٌ وِزْرَ أُخْرَى

Children, therefore, should not obey their parents if asked to deviate from living according to their belief in the oneness of God.

> *But if they strive to make you join in worship with Me things of which you have no knowledge, obey them not; yet bear them company in this life with justice (and consideration), and follow the way of those who turn to Me (in love). In the End the*

return of you all is to Me, and I will tell you the truth (and meaning) of all that you did. (Qur'ān 31:15)

وَإِنْ جَاهَدَاكَ عَلى أَنْ تُشْرِكَ بِي مَا لَيْسَ لَكَ بِهِ عِلْمٌ فَلَا تُطِعْهُمَا وَصَاحِبْهُمَا فِي الدُّنْيَا مَعْرُوفًا وَاتَّبِعْ سَبِيلَ مَنْ أَنَابَ إِلَيَّ ثُمَّ إِلَيَّ مَرْجِعُكُمْ فَأُنَبِّئُكُمْ بِمَا كُنْتُمْ تَعْمَلُونَ

Moreover, children are asked to pray for their parents, whether they are alive or have passed away. In the Qur'ān, Abraham addresses his father, saying:

"Peace be on you. I will pray to my Lord for your forgiveness; for He is to me Most Gracious." (Qur'ān 19:47)

سَلَامٌ عَلَيْكَ سَأَسْتَغْفِرُ لَكَ رَبِّي إِنَّهُ كَانَ بِي حَفِيًّا

Islam thus demonstrates the link between the virtue of honoring one's parents and belief in Allāh. Faith in Allāh is reflected in all man's behavior on this earth, the most important of which is the kindness shown those whom God chose to be one's parents.

The Value of Work: An Inner Connection

A balanced life, on the level of community, is that in which everyone has a share in working for the prosperity of all, guided by inner connections that make each individual one with the whole. That kind of attachment supports one in overcoming one's egoistic endeavors and in working with sincerity and honesty. The Prophet says,

The honest and sincere merchant is (resurrected to be) among the righteous, the martyrs, and Prophets.[24]

التاجر الصدوق الأمين مع النبيين والصديقين والشهداء

Rather than competing for individual gain, people attached by bonds of love and connection compete to support the needy. As a sign of

[24] Narrated by Tirmidhī and Abū Dā'ūd.

selflessness, they are guided to give the needy that which they value most. The Holy Qur'ān asserts that meaning:

By no means shall you attain righteousness unless you give (freely) of that which you love. (Qur'ān 3:92)

لَنْ تَنَالُوا الْبِرَّ حَتَّى تُنْفِقُوا مِمَّا تُحِبُّونَ

In the Prophet's lifetime, the residents of Medina shared their homes and income with the immigrants from Mecca. They willingly and happily welcomed them and made their life in Medina possible.

Balancing the Relationship between Earth and Heaven through Work

Work is a sacred act if it is motivated by the desire to fulfill one's goal on earth. Appreciating life makes every moment very precious, needing to be directed to what is useful for oneself and for others. The Prophet Muḥammad frequently reminded people of their responsibility for all that is bestowed on them in this life.

On Resurrection Day a human being is questioned about how he made use of the time he spent on earth; what he did with the knowledge he acquired; whence he earned his money and in what he spent it; and in what affairs his physical body was used. (PH)[25]

لا تزول قدما عبد يوم القيامة حتى يسأل عن عمره فيما أفناه وعن علمه ما فعل به وعن ماله من أين اكتسبه وفيما أنفقه وعن جسمه فيما أبلاه

The Holy Qur'ān reminds man that believing in Allāh is accomplished when he understands the reason for being on earth and sets his goal accordingly.

"O my People! worship Allāh; you have no other god but Him. It is He Who has produced you from the earth and settled you therein." (Qur'ān 11:61)

يَاقَوْمِ اعْبُدُوا اللَّهَ مَا لَكُمْ مِنْ إِلَهٍ غَيْرُهُ هُوَ أَنْشَأَكُمْ مِنَ الْأَرْضِ وَاسْتَعْمَرَكُمْ فِيهَا

[25]Narrated by Tirmidhī and Dārimī.

The expression "settled you therein" is expressed in one word in Arabic, *istaʿmarakum*, derived from the root *ʿa-ma-ra*. The root is also used as a verb connoting many meanings, among which is "to make of a desert a place suitable for life." Working to change the place one inhabits is required before it can be ready to live in; this is the figurative meaning of the verb. It also connotes the ability to build civilizations or to establish cultural entities. In short, it implies various aspects of our earthly life. Within the context of the above verse, man appears to have a very special position among all creatures. He alone interacts with awareness of what he does, building and investing.

This verse is related to the one in which the Divine tells the angels that He is making a representative on earth. The human being is capable of transforming earth, making it suitable for living, because God gave him the capabilities to do so as His representative. His special rank allows him to use the Trust placed in him to develop the earth. In body, he is part of the physical world, and in spirit, he represents the Divine. Once man understands his position, he is ready to *"work righteousness."* [26]

To *"work righteousness"* is a very broad term that cannot be defined precisely; in general, it means an "approach that balances benefits to man and honoring Allāh." This kind of balance is not only an individual task, but that of groups who work together to build, reform, and survive.[27] Yet man always needs to reach beyond the immediate fulfillment of his physical needs. He must search for meaning in his work and life and add value to what he is doing.

When a person works to enhance his material status only, heedless of the spiritual dimension, his life becomes pointless.

> *Know you all, that the life of this world is but play and amusement, pomp and mutual boasting and multiplying, in rivalry among yourselves, riches, and children. Here is a similitude; how rain and the growth which it brings forth delight the*

[26]Many verses in the Holy Qur'ān mention *"those who believe and work righteousness."*

[27]Working to survive entails various activities that have enhanced humanity's development up to the modern age. Through the struggle to survive and develop, we discover the world and expand our knowledge.

> *tillers; soon it withers; you will see it grow yellow; then it becomes dry and crumbles away. But in the Hereafter is a severe penalty (for those devoted to wrong-doing) and forgiveness from Allāh and His Good Pleasure (for those devoted to Allāh). And what is the life of this world, but the enjoyment of illusion? (Qur'ān 57:20)*
>
> اعْلَمُوا أَنَّمَا الْحَيَاةُ الدُّنْيَا لَعِبٌ وَلَهْوٌ وَزِينَةٌ وَتَفَاخُرٌ بَيْنَكُمْ وَتَكَاثُرٌ فِي الْأَمْوَالِ وَالْأَوْلَادِ كَمَثَلِ غَيْثٍ أَعْجَبَ الْكُفَّارَ نَبَاتُهُ ثُمَّ يَهِيجُ فَتَرَاهُ مُصْفَرًّا ثُمَّ يَكُونُ حُطَامًا وَفِي الْآخِرَةِ عَذَابٌ شَدِيدٌ وَمَغْفِرَةٌ مِنَ اللَّهِ وَرِضْوَانٌ وَمَا الْحَيَاةُ الدُّنْيَا إِلَّا مَتَاعُ الْغُرُورِ

The Prophet taught that misery is the outcome of attachment to worldly pleasures. Those who make themselves slaves to money and desires, seeking more and more, gain nothing but misery.

> *Miserable is the servant of dinar and dirham (money). (PH)*[28]
>
> تعس عبد الدينار وعبد الدرهم

The Prophet demonstrated his concern for those who compete for more money and pleasure, losing themselves in the process.

> *It is not poverty that makes me worry about you. What worries me most is that when wealth and allurements of the earthly life are available to you, as happened with those who preceded you, you will compete to have more and more. So, the earthly life will lead you, as it did them, to destruction. (PH)*[29]
>
> فو الله ما الفقر أخشى عليكم ولكن أخشى أن تبسط عليكم الدنيا كما بسطت على من كان قبلكم فتنافسوها فتهلككم كما أهلكتهم

Approaching the temporal from a spiritual perspective allows human beings to retain their humanness. Without this spiritual perspective, an individual treats himself as a mere physical body, as a

[28]Narrated by Bukhārī.
[29]Narrated by Bukhārī, Muslim and others.

machine. Consequently he loses the meaning of being truly alive. The spiritual perspective gives work new dimensions, making it an opportunity to add to one's good deeds, to be counted in the Hereafter.

> *Seek, through all that Allāh has bestowed on you, the Home of the Hereafter. Do not forget your portion in this world, but do good, as Allāh has been good to you, and seek not mischief in the land, for Allāh loves not those who do mischief.* (Qur'ān 28:77)
>
> وَابْتَغِ فِيمَا ءَاتَاكَ اللَّهُ الدَّارَ الْآخِرَةَ وَلَا تَنْسَ نَصِيبَكَ مِنَ الدُّنْيَا
> وَأَحْسِنْ كَمَا أَحْسَنَ اللَّهُ إِلَيْكَ وَلَا تَبْغِ الْفَسَادَ فِي الْأَرْضِ إِنَّ اللَّهَ
> لَا يُحِبُّ الْمُفْسِدِينَ

Imbalance

The Prophet's teachings made it clear that earning one's living is a sacred task. Even a humble occupation is better than begging or depending on others for support. The value of work is not measured by how much power or prestige it provides, but how it is done.

A significant story explains how the Prophet encouraged people to earn their living and be dignified. It was said that one of the Prophet's followers devoted all his time to meditation and worshipping God. The Prophet asked who supported this man and discovered that the man's brother provided for him. The Prophet did not approve of the man's behavior, but praised the brother who worked. The story clearly shows that no excuses should be made to justify dependence on others' efforts. To follow the spiritual training system should not keep a person from pursuing his struggle in life. Moreover, the Prophet deemed the struggle to earn one's living a compulsory requirement for a Muslim. The Prophet praised those who fulfill their needs through work, pointing to the example of the Prophet David, who had earned his own living.

It is most preferable that one earns one's living by work. (PH)[30]

ما أكل أحد طعاما خيرا من أن يأكل من عمل يده

While honesty and sincerity stem from the awakened conscience and the realization of the oneness of all, dishonesty is the reflection of a tainted soul and misguided behavior. The Holy Qur'ān warned those who cheat or use usury to increase their capital.

> *O you who believe! Devour not usury, doubled and multiplied, but fear Allāh, that you may prosper. (Qur'ān 3:130)*

يَاأَيُّهَا الَّذِينَ ءَامَنُوا لَا تَأْكُلُوا الرِّبَا أَضْعَافًا مُضَاعَفَةً وَاتَّقُوا اللَّهَ لَعَلَّكُمْ تُفْلِحُونَ

The Prophet affirmed that Islam commands people not to harm each other.

> *One should not cause damage to oneself, nor to others, according to Islām. (PH)*[31]

لا ضرر ولا ضرار في الإسلام

> *An investor is supported (by God); a monopolist is damned. (PH)*[32]

الجالب مرزوق والمحتكر ملعون

When individuals are just to themselves, they become just to others, and becoming just to others will reflect on them, as well. When the Prophet advised his followers to be just, he guided them to the way to be better human beings and to realize an inner balance.

> *And come not near to the orphan's property, except to improve it, until he attains the age of full strength; give measure and weight with justice. (Qur'ān 6:152)*

وَلَا تَقْرَبُوا مَالَ الْيَتِيمِ إِلَّا بِالَّتِي هِيَ أَحْسَنُ حَتَّى يَبْلُغَ أَشُدَّهُ وَأَوْفُوا الْكَيْلَ وَالْمِيزَانَ بِالْقِسْطِ

---

[30] Narrated by Bukhārī.
[31] Narrated by Aḥmad, Malik and Ibn Mājah.
[32] Narrated by Ibn Mājah and Dārimī.

Give just measure and weight, nor withhold from the people the things that are their due; and do no mischief on the earth after it has been set in order; that will be best for you, if you have faith. (*Qur'ān 7:85*)[33]

فَأَوْفُوا الْكَيْلَ وَالْمِيزَانَ وَلَا تَبْخَسُوا النَّاسَ أَشْيَاءَهُمْ وَلَا تُفْسِدُوا فِي الْأَرْضِ بَعْدَ إِصْلَاحِهَا ذَلِكُمْ خَيْرٌ لَكُمْ إِنْ كُنْتُمْ مُؤْمِنِينَ

A Social System that Liberates Man from Idolatry

The *Sharī'ah*, as a source of legal systems, was not introduced to impose a fixed framework on a particular society; rather, it introduced principles to improve the status quo of any society, at any time, and in any place. The implementation of the *Sharī'ah* in the Prophet's lifetime approached existing problems in a realistic way. For example, Islam is against slavery, yet it was not possible, for various reasons, to ban slavery at that time. Instead, the *Sharī'ah* encouraged the liberation of slaves by various means.

The oneness of God, expressed in the oneness of life and the oneness of humanity, is the core around which the Islamic system builds its call. Yet we have to confront the fact that within each human being there is a hidden idol. The individual discovers that hidden idol when interacting with his fellow man. One is vulnerable to being trapped as a result of worldly attraction. We can easily make a god of ourselves if we have the power of money or authority. We transgress our limits if we think ourselves to be perfect beings or if we confuse doing assigned tasks out of a sense of responsibility with dominating or controlling others out of vanity and pride. On the other hand, the less privileged in society are apt to forget that the Supreme can defend them against exploiters. They deviate from the straight path when thinking that people like themselves are autonomous and in full control of their destiny.

The political and economic systems in an Islamic-oriented soci-

[33]The authors have stressed this phrase in order to highlight the implicit meaning.

ety should support man in overcoming this tendency. They should protect marginal people and exert all efforts necessary to satisfy their needs and liberate them from exploitation. They should also protect powerful people from their tendency to transgress.

An Economic System that Aims for Liberty and Prosperity for All

By emphasizing the spiritual value of work, the Islamic teachings eliminate the propensity to accumulate money. Earning one's living through work is most respected and spiritually rewarded.

The principle behind the role of money is that human beings, transcendentally speaking, do not own, but are given the responsibility to invest. What they "have" is merely on loan from Allāh. The way that they approach that loan describes what resides in their hearts; whether they surrender to Allāh or are deceived by the temporary feeling of power they have, persuaded that they have a free hand to do what their lower selves tell them to do. From this perspective, wealth is considered a trap and should be approached carefully. In the Holy Qur'ān there is a parable of two persons, one who possessed two gardens and had children, while the other owned nothing. The rich person was deceived by what he had, thinking that his good fortune would be eternal. His colleague reminded him that in feeling this way, he was losing faith in the One that gives life to all. The parable is as follows:

> *Set forth to them the parable of two men: for one of them We provided two gardens of grape-vines and surrounded them with date-palms; in between the two We placed a sown field. Each of those gardens brought forth its produce, and failed not in the least therein. In the midst of them We caused a river to flow. Abundant was the produce this man had; he said to his companion, in the course of a mutual argument: "More wealth have I than you, and more honor and power in (my following of) men." He went into his garden in a state unjust to his soul. He said, "I do not think that this will ever perish, and neither do I think that the Hour (of Judgment) will ever come. Even if I am brought back to my Lord, I shall surely find*

something better in exchange." His companion said to him, in the course of the argument with him: "Do you deny Him Who created you out of the dust, then out of a sperm-drop, then fashioned you into a man? But I think for my part that He is Allāh, my Lord, and none shall I associate with my Lord." (Qur'ān 18:32-38)

وَاضْرِبْ لَهُمْ مَثَلًا رَجُلَيْنِ جَعَلْنَا لِأَحَدِهِمَا جَنَّتَيْنِ مِنْ أَعْنَابٍ
وَحَفَفْنَاهُمَا بِنَخْلٍ وَجَعَلْنَا بَيْنَهُمَا زَرْعًا، كِلْتَا الْجَنَّتَيْنِ ءَاتَتْ أُكُلَهَا
وَلَمْ تَظْلِمْ مِنْهُ شَيْئًا وَفَجَّرْنَا خِلَالَهُمَا نَهَرًا، وَكَانَ لَهُ ثَمَرٌ فَقَالَ لِصَاحِبِهِ
وَهُوَ يُحَاوِرُهُ أَنَا أَكْثَرُ مِنْكَ مَالًا وَأَعَزُّ نَفَرًا، وَدَخَلَ جَنَّتَهُ وَهُوَ ظَالِمٌ
لِنَفْسِهِ قَالَ مَا أَظُنُّ أَنْ تَبِيدَ هَذِهِ أَبَدًا، وَمَا أَظُنُّ السَّاعَةَ قَائِمَةً
وَلَئِنْ رُدِدْتُ إِلَى رَبِّي لَأَجِدَنَّ خَيْرًا مِنْهَا مُنْقَلَبًا، قَالَ لَهُ صَاحِبُهُ
وَهُوَ يُحَاوِرُهُ أَكَفَرْتَ بِالَّذِي خَلَقَكَ مِنْ تُرَابٍ ثُمَّ مِنْ نُطْفَةٍ ثُمَّ
سَوَّاكَ رَجُلًا، لَكِنَّا هُوَ اللَّهُ رَبِّي وَلَا أُشْرِكُ بِرَبِّي أَحَدًا.

Vanity and lack of gratitude to Allāh are related, and they are the most common symptom of imbalance that human beings have suffered from throughout the ages.

The *Sharī'ah* does not limit what can come under a person's responsibility, commonly known as his property. The individual is not controlled by the power of the legal system alone, but should make decisions on the basis of complete free will. The legal system is designed to stop aggression and violence, not to limit a person's choices. Unlike the communist system, in which individuals do not have access to private property, the *Sharī'ah* does not ban private property. Yet there is a constant reminder of the deeper meaning of life, whereby one will leave everything behind and all that remains will be one's good deeds.

Remembering that death is the ultimate fact that humans face adds meaning to life. Those constantly aware of this are likely to look for what is good for the whole community, as they recognize that they do not own things, but are entrusted with responsibilities.

> *And do not consume your property among yourselves for vanities, nor use it as bait for the judges, with intent that you may consume wrongfully and knowingly property that belongs to other people.* (*Qur'ān 2:188*)
>
> وَلَا تَأْكُلُوا أَمْوَالَكُمْ بَيْنَكُمْ بِالْبَاطِلِ وَتُدْلُوا بِهَا إِلَى الْحُكَّامِ لِتَأْكُلُوا فَرِيقًا مِنْ أَمْوَالِ النَّاسِ بِالْإِثْمِ

Unlike the capitalist system, accumulation of wealth is of no use in a society that does not encourage an extravagant lifestyle, but encourages modesty. While an individual is free to expand his wealth without limit, he is asked not to freeze his money, so that he puts it to use, by either investing or spending it.

> *. . . those who bury gold and silver and spend it not in the Way of Allāh.* (*Qur'ān 9:34*)
>
> وَالَّذِينَ يَكْنِزُونَ الذَّهَبَ وَالْفِضَّةَ وَلَا يُنْفِقُونَهَا فِي سَبِيلِ اللَّهِ

At the same time, the individual is asked to be modest and humble. He abides by this guidance by using his money in ways that benefit the community.

Guided by Islam's main principles, economic regulations could intercede for the benefit of all and even eradicate poverty.

By establishing a system for inheritance, the *Sharī'ah* gives responsibility for property to the community, while providing instructions as to how to distribute the deceased's wealth. During a person's lifetime, they are free to give from their fortune to anyone. Once they pass away, their wishes, stipulated in a written will as to the distribution of their fortune, are taken into consideration, but only for a third of it. The wisdom behind this rule lies in the balance between a person's right to decide what should be done with their property and a reminder that their property goes back to its true Owner and the responsibility for it passes on to others. When a believer is aware of that truth, they think deeply about their motivations when writing a will or distributing their fortune while still alive. To wit, when deciding what to do with their property, they ask themsleves whether they are motivated by unfair preferences or by their devotion to Allāh.

System of Retribution: Justice for All

A person is responsible for their wealth, time, and work; they can either invest them or waste them. Revelations give them general principles and teachings to guide the way. Again, they can either abide by those teachings or ignore them. No social control can regulate a person's commitment to those teachings, as it is related to inner spiritual development. Each person is rewarded according to their intention and sincerity.

Those who are deceived by the illusions of the earthly world are vulnerable to the temptation to do injustice to themselves by harming others. When there is aggression, the use of violence, or theft, legal institutions intercede to ensure the safety of society's members and to treat those who violate the legal system, helping them to correct their ways and liberating them from false deities.

It is well known that punishment in any legal system is intended to protect people from criminals. In addition to that, Islamic philosophy considers the criminal to be a victim of his own bad deeds. It is his deviation from the straight path that empowers his evil side. He falls into the trap of worshipping false idols of various shapes. It is out of mercy that he should be punished in this world rather than waiting for the far greater punishment of the Divine. It is one of the basic beliefs in Islamic teachings that everything that a person does is counted and rewarded.

> *Then shall anyone who has done an atom's weight of good see it; and anyone who has done an atom's weight of evil, shall see it. (Qur'ān 99:7, 8)*
>
> فَمَنْ يَعْمَلْ مِثْقَالَ ذَرَّةٍ خَيْرًا يَرَهُ، وَمَنْ يَعْمَلْ مِثْقَالَ ذَرَّةٍ شَرًّا يَرَه

Based on that belief in divine justice, punishment on earth aims to help and support the person who has committed a crime by granting him the opportunity to be punished here rather than in the afterlife, where he will no longer be able to modify his attitude.

One of the primary objectives of the *Sharī'ah* is to awaken the individual conscience by comparing the earthly punishment to the Divine punishment. Justice according to the *Sharī'ah* focuses on how to make criminals and other members of society aware of their eternal accountability.

For example, cutting off a thief's hand may seem to be a severe punishment, but it conveys a message to the entire society that our hands are created to work for honest purposes and that if they do not do their work properly, then they are no longer needed. This deeper meaning behind each punishment should be considered in light of how the implementation of such a law requires many procedures to prove the crime.

A person who picks fruit from a tree within reach to eat out of hunger, for instance, is not a thief. Nor is a person who finds something by chance and takes it because he fails to recognize its owner. Unless the "theft" is carried out as an aggressive act against another person's right and without any legitimate excuse, the severe punishment of cutting off the hand is not valid. The Prophet advised that punishment should only be implemented when there is clear proof that a person committed a crime. If the judge is uncertain, the "thief's" hand, for example, should not be cut. The Prophet guides his followers:

> *Hold implementation of legal punishments until you have sent away all doubts (about whether or not the alleged person is the one for whom the legal punishment is fully applicable). (PH)*[34]
>
> ادرءوا الحدود بالشبهات

According to the Islamic system of justice embedded in the *Sharī'ah*, considering an offender as subject to the legal punishments (*Ḥudūd*) outlined in the Holy Qur'ān is a very complicated process requiring intense investigation. Judges, therefore, are commanded to study the social, economic, political, and psychological contexts that have led someone to commit an offense before punishing them. For that reason, Prophetic teachings command those responsible for maintaining justice and security to be motivated by mercy when considering a case. In this respect, the Prophet says,

> *It is better that a judge mistakenly declare someone as innocent, than misguidedly implement a legal punishment on an*

[34] Narrated by Ibn Mājah.

innocent. (PH)[35]

إن الإمام أن يخطئ في العفو خير من أن يخطئ في العقوبة

This is not a call for laxity that risks encouraging people to commit unlawful deeds. The logic behind this is that retribution should be respected and one who transgresses should be stopped. But in certain circumstances, the legal punishments outlined in the *Sharī'ah* may be unacceptable to a society; for instance if that society suffers problems that make people more prone to commit certain offenses. In this case other forms of punishment can be instituted. For instance, the second, well-guided caliph, 'Umar ibn al-Khaṭṭāb, forbid the punishment of cutting off a thief's hand during famines. Here, then, *Ijtihād* determines the best way to preserve the principle while modifying the actual punishment.

Capital punishment is a subject of debate in modern times. Some are inclined to give the criminal the opportunity to live following being found guilty for a period of time. From the Islamic perspective, a person who kills another for no rightful reason is considered a killer of all humanity; his punishment in the afterlife will thus be terribly severe. Making him face what he did may awaken his conscience to the gravity of his crime. He may regret his deed and repent, thereby opening a door of mercy.

Various punishments are meant to remind man of his mission on earth as God's representative and to liberate him from false goals.

A Political System: Shared Responsibility and Freedom for All

According to the Islamic teachings, every human being has duties to fulfill and rights to enjoy. When rights and duties are well balanced, people have the opportunity to lead dignified and secure lives. The leader or ruler of a community is no exception; he is chosen by the community to serve them and should not use his position to dominate them.

In Islām, as in other revelations, one's life in this world is evaluated from a spiritual perspective that looks to the eternal life beyond

[35]Narrated by Tirmidhī.

physical death; one should rule or lead a community according to this perspective. The ruler's actions affect not only a small circle of people, but the entire community and its future. This immense responsibility has great impact on the leader's spiritual future.

Deceived by the temporal power he wields, a leader is liable to consider himself a Lord to be obeyed blindly. If he dominates and oppresses people, he is, in fact, committing the gravest sin, that of mistaking himself for a god equal to Allāh, which will be punished on Judgment Day. The Prophet warns against that propensity.

> *To be a leader (of a nation) is as if receiving a trust. On the Day of Judgment, it might cause great shame and guilt, except for those who managed it truthfully, fulfilling their duties properly. (PH)*[36]
>
> إنها أمانة وإنها يوم القيامة خزي وندامة إلا من أخذها بحقها وأدى الذي عليه فيها

On the other hand, if he fulfills his duties out of piety, makes himself a model of how to serve people, seeks only to get closer to Allāh and to purify himself from the illusion of power, spreads spiritual awareness, and guides people to the straight way, his reward will be immense.

> *The Imām (the leader) is a source of exposing subjects to (certain moral) tests; they follow him in wars, and they take him as an exemplar. If he guided them to the way of Allāh, he will be rewarded for it; if not, he will reap what he has sown. (PH)*[37]
>
> إنما الإمام جُنة يُقاتَل من ورائه ويتقى به لئن أمر بتقوى الله عز وجل وعدل كان له بذلك أجر وإن يأمر بغيره كان عليه منه

> *To maintain justice for one day is more rewarding (spiritually) than sixty years of worship. (PH)*[38]
>
> عدل يوم واحد أفضل من عبادة ستين سنة

[36] Narrated by Muslim and Abū Dā'ūd.
[37] Narrated by Bukhārī and Muslim.
[38] Narrated by Suyū textsubdottī.

Within this context, the Prophet assured us that

> *The most beloved person to Allāh, the closest to Him on the Day of Reckoning, is a just leader (imām), while the most remote and cursed is the unjust leader. (PH)*[39]
>
> إن أحب الناس إلى الله يوم القيامة وأدناهم منه مجلسا إمام عادل وأبغض الناس إلى الله وأبعدهم منه مجلسا إمام جائر
>
> *A person who governs Muslims and cheats them will be forbidden to go to Heaven. (PH)*[40]
>
> ما من والٍ يلي رعية من المسلمين فيموت وهو غاش لهم إلا حرم الله عليه الجنة
>
> *Seven types of people will enjoy being in the Shade of Allāh on a Day when no other shade exists; (among them is) a ruler who adhered to justice. (PH)*[41]
>
> سبعة يظلهم الله بظله يوم لا ظل إلا ظله: الإمام العادل ...

The Prophet set a valuable example of how to lead a community with justice and piety. He was tolerant of people of different creeds, founding a principle fundamental to any society — that its members should be free to choose their beliefs and to express their ideas.

He referred to Islamic legislation for his followers alone, asking Jews and Christians to use their own legal systems. In this way, he avoided imposing on them a legal system that they might not accept. He recognized the right of ethnic groups within the larger community to have a degree of autonomy.

> *It was We who revealed the Law (to Moses); therein was guidance and light. By its standard have been judged the Jews, by the Prophets who bowed (as in Islam) to Allāh's Will, by the Rabbis and the Doctors of Law; for to them was entrusted the*

[39] Narrated by Tirmidhī.
[40] Narrated by Bukhārī and Muslim.
[41] Narrated by Bukhārī, Muslim and Tirmidhī.

protection of Allāh's Book, and they were witnesses thereto. (Qur'ān 5:44)

إِنَّا أَنْزَلْنَا التَّوْرَاةَ فِيهَا هُدًى وَنُورٌ يَحْكُمُ بِهَا النَّبِيُّونَ الَّذِينَ أَسْلَمُوا لِلَّذِينَ هَادُوا وَالرَّبَّانِيُّونَ وَالْأَحْبَارُ بِمَا اسْتُحْفِظُوا مِنْ كِتَابِ اللَّهِ وَكَانُوا عَلَيْهِ شُهَدَاءَ

Let the People of the Gospel judge by what Allāh has revealed therein. (Qur'ān 5:47)

وَلْيَحْكُمْ أَهْلُ الْإِنْجِيلِ بِمَا أَنْزَلَ اللَّهُ فِيهِ

While the Prophet was responsible for making all important decisions, he sought advice from his companions, taking their suggestions into consideration. A Persian Muslim enlightened him on the subject of Persian experience in wars. He was also ready to admit his mistakes, thereby providing humankind an example. All of this demonstrated that a political leader should not wield authority alone.

Consult them in affairs (of moment). Then, when you have taken a decision, put your trust in Allāh. For Allāh loves those who put their trust (in Him). (Qur'ān 3:159)

وَشَاوِرْهُمْ فِي الْأَمْرِ فَإِذَا عَزَمْتَ فَتَوَكَّلْ عَلَى اللَّهِ إِنَّ اللَّهَ يُحِبُّ الْمُتَوَكِّلِينَ

Those who hearken to their Lord, and establish regular prayer . . . (conduct) their affairs by mutual consultation. (Qur'ān 42:38)

وَالَّذِينَ اسْتَجَابُوا لِرَبِّهِمْ وَأَقَامُوا الصَّلَاةَ وَأَمْرُهُمْ شُورَى بَيْنَهُمْ

A companion of the Prophet, Abū Hurayrah, said,

"I have never seen a person who is keener to consult his fellows than the Prophet."[42]

يقول أبو هريرة ما رأيت أحدا أكثر مشورة لأصحابه من رسول الله

[42] Narrated by Tirmidhī.

A leader has the responsibility to choose worthy consultants, who can then help shoulder his great responsibilities; together they provide a good life for the citizens of the community.

If a ruler were on a straight path he would be keen to choose a good minister; if the ruler forgot (a good thing), he would remind him. And when the ruler wants to do goodness, he would support him in fulfilling it. If the ruler were not on the straight path, he would choose a corrupt minister; if the ruler forgot, he would not remind him. And if ever the ruler remembered (a good thing to be done), he would not support him in putting it into practice. (PH)[43]

إذا أراد الله بالأمير خيرا جعل له وزير صدق إن نسي ذكّره وإن ذكَرَ أعانه وإذا أراد به غير ذلك جعل له وزير سوء إن نسي لم يُذكّره وإن ذكَرَ لم يعنه.

In an Islamic society, the community should penalize its leader if he has deviated from the principles that they set together. Fear should not enter the heart of a person of faith, who does not rely on any power but the Supreme. Courageously standing up to an unjust leader is considered a divine struggle.

The best of struggles is declaring a word of truth before a despotic leader. (PH)[44]

أفضل الجهاد كلمة حق عند سلطان جائر

One who fears a leader's power or supports him out of self-interest will be called to account in the Hereafter. It will be his responsibility if the community suffers from unjust rule. Therefore, if an unjust ruler is allowed to continue to rule, the community is to blame. The Prophet Muḥammad told a parable of three types of persons to whom God would not speak on Judgment Day; one of them is:

[43]Narrated by Abū Dā'ūd and Nasā'ī.
[44]Narrated by Aḥmad.

> *he who gives his vote to a nominated ruler for the mere interest in the earthly life. If the ruler gave him what he elected him for, he would keep on being loyal to him; if not, he would end his fidelity.* (PH)[45]
>
> وفي وصفه لثلاثة لا يكلمهم الله يوم القيامة: رجل بايع إماما لا يبايعه إلا للدنيا فإن أعطاه ما يريد وفى له وإلا لم يف له

The role of the Prophet as a ruler and political leader was a temporal one. The people of Medina could have respected him only as a Prophet and not elected him their ruler, but this would not have changed his power as a Prophet. He could have advised whoever became leader, as much as any citizen in the community. As a Prophet, Muḥammad was inspired and asked to lead his community spiritually, which in turn affected the people's direction in life, including their lifestyle.

In his spiritual leadership, people could not interfere with the Prophet's decisions. In his political leadership, members of the community are responsible for choosing their ruler and must supervise his decisions, style, and deeds, criticizing or praising him according to public, not private, interests.

Knowing the burdens that await a ruler, a wise person would not seek such great responsibility, whereby he must consider the spiritual dimension when making decisions and act accordingly. Being attracted to the power and the prestigious position that he enjoys, a leader is susceptible to "taking gods with God." A truly pious person refrains from competing for such a position. That may explain why the Prophet, as political leader, said that he would not designate as governor of a community a person seeking leadership for its own sake.

> *We do not give authority (of government) to someone who asks for it, or someone who seeks it earnestly.* (PH)[46]
>
> إنا والله لا نولي على هذا العمل أحدا سأله ولا أحدا حرص عليه

---

[45]Narrated by Bukhārī, Muslim, Abū Dā'ūd, and others.

[46]Narrated by Bukhārī, Muslim, and Abū Dā'ūd.

In an Islamic society, each individual is responsible for the whole community and should participate in the decision-making process. Every citizen has the right to choose his political leader and to participate in founding a system that supports him in realizing his dreams. Every person should be allowed a decent life in which his basic needs are satisfied. While the ruler is responsible for leading his community toward a balanced way of living in which each enjoys a good life and is encouraged to grow spiritually, each individual is responsible for observing, sponsoring, and correcting the direction of the political leadership. The responsibility of advising one another in a Muslim society is an obligation, not a choice. The Prophet advised his followers to consult one another, to take advice from others, and to direct and offer their advice to their fellows, without, however, imposing their views.

That system of shared responsibility may be realized through different political models; each community may create the model best suited to it, according to its needs, its aspirations, and its creativity. There are thus a variety of political models possible under the Islamic principles set by the *Sharīʿah*.

Summary

The Revelation to the Prophet Muḥammad guides man to lead a balanced life in which he can fulfill his spiritual needs through earthly activities, without a dichotomy between the body and the spirit. The harmony that can be realized during a person's lifetime is achieved by believing in the Divine Law that gives order to everything. The Prophet Muḥammad's life demonstrated how to live in harmony with the Divine Order. His *Sunnah*, therefore, is a source of inspiration for those who follow him; it is part of the *Sharīʿah* as a divine path tailored by divine inspiration and included in the Holy Qur'ān.

The *Sharīʿah* is intended to be a source of inspiration for humankind; its ultimate goal is the realization of justice on earth. That can only be achieved if man is just to himself by being in harmony with the Divine Order, so that a balanced way of life can be attained. That is the living aspect of faith, for while it is true that faith is a private matter between an individual and Allāh, that relationship is reflected in man's behavior and ethics.

A balanced life starts on the individual level, when we recognize our place in the universe and become aware of the continuation of life, so that we resist the tendency to give absolute values to false goals. In doing so, we will be just to ourselves. In this respect, a balanced life means that we can make every moment on earth fruitful by relating our deeds in this life to the harvest that awaits us in the Hereafter. Our endeavors would be directed toward purifying our intentions, in order to be honest and sincere in acquiring spiritual, rather than material, rewards. To awaken to this reality reduces our vanity and increases our readiness to move forward in spiritual development. That awareness means that we are continuously attempting to restore and retain balance.

Because human beings live on earth, their relation with the natural world should also be balanced. That balance is only achieved when humans realize the unity of life, that they are part of the whole, a reflection of it. Man's body is just part of the natural world and he should respect it and fulfill its needs without indulging in desires. When he attempts to fulfill those needs he encounters nature. Approaching nature with respect and appreciation guarantees bounty for all. When human beings are careful not to take more than they require, and not to destroy a plant, shoot birds for pleasure, or pollute the environment, Mother Nature prospers and continues to give. On the other hand nature, manifesting the Mightiness of Allāh, sends man a message. Nature is a source of inspiration and a mirror that reflects the Presence of the Unseen. Art is nothing but an expression of that relationship. Man is curious to know the secrets of creation and the order inherent in the natural world. The Islamic teachings encourage human beings to look around themselves and discover the world and also to observe it as a series of Signs that point to the Creator. The development of science is an outcome of following those teachings.

On a third level, Islamic teachings reveal to human beings that they are created from one soul and that to Allāh they will all return. When a person experiences the oneness of humanity's Origin, he does not see himself as an individual separated from his fellow human beings. That awareness brings humanity together to seek what is best for all. From this perspective, it is the responsibility of all to support their fellow human beings, irrespective of national, ideological, cultural, racial, sexual, or any other affiliation. In a world guided by discovering the human connection, each individual is part of a marvelous symphony. The relationships between man and woman, poor and rich, rulers and subjects take on different meanings when the oneness of humanity serves as a framework. The aspiration of humanity is to give all individuals an equal opportunity to realize their potential. Equality does not translate into uniformity, as diversity is in the nature of things. And when each person has the opportunity to realize their potential without social constraints, they discover that they each have a role to play and can be respected for what they do; a street-cleaner and a minister would both receive due respect. Balance is achieved and justice prevails.

Justice is achieved when a balanced life is realized on various levels. Economic, legal, and political systems are indispensable to the maintenance of order in society. In the Islamic teachings, these systems are inspired by the basic principles of Islam as shaped by the *Sharīʿah*. In economic matters, Islam sets general principles, leaving each society free to implement them according to its respective requirements. The *Sharīʿah*, unlike communist law, does not forbid private property, but unlike the capitalist system, it requires modesty and frowns on extravagant accumulation of wealth. While individuals are free to increase their wealth, they should use it for investment and expenditure rather than saving it uselessly. Guided by Islam's main principles, economic regulations should benefit all, eradicating poverty in the process.

Because justice should also benefit all, legal institutions intervene to ensure a safe environment. In punishing those who violate the legal system, the *Sharīʿah* seeks to help them mend their ways. Because Islam teaches that man's every action is counted and rewarded, earthly punishment aims to support the criminal by giving him the opportunity to be punished here and now rather than in the afterlife.

According to Islamic *Sharīʿah*, a political system should reflect shared responsibility and freedom for all. Every human being has a duty to fulfill and rights to enjoy. When rights and duties are well-balanced, people have the opportunity to live a dignified and secure life. This holds true for a community's leader as well. Chosen by the community to serve them, he should not use his position to exploit them. But if he fulfills his duties out of piety, serving people as a servant of Allāh, free of the illusions of power, his reward will be great. In an Islamic society, the community should discipline their leader if he deviates from the principles agreed upon; courageously confronting the unjust leader is considered a divine struggle. Various political models can be used to realize this shared responsibility between ruler and ruled; each community creates the model most appropriate for it, developing it according to its needs, its aspirations and its creativity.

6
The Islamic Call

The Islamic Call is based on loving others as one loves oneself. It therefore targeted the whole world out of love and mercy.

> *We sent you only as a mercy for all the worlds.* (Qur'ān 21:107)
>
> وَمَا أَرْسَلْنَاكَ إِلَّا رَحْمَةً لِلْعَالَمِينَ
>
> *We have sent you to all mankind.* (Qur'ān 34:28)
>
> وَمَا أَرْسَلْنَاكَ إِلَّا كَافَّةً لِلنَّاسِ
>
> *O Messenger, convey that which has been revealed to you from your Lord, and if you do not, then you will not have delivered His message. And God will protect you from the people, and God does not guide the unbelieving people.* (Qur'ān 5:67)
>
> يَاأَيُّهَا الرَّسُولُ بَلِّغْ مَا أُنْزِلَ إِلَيْكَ مِنْ رَبِّكَ وَإِنْ لَمْ تَفْعَلْ فَمَا بَلَّغْتَ رِسَالَتَهُ وَاللَّهُ يَعْصِمُكَ مِنَ النَّاسِ إِنَّ اللَّهَ لَا يَهْدِي الْقَوْمَ الْكَافِرِينَ

Spreading the word of truth was a task assigned to the Prophet (Peace be upon him) by the Divine. The message he was to convey reached his heart even before the Revelation.

Before the Revelation, the Prophet isolated himself in the Cave of Ḥirā'[1] to ponder the meaning of life. During his stay there, the Revelation came to him to answer his quest.

> *Recite: By the name of your Lord who created; He created man from a connecting cell. Recite, for your Lord is the Most*

---

[1] A small cave in Mount Ḥirā', near Mecca. (Ibn Hishām, 1: 224, 225).

Generous. He taught the human being all that he did not know before. (Qur'ān 96:1-5)

اقْرَأْ بِاسْمِ رَبِّكَ الَّذِي خَلَقَ ،خَلَقَ الْإِنْسَانَ مِنْ عَلَقٍ، اقْرَأْ وَرَبُّكَ الْأَكْرَمُ، الَّذِي عَلَّمَ بِالْقَلَمِ ، عَلَّمَ الْإِنْسَانَ مَا لَمْ يَعْلَمْ.

Following the Revelation, the Prophet was commanded by the Divine to convey His call to the Prophet's nearest relatives.

And admonish your nearest kinsmen. (Qur'ān 26:214)

وَأَنْذِرْ عَشِيرَتَكَ الْأَقْرَبِينَ

Then the Messenger of Allāh was commanded to spread the word of truth to others. The principal aim of the Call was to reach those who search for truth and enlighten those going astray. As a messenger of Allāh, he was obligated to convey the message as widely as possible.

The core of the Revelation was to educate people as to the purpose of their own existence and to teach them how to relate to Allāh. The Prophet never used power to force those closest to him to follow the teachings.

Let there be no compulsion in religion. (Qur'ān 2:256)

لَا إِكْرَاهَ فِي الدِّينِ

Out of the conviction, as the Holy Qur'ān revealed, that all Revelations are considered diverse expressions of the one Religion of Islām,[2] it was not the primary goal of the Prophet to convert the People of the Book[3] to his creed; rather, he intended to explain to them the original teachings of Moses and Jesus as revealed to him by the Divine.

The confusion prevailing in the minds of Muslims and non-Muslims as to Islām's approach to other revelations is due, among other things, to a misguided understanding of the Prophet's life. A cursory reading of the Prophet's life misconstrues various situations, focusing on certain aspects and neglecting others.

---

[2]This is the theme of Chapter One.

[3]This is the term used in the Qur'ān to refer to Jews and Christians.

With the reading presented herein, those who claim that the main goal of the Call was to establish an Islamic power can understand that power was never the objective of the Prophet. And those who think that the stage of Mecca represented a temporary peace strategy may discover the gravity of their mistake.

That the Islamic Call conveyed by the Prophet gained more ground and became more powerful with time was a natural outcome of a religion that gives faith in Allāh a living dimension. By the very nature of faith in Allāh, the individual can challenge political authority and may also attempt to change the mores of his society, fearing nothing but the power of Truth. Naturally, rulers who dominate their subjects despise discovering their loss of control over them. Hence the leaders of the Quraysh[4] perceived the call that Muḥammad conveyed as a threat to their power. Consequently, they ignored the core of the message, focusing on the political.

For them, the Muslims' opening of Mecca was a political victory for the Prophet and they acknowledged their defeat by converting to Islām. The Prophet did not intend to take revenge or force them to convert to Islām. When he told the inhabitants of Mecca, *"Go, you are set free,"* [5] he meant it, regardless of whether or not they became Muslims.

In this chapter, we introduce our approach to the Prophet's life, pointing out common mistakes that have led to distorted understanding of Islām's teachings. In our efforts to understand the basic principles of that Call, we discuss three themes that we consider crucial in appreciating it. First, we consider that witnessing that there is no god but God is the cornerstone of the Call, the way for a person to reach his or her highest rank as a servant of God.[6] This is the call common to all revelations and therefore the basis for a "reconciling principle," *al-kalimah as-sawā'*, and forms the basis for the Prophet's

---

[4]This is the name of the tribe to which the Prophet Muḥammad belonged, the most powerful tribe in Arabia at that time.

[5]This event took place in the eighth year following the emigration of the Prophet to Medina. The people of Mecca were very frightened, as they thought that the Prophet would punish them for what they had done to him and his followers (Haikal, 426). See also the Appendix, "The Prophet Accepted a Peace Treaty with the Quraysh" and "Opening Mecca Served to Spread Peace."

[6]The implications of being a servant of God are discussed in Chapter Three.

dialogue with Jews, Christians, and even the pagans of Mecca. It intended to bring the entire world together to live in peace; this reason motivated the decision to send envoys to the great empires of the time.

This leads to the second theme: the result of gathering people around a "reconciling principle" leads to peace among all nations. Peace in the Islamic Call is not limited to the political sphere, as it is the fruit of spiritual achievement; that is, peace envelops the world when it spreads from within each human soul. This can happen if human beings liberate themselves from illusion in all its forms; that is, when they practice faith in the One God. It is for this reason that peace is connected to the greater struggle *(al-jihād al-akbar)*, which is directed to overcome the lower self. Struggle *(jihād)* is intrinsically related to peace—not war, as is commonly asserted. Even when one is obliged to defend oneself against aggression, one should purify one's heart from hatred, lust for revenge, and anger, and interpret the act of fighting as an obligation to defend Truth, with the ultimate goal of spreading peace. Indeed, Islām came to end the prejudice based on "tribal pride" *('aṣabīyyah)*, the cause of countless wars that would never have ended if Islām had not come with its call for peace. Because of this emphasis on peace, one should treat people of other religions with love and tolerance.

Tolerance as an essential aspect of the Islamic Call is the third theme discussed in this chapter. A Muslim should transcend differences and look for what he has in common with others when he seeks friendship with people belonging to other cultures or beliefs. Even when conquering nations that choose to fight Muslims, Muslims should be compassionate and understanding and attempt to erase bitterness and hatred from the hearts of those conquered. In a society in which people of different beliefs live alongside Muslims, they should be allowed to practice their rites freely and their way of life should be respected.

Before exploring these three themes, it is of paramount importance to review our approach to reading the dimensions of the Prophet's way of conveying the Call. We begin with the belief that, first, it is only possible to grasp the true meaning of the Prophet's sayings and deeds by awakening one's capacity to perceive sayings and actions beyond their literal level. To read the life of the Prophet thus involves a spiritual dimension, not merely academic discipline. The understanding thereby gained does not pretend to be final, as the more one seeks purity of the heart, the more one can see. Reading the life of the Prophet is thus a continuous struggle to gain knowledge.

Second, although reflecting upon the Prophet's life is primarily accomplished through continuous purification of the heart, the credibility of the knowledge gained is subject to its consistency with the teachings of the Holy Qur'ān and the coherence of all the Prophet's sayings and deeds. In other words, the Prophet's life, his sayings, and the Holy Qur'ān are interrelated and describe one another. The interconnection can be found if we sincerely and purely search for it. Once an event, a holy verse, or a Prophetic saying is taken out of context and examined separately, the message is twisted and the meaning distorted. What we mean by "context" here is not limited to the textual, social, and political spheres, but includes the spiritual evolution of the Call, its core guidance, and its ultimate goal.[7]

It is of crucial importance to understand the Prophet's sayings or actions in the context of the core of the Call. This is an intense spiritual training in which the core of one's existence should be reached in order to find the whole; the scattered guidance is then integrated from within. That struggle to understand from within diminishes what seemingly appear to be contradictory statements or conflicting events.

---

[7]Examples are numerous; many issues that still cause confusion are the result of ignorance of the integrative and holistic nature of the Prophet's life, his sayings, deeds, and the Holy Qur'ān's teachings. For example, it is frequently argued that the Prophet's call was intrinsically political and that its ultimate goal was to establish an Islamic state, which he would lead. This argument is discounted easily, as the Prophet, who conveyed a Call seeking to liberate humanity from illusions, could not fight for political reasons. Those who interpret the core of the Islamic Call as conveyed to Muḥammad to be the establishment of a state overlook the development of the Call and the process taking place before the emigration to Medina. Those who focus on a particular saying that highlights war as a means to spread the Call, disregarding how patient and tolerant Muḥammad could be with his opponents, are unable to recognize the core of the Call. It was peace, not war, that the Prophet spread within and without.

Third, no generalization should be made as a result of a literal understanding of texts or events. That can cause more harm than benefit. Those who depend on specific verses or sayings of the Prophet to justify the use of violence against non-Muslims, for example, twist the meanings of those verses and sayings by overlooking the main principles of which Muḥammad was a living example. It should be clear that each advice of the Prophet is valid for particular circumstances; no advice should be generalized absolutely or ignored completely. In any case, one should always remember that in Muḥammad's time, people joined Islām out of free will.

Fourth, it must be understood that the Prophet's life, like that of many people, took place in phases and that the phases did not contradict each other; rather, each one provides us with messages and visions that integrate with the main principles of the Call. Many people tend to ignore the Prophet's life in Mecca, focusing instead on the establishment of the Islamic state in Medina; thus they reach false conclusions as to the goals of the Call.

The "Reconciling Principle" Emphasizes Inner Freedom

Islām, as the Religion of *fiṭrah*, respects diversity as characteristic of both the natural world and the human world. Yet the Islamic Call invites the entire world to a "reconciling principle"[8] according to which the ultimate goal of creation is clear: to be worthy of being human and, in Islamic terminology, of being a servant of Allāh. If the world unites in this goal, and every nation is trusted to achieve the goal in its own way and according to the guidance provided by Allāh's Messengers and other wise individuals, peace will prevail and love will unite the whole world in one big family.

In short, to come to a "reconciling principle," with humankind in general and with the People of the Book in particular, forms the basis of the Islamic Call. It is linked to the invitation to witness, "There is no god but God." Witnessing the oneness of God is the

---

[8] *Al-kalimah as-sawā'*, is variously translated as reconciling principle, common principle, and common term. See the glossary.

cornerstone of the Islamic Call, because it is the way to be a servant of God.

> *Say: "This is my Way: I invite unto Allāh, on evidence and conscious insights as clear as seeing with one's eyes, I and whoever follows me. Glory to Allāh! And never will I join gods with Allāh!" (Qur'ān 12:108)*
>
> قُلْ هَذِهِ سَبِيلِي أَدْعُو إِلَى اللَّهِ عَلَى بَصِيرَةٍ أَنَا وَمَنِ اتَّبَعَنِي
> وَسُبْحَانَ اللَّهِ وَمَا أَنَا مِنَ الْمُشْرِكِينَ

> *Say: "O People of the Book! Come to 'common terms' between you and us: that we worship none but Allāh; that we associate no partners with Him; that we erect not, from among ourselves, Lords and patrons other than Allāh." If then they turn back, say: "Bear witness that we (at least) are Muslims (surrendering to Allāh's Will)." (Qur'ān 3:64)*
>
> قُلْ يَاأَهْلَ الْكِتَابِ تَعَالَوْا إِلَى كَلِمَةٍ سَوَاءٍ بَيْنَنَا وَبَيْنَكُمْ أَلَّا نَعْبُدَ
> إِلَّا اللَّهَ وَلَا نُشْرِكَ بِهِ شَيْئًا وَلَا يَتَّخِذَ بَعْضُنَا بَعْضًا أَرْبَابًا مِنْ دُونِ
> اللَّهِ فَإِنْ تَوَلَّوْا فَقُولُوا اشْهَدُوا بِأَنَّا مُسْلِمُونَ

For the most part, to witness the oneness of Allāh implies that man has faith in the One Transcendent, Supreme, Unseen and Manifest Being. To Him alone man surrenders. Man's faith should be reflected in his earthly life in such a way that he does not make a god of any physical, limited, transient thing. In the Prophet's time, as in other eras, people had many gods: power, money, physical desires, political authority, etc. The 360 idols placed around the *Ka'bah* were but one aspect of the illusory way of life to which they conformed. Mistaking illusions for gods leads man to slavery, as he loses his inner freedom. Witnessing that there is only one Origin of Life, which transcends all the known and seen power of the world, liberates man from the confusion of the conflicting gods that he creates and supports him in retaining his inner freedom.

The Common Principle and the Inhabitants of Mecca

In the Prophet's time, the Call to witness the oneness of God represented the "common principle" around which the inhabitants of Mecca could have gathered. It could have solved many problems in the corrupt social environment. Faith in the Supreme Being would have meant that people would not associate partners with Him, taking them as their lords, fearing them and surrendering to them. It could have meant that those who enjoyed political and economic power would not control, dominate, and exploit those less privileged. This faith could have liberated the helpless, ridding them of their desolate self-image, as they could have experienced Allāh's support and protection.

The "common principle" between the Prophet Muḥammad and the inhabitants of Mecca could have been achieved if the majority of Mecca's inhabitants had not overemphasized the importance of their following an ancient heritage, a source of false self-pride. Peaceful co-existence could have been realized if they had been able to change their orientation in life. Denying the continuation of life after physical death, they were keen to realize the utmost in worldly pleasures on earth, competing to achieve the most wealth and power, regardless of their transgressions and injustices to others. In this context, Muḥammad's call was a disruption of their way of life.

For the Prophet Muḥammad, the "common principle," as he defined it, was necessary to settle any conflict. For the inhabitants of Mecca, what the Prophet asked for was deemed unattainable. They were bound to their lifestyle and the beliefs that justified it. To reject paganism was to reject the entire illusory value system of their society. That was too difficult for them to accept.[9]

---

[9]Some researchers misinterpret the Islamic Call as one that does not accept pluralism. They justify their interpretation by citing the episode in which the heads of the tribes in Mecca said to the Prophet, "Leave us with our gods and we leave you with your God." The Prophet then told them: "If I accepted this (offer) would you say something that is apt to make you distinct not only among the Arabs but also the rest of the world?" They said, "What is it?" The Prophet said, "Say there is no god but God, *Lā ilāha illā Allāh.*" Thinking that the Prophet was deceiving them, they became furious, announcing that they would never again seek to negotiate with Muḥammad and vowed to assassinate him. (Ibn Saʿd, 1: 187). At that time, the Prophet Muḥammad did not have the political or economic power to prevent

For thirteen years in Mecca, the Prophet spread the Divine's Call steadily and with great faith in Allāh. His insistence on coming to the "common principle" and on calling for a better life was not an expression of prejudice, as some historians came to interpret it. His perseverance in proclaiming the oneness of God came from the conviction that faith in Allāh would liberate the exploited from fear and liberate exploiters from false ideas. In the darkest times, when his followers fell under the tyranny of the unbelievers, he did not compromise or fear any power.[10] He realized complete inner freedom, as did his followers, who sacrificed their lives.

The Common Principle and the People of the Book

During the Prophet's time in Medina, the core meaning of the "common principle" remained the same,

> *"that we worship none but Allāh; that we associate no partners with Him; that we erect not, from among ourselves, Lords and patrons other than Allāh." (Qur'ān 12:108)*
>
> أَلَّا نَعْبُدَ إِلَّا اللَّهَ وَلَا نُشْرِكَ بِهِ شَيْئًا وَلَا يَتَّخِذَ بَعْضُنَا بَعْضًا أَرْبَابًا مِنْ دُونِ اللَّهِ.

For the People of the Book, the oneness of God signified the revival of the original call that Abraham had conveyed and which had been perpetuated in the messages of Moses and Jesus. The Prophet invited them to Islām, not as a special or new religion, but as their original religion.[11] To accept the "common principle" is to

---

them from doing anything. They were entirely free to do as they liked, as they had greater power and authority in every respect. Thus when they told him to leave them with their gods, they were trying to force him to recognize their beliefs or at least to overlook their transgressions, something that contradicted the basis of the Revelation he conveyed. From his perspective, the Prophet was trying to make them realize that the spiritual gains that a person enjoys as a fruit of witnessing that "there is no god but God" surpass any other earthly authority to which they were devoted.

[10]See the Appendix, "The Islamic Call Should Be Free of any Earthly Aspirations."

[11]The guidance to serve God alone is the first of the Ten Commandments revealed to Moses; all other commandments follow. Moses, quoting God, told his

understand anew the Call that all the Prophets conveyed. The Holy Qur'ān put it clearly and concisely:

> *And they have been commanded no more than this: to worship Allāh, offering Him sincere devotion, by being Ḥunafā' (ever seeking the Religion of Uprightness). (Qur'ān 98:5)*[12]
>
> وَمَا أُمِرُوا إِلَّا لِيَعْبُدُوا اللَّهَ مُخْلِصِينَ لَهُ الدِّينَ حُنَفَاءَ

To come to a "common principle" meant that they could keep their own rituals, rather than be required to declare their commitment to perform Muslim rites. It sufficed that they believed that Muḥammad was honest and sincere, so that they could take his teachings seriously and reconsider their misunderstandings of the teachings of Moses and Jesus. Such people existed at the time of Muḥammad just as they have always existed. The Holy Qur'ān says of them,

> *And there are, certainly, among the People of the Book, those who believe in Allāh, in the revelation to you, and in the revelation to them, bowing in humility to Allāh. They will not sell the Signs of Allāh for a miserable gain! For them is a reward with their Lord, and Allāh is swift in account. (Qur'ān 3:199)*
>
> وَإِنَّ مِنْ أَهْلِ الْكِتَابِ لَمَنْ يُؤْمِنُ بِاللَّهِ وَمَا أُنْزِلَ إِلَيْكُمْ وَمَا أُنْزِلَ إِلَيْهِمْ خَاشِعِينَ لِلَّهِ لَا يَشْتَرُونَ بِآيَاتِ اللَّهِ ثَمَنًا قَلِيلًا أُولَٰئِكَ لَهُمْ أَجْرُهُمْ عِنْدَ رَبِّهِمْ إِنَّ اللَّهَ سَرِيعُ الْحِسَابِ

To revive the belief in the oneness of God could have allowed the People of the Book, including the followers of Muḥammad, to

---

people: *"You shall have no other gods before me. You shall not make for yourself any graven image, or any likeness of any thing ... You shall not bow down to them, nor serve them." (Ex. 20:3-5)* Jesus said, *"You shall worship the Lord your God, and Him only shall you serve." (Matt. 4:10)* Both Moses and Jesus told their people: *"You shall love the Lord your God with all your heart, and with all your soul, and with all your mind." (Deut. 11:13)(Matt. 22:37)*

[12] *Ḥunafā'* is the plural of *ḥanīf*: one who seeks uprightness and purity consistently and constantly. Our translation.

approach life from a similar perspective, so that they could be honest, loyal to one another, and able to co-exist in peace. When the Jewish tribes broke their treaty with the Prophet,[13] they violated the ethical code of all heavenly Revelations. They chose to deviate from the "common term" that could have connected them to Muslim society. Thus they left no space for the Prophet to accept them within the community. They took Muḥammad to be their enemy because they did not accept his spiritual call, seeing him as a mere political leader eager to steal their power.

To Come to a Common Principle is the Basis for Relations Between Nations

To come to a "common principle" appears to be the basis according to which human relationships can be constructed. Without that basis, it is easy for an individual or a group to use malicious means to achieve goals. It is easy to be obsessed by egoistic desires and to submit to any power (taking gods with God).

If man can free himself from any dominant temporal power and pursue only the values of truth and justice, he can be considered one who is committed to the "common principle." *"We erect not, from among ourselves, Lords and patrons other than Allāh."* The absolute values of Truth, Goodness and Justice are manifestations of God. Those who seek to enlighten their way by following these principles are on their way to believing in the Unseen, the Transcendent.

The continuous call to the "common principle" was essential to the Islamic Call. Yet no enforcement was practiced. *If then they turn back, say ye: "Bear witness that we (at least) are Muslims (surrendering to Allāh's Will)."*

The Call for the "common principle" explains the Prophet's messages to the emperors of his time, in Rome, Abyssinia, Persia, and

---

[13]This occurred at a time when the Prophet was selected by the majority of Medina's inhabitants to be their ruler. He signed a treaty with the Jewish tribes to live "as one nation" whereby each should keep their faith freely. In the treaty, the Jews agreed not to support the Arabs of Quraysh if they attacked the Prophet and his followers in Medina. Jews violated the treaty when they helped Muḥammad's enemies. (The text of the treaty is published in Haikal, 239-241). See more in the Appendix.

Egypt. When addressing Christian emperors, the Prophet's message included the phrase *"O People of the Book! Come to common principles between you and us."* The Prophet intended to underline the "common principles" that gather Muslims and Christians in the following message to the "Negus," or emperor, of Ethiopia:

> *In the name of God the most Gracious and Merciful.*
> *From: Muḥammad, the Messenger of God.*
> *To: Negus, the king of Ethiopia.*
> *I praise Allāh, the Holy, Peace, the Guardian of Faith, the Almighty. I witness that Jesus, the son of Mary, is the Spirit of God and His Word that He bestowed on the Virgin Mary, the pure and kind. God created Jesus from His Spirit and breathed into him, and He created Adam as well. I invite you to God the One Who has no partners, to obey Him and believe what has been revealed to me. I am a messenger of God. I call you and your subjects to Him, the Most Supreme. Here I have conveyed (what I had to) and (only) sent my advice. Peace is upon those who are well guided.*[14]
>
> بسم الله الرحمن الرحيم، من محمد رسول الله إلى النجاشي ملك الحبشة. فإني أحمد الله تعالى إليك، الله الذي لا إله إلا هو الملك القدوس السلام المؤمن المهيمن، وأشهد أن عيسى ابن مريم روح من الله وكلمته ألقاها إلى مريم البتول الطيبة الحصينة، حملت عيسى فخلقه الله تعالى من روحه، ونفخه كما خلق آدم بيده، وإني أدعوك إلى الله وحده لا شريك له، والموالاة على طاعته، وأن تتبعني وتؤمن بالذي جاءني، فإنني رسول الله، وإني أدعوك وجنودك إلى الله عز وجل، وقد بلغت ونصحت، فاقبلوا نصيحتي، والسلام على من اتبع الهدى

[14]This message is documented in most biographies of the Prophet. However, the text here is quoted from Abū Ẓahra's *The Seal of Prophets*, 3:864.

Historians disagree on whether the Negus[15] of Ethiopia converted to Islām or not, but it is agreed that he supported Muḥammad when he received the Muslims who migrated to his kingdom, refusing to send them back to Muḥammad's enemies as the latter requested. Muqawqas of Egypt paid a courtesy to the Prophet by sending him presents from Egypt. He politely expressed his inclination to remain Christian. Both emperors responded positively to the Prophet's letters.

Heraclius, the king of the Romans, may have been convinced that Muḥammad was a Prophet, but was preoccupied by the destiny of his reign. He thought that once he declared his belief in Muḥammad, he would be obliged to acknowledge his political leadership and submit to him. And if he allowed the growing Call to spread among his people and the regions he dominated, he risked facing resistance to his authority. He chose to uproot that call before it became a real threat. Khusrau of Persia was even more hostile to Muḥammad's missive, going as far as sending agents to assassinate the Prophet.[16] Those emperors who refused to come to "common terms" chose to be enemies of the Islamic Call, reacting in the same way that the tribes of Quraysh had before—attacking the Prophet militarily.

Spreading Peace is the Core of the Islamic Call

A common stereotype dominates the minds of some Muslims and non-Muslims: they think that Islām calls for wars against those who do not hold Islamic beliefs. The fallacy of that notion is made clear if one looks to the struggle that Muḥammad and his followers went through in order to spread peace.

---

[15] The Ṇegus reacted to the Prophet Muḥammad's call with purity and wisdom. On hearing the verses of the Holy Qur'ān, he commented, "These words and those of Jesus are glimpses of Light that come from the same Lamp." Hence the Negus received the message of the Prophet. Whether he converted to Muḥammad's creed or not is unimportant. (Ibn Hishām, 1:303-305)

[16] Abū Ẓahra, 1993, pp. 861-867.

How to Realize Peace

"S-l-m" is the root from which the words Islām and *salām* (peace) derive. Muḥammad's followers greet each other every day with *Salām*. *As-Salām* is one of Allāh's names mentioned in the Holy Qur'ān. And *salām* (peace) is the state of a person who becomes worthy of being a servant of Allāh, an *'abdullāh*.

> *Servants of Allāh the Most Compassionate are those who walk on earth in modesty and if ignorant people address them, they say, "Peace." (Qur'ān 25:63)*
>
> وَعِبَادُ الرَّحْمَٰنِ الَّذِينَ يَمْشُونَ عَلَى الْأَرْضِ هَوْنًا وَإِذَا خَاطَبَهُمُ الْجَاهِلُونَ قَالُوا سَلَامًا

Peace has a very special meaning in the Call that the Prophet conveyed. Without discerning that meaning, we are not able to understand the changing events in his life that seem contradictory at times and are thus subject to misinterpretation.

Peace is not merely a political ideal whereby people simply live together without disputing. Nor is it an imposed state to prevent the weak from fighting the strong. When peace spreads in people's hearts and pervades human relations, freedom will be established and protected.

Peace is a spiritual state that reflects inner freedom. Once a person has nothing to fear and no longer attributes absolute value to things, peace and serenity fill his soul and his own existence will spread the energy of love.

Peace on the societal level cannot be realized fully and truly without inner peace. Wars spread because we create an enemy to release the conflicts that fill our souls. We invent reasons that may appear logical and acceptable in order to justify our attacks, aggression, and violence. Differences in beliefs, ideas, traditions, and thoughts can never be legitimate reasons for wars and aggression. Life, according to the teachings of Islām, is a very precious gift and should be cherished with great respect. Wars, therefore, should be avoided and violence should not be practiced against any person.

> . . . *if anyone kills a person who is not guilty of murder,*

and did not commit evil on earth, it would be as if he killed all human beings. And if anyone saves the life of one person, it would be as if he saved the life of all human beings. (Qur'ān 5:32)[17]

مَنْ قَتَلَ نَفْسًا بِغَيْرِ نَفْسٍ أَوْ فَسَادٍ فِي الْأَرْضِ فَكَأَنَّمَا قَتَلَ النَّاسَ جَمِيعًا وَمَنْ أَحْيَاهَا فَكَأَنَّمَا أَحْيَا النَّاسَ جَمِيعًا

The Islamic Call came to teach human beings to know their true self so that they can control their lower self, with all its desires and egoistic endeavors. To tame this animal-like ego is a very real challenge, referred to as the greater struggle, *al-jihād al-akbar*. The smaller struggle, *al-jihād al-aṣghar*, is that of entering into physical battle when there are no other alternatives. One does this for an ultimate goal: not simply to defend one's own individual life, but also to face courageously any power that aims to conquer the Truth. In the heat of the battle, the martyr's motive is not revenge but the defense of a higher cause. Unless his heart is full of peace, he is not considered a Muslim and martyrdom would not be achieved. The lower self should not take the lead in defending the cause of Allāh, which can only be possible if the battle is undertaken for the sake of peace.

The warrior controls his lower self owing to his remembrance of Allāh. In the Holy Qur'ān, the phrase "Be conscious of Allāh" (*ittaqūllāh* appears repeatedly, aiming to make one consciously aware of the Divine Presence. Achieving that awareness supports the state of peace within one's soul and overcomes the tempting aggressiveness of the self.[18]

The Prophet Counters Qurayshi Enmity with Peace

Throughout the Prophet's life, his call for the oneness of Allāh was linked to the spread of peace. In Mecca, the community that the Prophet Muḥammad aimed to establish was one of peace. Because the Islamic Call was based on peace, he did not want to become

[17] Our translation.

[18] See the Appendix.

embroiled in disputes with the Meccans regarding their beliefs.

> *Say: "Oh deniers (ungrateful to Allāh), I worship not that which you worship. Nor will you worship that which I worship. And I will not worship that which you have been wont to worship. Nor will you worship that which I worship. To you be your Way, and to me mine." (Qur'ān 109:1-6)*
>
> قُلْ يَاأَيُّهَا الْكَافِرُونَ، لَا أَعْبُدُ مَا تَعْبُدُونَ، وَلَا أَنْتُمْ عَابِدُونَ مَا أَعْبُدُ، وَلَا أَنَا عَابِدٌ مَا عَبَدْتُمْ، وَلَا أَنْتُمْ عَابِدُونَ مَا أَعْبُدُ، لَكُمْ دِينُكُمْ وَلِيَ دِين

The enmity in the hearts of the people of Quraysh came from their fear of Muḥammad's emerging power, which risked weakening their position. The Prophet defended the Call regardless of the danger he faced. It was not out of enmity that he refused to compromise with the leaders of Quraysh, but because he wanted his position to be clear and the call to be pure. The Qurayshi leaders proposed that he rule them, or that they make him as rich as they were if, and only if, he forsook spreading his belief. The Prophet refused and made the famous statement to his uncle who had urged him to accept their offer.

> *I swear that if even they brought the Sun and the Moon and put them on my right and left hands in order to make me give up this Call, I would not abandon my way until God makes it rise, or I am led to my end while working for it.*[19]
>
> والله لو وضعوا الشمس في يميني والقمر في يساري على أن أترك هذا الأمر حتى يظهره الله أو أهلك فيه ما تركته

Further aggression was directed against Muḥammad and his followers. In response to the Qurayshi hostility, his followers were asked to stand fast. They were able to bear the unbearable because they had reached that inner freedom which brought peace to their hearts. They did not fear death, nor feel that any person could harm them. Their goal was neither to be saved nor killed, but to fulfill

[19]Haikal, 164.

the purpose of their existence and to prepare themselves for Allāh. To Him they surrendered. This brought peace to their hearts and strengthened their will.

> *Forgive and tolerate, until Allāh accomplishes His purpose, for Allāh has power over all things. (Qur'ān 2:109)*[20]
>
> فَاعْفُوا وَاصْفَحُوا حَتَّى يَأْتِيَ اللَّهُ بِأَمْرِهِ إِنَّ اللَّهَ عَلَى كُلِّ شَيْءٍ قَدِيرٌ

The Qurayshi tribes exerted further pressure on the Prophet when they decided to boycott any commerce with Muḥammad and his followers, but he did not exchange hatred for hatred, aggression for aggression. He was forced to leave Mecca when he realized that his life was in danger. Emigration was not his choice, but the only alternative left to him once the tribal leaders had decided to kill him. When he left for Yathrib he had no inkling whether he would ever return to his birthplace. Emigration, then, was not a strategic plan, but a reasoned choice to continue the Call.

The attitude of the Prophet and his followers was not the strategy of a weak group that could not face the powerful majority. Indeed, he would later fight with small troops against much greater troops. His peaceful approach towards his opponents remained unchanged in Medina.

The Prophet Struggles for Peace in Medina

The Prophet sought to spread peace and to live in peace. When he migrated to Medina, he brought peace to opposing tribes there.[21] It was clear that peace was the goal to be realized among people of different faiths and races. The responsibility of spreading peace and absorbing the enmity of others fell upon the Muslims, as a Muslim can diminish hatred by spreading love, dispel darkness by radiating light, and dissolve aggressiveness by embodying peacefulness.

[20] Our translation.

[21] The two biggest tribes in Medina, the Aws and the Khazraj, were age-old enemies. When they accepted Islām, they ended their hostilities and became like brothers, who cooperated rather than competed.

Nor can goodness and evil be equal. Repel (evil) with that which is better; then will he between you and whom there was hatred become your friend and intimate! (Qur'ān 41:34)

وَلَا تَسْتَوِي الْحَسَنَةُ وَلَا السَّيِّئَةُ ادْفَعْ بِالَّتِي هِيَ أَحْسَنُ فَإِذَا الَّذِي بَيْنَكَ وَبَيْنَهُ عَدَاوَةٌ كَأَنَّهُ وَلِيٌّ حَمِيمٌ

From that core principle, the Prophet established the necessity to live in peace with citizens in the same community and to conform to its legal system, whether Muslims form the majority or the minority of that community.

During this period, Muslim power grew, not because they intended to be more powerful, but because they were attacked and, unexpectedly, won nearly every battle they were obliged to enter. Every battle they fought was in defense.[22]

Muḥammad and his followers also fought when people with whom he had made a covenant or treaty broke it. Muslims were asked to be alert, ever ready to fight such people.

But if they violate their oaths after their covenant, and taunt you for your faith, fight the leaders of the deniers—for their oaths are nothing to them—that thus they may be restrained. (Qur'ān 9:12)[23]

وَإِنْ نَكَثُوا أَيْمَانَهُمْ مِنْ بَعْدِ عَهْدِهِمْ وَطَعَنُوا فِي دِينِكُمْ فَقَاتِلُوا أَئِمَّةَ الْكُفْرِ إِنَّهُمْ لَا أَيْمَانَ لَهُمْ لَعَلَّهُمْ يَنْتَهُونَ

The Prophet's sojourn in Medina was somewhat different from his stay in Mecca. The Prophet of Allāh became a ruler of a community, which placed various responsibilities on his shoulders.[24] He had to settle various conflicts among the tribes of Medina and

[22]See the Appendix, "The Quraysh Tribe Extended its War Against Muslims Following their Emigration to Medina" and "The Prophet Accepted a Peace Treaty with the Quraysh."

[23]See the Appendix, "The Jews in Medina Refrained from Living in Peace with the Prophet Muḥammad."

[24]The people of Medina made this choice, asking the Prophet to accept their wish; that is, the Prophet did not initiate that process while trying to spread the word of truth. He told the delegation from Yathrib, visiting him in Mecca: *"I just*

sought to establish a harmonious community. Supported by the Revelation, he succeeded in founding a just society in which people of diverse ethnic origins and varied religious affiliations were treated equally and given the right to use their Holy Books as their legal frame of reference in their disputes.

> *Let the People of the Gospel judge by what Allāh has revealed therein. (Qur'ān 5:47)*
>
> وَلْيَحْكُمْ أَهْلُ الْإِنْجِيلِ بِمَا أَنْزَلَ اللَّهُ فِيهِ

> *But why do they come to you for decision, when they have (their own) Law before them? Therein is the (plain) command of Allāh. (Qur'ān 5:43)*
>
> وَكَيْفَ يُحَكِّمُونَكَ وَعِنْدَهُمُ التَّوْرَاةُ فِيهَا حُكْمُ اللَّهِ

Because the Prophet became a political leader, many historians, both Muslim and non-Muslim, confound the religious call and the political status of the Prophet, positing that the establishment of an Islamic society was the primary goal of the call, and thus transform religion into politics. From this perspective, they mistakenly interpret that the Prophet's battles were for power and authority.

Peace for the Whole World

While it is true that the Prophet played a political role as the leader of a community, the religious Call he conveyed remained clear and distinct. As a ruler he conveyed a message that is part of the Islamic Call. He intended to establish an example of how the temporal and the sacred are not separate. Being a Prophet did not require him to abandon a task he was chosen to accomplish. It is true that he used his position as a ruler to establish a community infused with Islamic principles and that he had to defend those principles by strengthening his position. Yet no force was used to convert

---

want you to support me until I convey the message that my Lord has charged me with." (Ibn Sa'd, 1:203)

تمنعون لي ظهري حتى أبلغ رسالة ربي

people to Islām. His ambitions were not political, but religious, as his Call was offered to the entire world.

Sending messengers to the great empires of the time was an extension of the primary principle of the Call, that one should love one's brother as one loves oneself. At that time, the most appropriate means—in fact, the only available means—to convey what had been revealed to the Prophet was to send envoys to the leaders of various tribes in Arabia and to the kings and emperors of neighboring areas. In the case of great nations such as Rome, Persia, and Abyssinia (Ethiopia), it would have been impossible to reach people without the permission of their rulers. If the ruler were open to the Call, that would be a great achievement for the message, as it could then reach people; whereas if the ruler did not accept the Call, his subjects would have no way to learn of it. As a messenger from Allāh, the Prophet was obliged to try the only available way.

When the rulers of the great empires of the time refused the Prophet's invitation, they were also seeking to protect themselves from the expansion of the call, which risked causing unrest in their countries. The Prophet understood that their refusal also meant that they would try to conquer his emergent Call. And try they did. Though militarily unprepared to face such enemies, Muḥammad took the risk, fulfilling the responsibility that he was given.[25]

The messages that the Prophet sent to emperors, kings and other rulers shared certain characteristics. In order to read them correctly, we must take into consideration the connotation of the very meticulously selected phrases, and relate them to the Holy Qur'ān's language, on the one hand, and to the core of the Islamic teachings, on the other. Because they were misinterpreted, they give the impression that the Prophet was threatening the power of these ancient empires.

The messages all included the same phrase:

> *"Peace is to whoever is well-guided."*
>
> السلام على من اتبع الهدى

The Holy Qur'ān mentions that this phrase was used by Moses when he asked the Pharaoh of Egypt to stop enslaving the children

[25]See the Appendix, "Confrontation with the Romans Was Unavoidable."

of Israel and grant them their freedom. Moses did not mean that if the Pharaoh did not listen to his advice he would fight him. Moses had two goals. On the one hand, he was calling the Pharaoh to believe in Allāh, the Supreme Transcendent who cannot be materialized in any shape or idea. On the other hand, he was asking him to be just. When the Pharaoh did not listen, Moses took the Children of Israel out of Egypt, fleeing across the Red Sea to the land of their fathers. The phrase *"Peace is to whoever is well guided"* should not be interpreted as a threat.

The other phrase common to these messages is

> *"I invite you to what Islām calls for. Accept Islām and you will be saved."*
>
> أدعوك بدعوة الإسلام، اسلم تسلم

This, too, sounds like a threat, as if Muḥammad were saying, "If you do not heed the Call, you will be crushed by the Muslim forces; in order to save yourself from that fate, you must convert to Islām." Such an interpretation supposes that Muḥammad was a madman who dared to challenge great powers with such naïve words, whereas this could not be true, as the Prophet led and ruled the community with wisdom and high moral standards. In fact, Muḥammad assumed those emperors to be wise and just leaders, so that they would allow Islamic teachings to spread among their people. Hence the following sentence:

> *"If you do not, you will be responsible for leading your whole nation astray."*
>
> إن توليت فإن عليك إثم أمتك

The goal of these messages is well defined.[26] It should be remembered that when the Prophet used the word "Islām," he was referring to all the Revelations that preceded him.[27]

---

[26]The majority of his messages included similar ideas, but in addressing the Negus the Prophet began his message by praising Allāh and then declaring his faith in Jesus as the Spirit of God and His Word that He bestowed on Virgin Mary. The focus was on the "common terms" that gather the People of the Book. Texts of those messages are in Abū Ẓahra, 1993, 3:858-867.

[27]See Chapter One.

The argument that the Prophet did not intend to threaten or to wage war against those empires is supported by the fact that he was not as powerful as they were. He had far less money, weapons, and people. Yet he found himself in a position in which he had to enter into battle against the stronger troops of great empires. At the same time, it was Muḥammad's task as a Prophet to reach human beings who were ready and waiting for the guidance, regardless of where they were, as is clear from the Prophet's guidance to Imām ʿAlī ibn Abī Ṭālib:

> *"Tell them what Islām is. If God made of you a tool for guiding one single human being to the path of Truth, that is better for you than having the whole world under your thumb."(PH)*[28]
>
> «ادعهم إلى الإسلام وأخبرهم بما يجب عليهم من حق الله فيه فوالله لأن يهدي الله بك رجلا واحدا خير لك من أن يكون لك حمر النعم»
>
> *"Never be the initiators of war. Even if they started, wait until they kill one of you, then tell them: cannot we have any other option than that (killing)? If even one of them was guided to the straight path, that will be one of the best things in the world." (PH)*[29]
>
> «لا تقاتلوهم حتى يبدءوكم ، فإن بدءوكم فلا تقاتلوهم حتى يقتلوا منكم قتيلا، ثم أروهم ذلك، وقولوا لهم هل إلى خير من هذا السبيل؟ فلأن يهدي الله بك رجلا واحدا خير مما طلعت عليه الشمس وغربت»

The Struggle to Reinforce Peace

In the lands newly conquered by Islām, the call to join Islām's teachings was smooth and peaceful. The Prophet provided his followers with instructions as to how to treat people.

---

[28] Narrated by Bukhārī and Muslim.
[29] Quoted in Abū Ẓahra, 1992, p. 48.

"Tell them first about the content of the message of Islām and give them the choice to become a Muslim. . . . If they do not, tell them that the second option is that they can, instead, pay ***jizyah*** *and we can live together in peace." (PH)*[30]

«««أدعهم إلى الإسلام فإن أجابوك فاقبل منهم وكف عنهم ... فإن أبوا فسلهم الجزية فإن هم أجابوك فاقبل منهم وكف عنهم»»»

Peace within this context implied that non-Muslims should accept that Muslims, who took on the responsibility of governing those areas following the defeat of their former rulers, would be their protectors. Non-Muslims were to pay an assigned amount of money called the *jizyah,* similar to a tax, to pay for the work of governing. Refusal to pay the *jizyah* would constitute a violation of Islamic rules and a sign of enmity.

In this context, we can understand the saying of the Prophet:

"I was commanded to fight people until they say: 'We witness that there is no god but God and Muḥammad is the Messenger of God;' turn their faces in the direction we do, offer Sacrifices the way we do, and perform prayers the way we do. Only then can they save their lives and money from me." (PH)[31]

أمرت أن أقاتل الناس حتى يشهدوا أن لا إله إلا الله وأن محمدا عبده ورسوله وأن يستقبلوا قبلتنا وأن يأكلوا ذبيحتنا وأن يصلوا صلاتنا فإذا فعلوا ذلك حرمت علينا دماؤهم وأموالهم

The literal meaning of that saying contradicts that of many others and that of verses in the Holy Qur'ān.

Let there be no compulsion in religion. (Qur'ān 2:256)

لَا إِكْرَاهَ فِي الدِّينِ

[30]Narrated by Muslim, Abū Dā'ūd, and Tirmidhī.

[31]Narrated by Abū Dā'ūd, Tirmidhī and Nasā'ī.

> *Say, "The Truth is from your Lord; let him who will, believe, and let him who will, reject (it)." (Qur'ān 18:29)*
>
> وَقُلِ الْحَقُّ مِنْ رَبِّكُمْ فَمَنْ شَاءَ فَلْيُؤْمِنْ وَمَنْ شَاءَ فَلْيَكْفُرْ
>
> *If it had been your Lord's Will, they would all have believed, all who are on earth! Will you then compel mankind, against their will, to believe? (Qur'ān 10:99)*
>
> وَلَوْ شَاءَ رَبُّكَ لَآمَنَ مَنْ فِي الْأَرْضِ كُلُّهُمْ جَمِيعًا أَفَأَنْتَ تُكْرِهُ النَّاسَ حَتَّى يَكُونُوا مُؤْمِنِينَ

The above-mentioned saying of the Prophet should not be taken literally, as it would contradict the basic principles of Islām. Certainly, the Prophet's intention was not to fight people in order to force them to convert to Islām. Instead, the *ḥadīth* should be thought of as a metaphor. It represented the Prophet's will to spread the word of Truth. His saying may be interpreted as a warning that spreading the word of Truth was not an easy task, but a struggle against the dark side in people. It was his mission as the messenger of the light and mercy of God to dispel that darkness, supporting people in their efforts to witness the oneness of God.

At that time, international laws did not exist, borders were not secured and a state's sovereignty was not respected. There was only one language, that of power. Throughout Muḥammad's mission, he was forced to fight for survival. The Prophet's mission was not to impose illusions, but to free people from them.

Briefly, our argument can be clarified with the help of the following points:

First, the Prophet did not choose to rule. He was chosen by the people of Medina to take on that responsibility. He then used his position to spread the Call bestowed on him by Allāh, not through violence or power, but by creating an atmosphere of peace and love.

Second, he did not choose the battles that he entered; there was no other option. The Holy Qur'ān addresses Muslims saying,

> *Fighting is prescribed for you, and you dislike it. (Qur'ān 2:216)*
>
> كُتِبَ عَلَيْكُمُ الْقِتَالُ وَهُوَ كُرْهٌ لَكُمْ

The term "prescribed for you," as read in context, suggests that fighting was the solution to a problem and thus purely the result of a temporal decision. The verse also speaks of Muslims disliking battle, as they were trained in the Call to live in peace. If another alternative had been available, the Prophet was inclined to prevent battles.

> *But if they incline towards peace, do you (also) incline towards peace, and trust in Allāh. (Qur'ān 8:61)*
>
> وَإِنْ جَنَحُوا لِلسَّلْمِ فَاجْنَحْ لَهَا وَتَوَكَّلْ عَلَى اللَّهِ إِنَّهُ هُوَ السَّمِيعُ الْعَلِيمُ

A verse allowing Muslims to confront those who fought them was revealed, explaining the reason for that permission:

> *To those against whom war is made, permission is given (to confront the aggressor), because they are wronged, and verily, Allāh is Most Powerful to aid them. (They are) those who have been expelled unjustly from their homes, (for no cause) other than that they say, "Our Lord is Allāh." (Qur'ān 22:39-40).*
>
> أُذِنَ لِلَّذِينَ يُقَاتَلُونَ بِأَنَّهُمْ ظُلِمُوا وَإِنَّ اللَّهَ عَلَى نَصْرِهِمْ لَقَدِيرٌ، الَّذِينَ أُخْرِجُوا مِنْ دِيَارِهِمْ بِغَيْرِ حَقٍّ إِلَّا أَنْ يَقُولُوا رَبُّنَا اللَّهُ

Third, the fighting assigned by the Holy Qur'ān was not against peace, in the sense that it was not authorized out of hatred or lust for domination. Those who fought did so not to earn a special status or to make material gains, but only for the sake of Allāh and in His name.[32]

Fourth, the battles during Muḥammad's lifetime were part of a struggle *(jihād)*. To participate in *jihād* required great faith in Allāh and a certain degree of inner freedom and inner peace. Unlike soldiers in other wars, the Muslim fighter was not defending his life; rather, he was defending the Call, willing to accept a martyr's death. The power of faith that he conveyed made one fighter equal many of his opponents.

---

[32] See the Appendix, "The path of Allāh Is an Inner Struggle for Purification."

> *"Never aspire to confront your enemies (in battle). Pray to God to be among those who seek to live peacefully with others. But if ever you confront them (in battle), be patient and know that Heaven is as close to you as the shadows of the swords."* (PH)[33]
>
> «أيها الناس لا تتمنوا لقاء العدو وسلوا الله العافية فإذا لقيتم فاصبروا واعلموا أن الجنة تحت ظلال السيوف»

Fighting was a struggle *(jihād)*, because victory was not guaranteed, the Muslim troops being almost always inferior in number. It was also *jihād* because it resulted from attacks by certain groups with the intention of oppressing or exploiting others, violating legitimate rights, or working to prevent the word of Truth from reaching others.

Fifth, one can safely say that whenever the Holy Qur'ān urged men to battle, this advice was tempered with advice to be just and to not exceed certain limits.

> *Fight in the cause of Allāh those who fight you, but do not transgress limits; for Allāh loves not transgressors.* (Qur'ān 2:190)
>
> وَقَاتِلُوا فِي سَبِيلِ اللَّهِ الَّذِينَ يُقَاتِلُونَكُمْ وَلَا تَعْتَدُوا إِنَّ اللَّهَ لَا يُحِبُّ الْمُعْتَدِينَ

> *O you who believe! Stand firmly for Allāh, as witnesses to fair dealing, and let not the others' hatred of you make you swerve to doing wrong and departing from justice. Be just—that is next to piety—and be conscious of Allāh. For Allāh is well-acquainted with all that you do.* (Qur'ān 5:8)
>
> يَاأَيُّهَا الَّذِينَ ءَامَنُوا كُونُوا قَوَّامِينَ لِلَّهِ شُهَدَاءَ بِالْقِسْطِ وَلَا يَجْرِمَنَّكُمْ شَنَآنُ قَوْمٍ عَلَى أَلَّا تَعْدِلُوا اعْدِلُوا هُوَ أَقْرَبُ لِلتَّقْوَى وَاتَّقُوا اللَّهَ إِنَّ اللَّهَ خَبِيرٌ بِمَا تَعْمَلُونَ

---

[33]Narrated by Bukhārī, Muslim, and Abū Dā'ūd.

And fight them until there is no more tumult or oppression, and there prevails justice and faith in Allāh altogether and everywhere; but if they cease, verily Allāh sees all that they do. (Qur'ān 8:39)

وَقَاتِلُوهُمْ حَتَّى لَا تَكُونَ فِتْنَةٌ وَيَكُونَ الدِّينُ كُلُّهُ لِلَّهِ فَإِنِ انْتَهَوْا فَإِنَّ اللَّهَ بِمَا يَعْمَلُونَ بَصِيرٌ

The Holy Qur'ān also guides Muslims to refrain from fighting inadvertently and from directing their attacks against innocent people:

... let there be no hostility except to those who practice oppression. (Qur'ān 2:193)

فَلَا عُدْوَانَ إِلَّا عَلَى الظَّالِمِينَ

It can also be said that Muslim fighters were guided to be alert to restore peace as soon as the transgressors showed serious intent to end their aggression.

But if they cease, Allāh is Oft-Forgiving, Most Merciful. (Qur'ān 2:192)

فَإِنِ انْتَهَوْا فَإِنَّ اللَّهَ غَفُورٌ رَحِيمٌ

Tolerance Towards People of Other Beliefs

The Prophet Muḥammad did not impose the Islamic teachings on others, tolerating diversity and accepting it as a fact of life. This is not surprising in a Prophet who made peace and love the core of his mission. His life is full of examples that demonstrate his tolerance. When ʿAsmā'a, the daughter of his companion Abu Bakr, asked him what she should do with her mother, who opposed the Islamic teachings, he answered that she should stay on good terms with the older woman. ʿAsmā'a was somewhat confused, as she could not understand one of the verses banning a Medina Muslim from having a denier as a friend. The verse says,

"O you who believe! Take not My enemies and yours as friends (or protectors), offering them (your) love ... (take them not as

> *friends), holding secret converse of love (and friendship) with them ... And any of you that does this has strayed from the straight path." (Qur'ān 60:1)*
>
> يَاأَيُّهَا الَّذِينَ ءَامَنُوا لَا تَتَّخِذُوا عَدُوِّي وَعَدُوَّكُمْ أَوْلِيَاءَ تُلْقُونَ
> إِلَيْهِمْ بِالْمَوَدَّةِ وَقَدْ كَفَرُوا بِمَا جَاءَكُمْ مِنَ الْحَقِّ يُخْرِجُونَ الرَّسُولَ
> وَإِيَّاكُمْ أَنْ تُؤْمِنُوا بِاللَّهِ رَبِّكُمْ إِنْ كُنْتُمْ خَرَجْتُمْ جِهَادًا فِي سَبِيلِي
> وَابْتِغَاءَ مَرْضَاتِي تُسِرُّونَ إِلَيْهِمْ بِالْمَوَدَّةِ وَأَنَا أَعْلَمُ بِمَا أَخْفَيْتُمْ وَمَا
> أَعْلَنْتُمْ وَمَنْ يَفْعَلْهُ مِنْكُمْ فَقَدْ ضَلَّ سَوَاءَ السَّبِيلِ

ʿAsmā'a came to understand that this verse referred to a certain incident. The verse criticized the behavior of a Muslim who had confided secret information to a person from Quraysh whom he considered a friend. This person had then delivered the information to the leaders of his tribe. As such, he chose to be an enemy of Muḥammad's message. A holy verse was revealed to support the Prophet's advice to ʿAsmā'a.

> *"Allāh does not forbid you from dealing kindly and justly with those who have not fought you on account of (your) faith and have not driven you out of your homes, for Allāh loves those who are just." (Qur'ān 60:8)*
>
> لَا يَنْهَاكُمُ اللَّهُ عَنِ الَّذِينَ لَمْ يُقَاتِلُوكُمْ فِي الدِّينِ وَلَمْ يُخْرِجُوكُمْ
> مِنْ دِيَارِكُمْ أَنْ تَبَرُّوهُمْ وَتُقْسِطُوا إِلَيْهِمْ إِنَّ اللَّهَ يُحِبُّ الْمُقْسِطِينَ

The holy verse dismisses any confusion by assuring that Muslims are free to choose their friends from among all peoples, regardless of their beliefs, as long as those people accept to live in peace with them.

Coexistence with People of Other Creeds

People of the Book are not considered enemies of Muslims and should be respected and honored.

And there are, certainly, among the People of the Book, those who believe in Allāh, in the revelation to you, and in the revelation to them, bowing in humility to Allāh. They will not sell the Signs of Allāh for a miserable gain! For them is a reward with their Lord, and Allāh is swift in account. (Qur'ān 3:199)

وَإِنَّ مِنْ أَهْلِ الْكِتَابِ لَمَنْ يُؤْمِنُ بِاللَّهِ وَمَا أُنْزِلَ إِلَيْكُمْ وَمَا أُنْزِلَ إِلَيْهِمْ خَاشِعِينَ لِلَّهِ لَا يَشْتَرُونَ بِآيَاتِ اللَّهِ ثَمَنًا قَلِيلًا أُولَئِكَ لَهُمْ أَجْرُهُمْ عِنْدَ رَبِّهِمْ إِنَّ اللَّهَ سَرِيعُ الْحِسَابِ

Those who had different beliefs, but did not attack Muslims or break covenants with them, could live peacefully within the Muslim community, even if they did not follow the heavenly guidance given to Muḥammad.

If one among the pagans asks you for asylum, grant it to him, so that he may hear the word of Allāh, and then escort him to where he can be secure. (Qur'ān 9:6)

وَإِنْ أَحَدٌ مِنَ الْمُشْرِكِينَ اسْتَجَارَكَ فَأَجِرْهُ حَتَّى يَسْمَعَ كَلَامَ اللَّهِ ثُمَّ أَبْلِغْهُ مَأْمَنَهُ ذَلِكَ بِأَنَّهُمْ قَوْمٌ لَا يَعْلَمُونَ

O you who believe! When you go abroad in the cause of Allāh, investigate carefully, and do not say to anyone who offers you a salutation of peace, "You are not a believer!" our of desire for the fleeting gains of this worldly life. (Qur'ān 4:94)

يَاأَيُّهَا الَّذِينَ ءَامَنُوا إِذَا ضَرَبْتُمْ فِي سَبِيلِ اللَّهِ فَتَبَيَّنُوا وَلَا تَقُولُوا لِمَنْ أَلْقَى إِلَيْكُمُ السَّلَامَ لَسْتَ مُؤْمِنًا تَبْتَغُونَ عَرَضَ الْحَيَاةِ الدُّنْيَا فَعِنْدَ اللَّهِ مَغَانِمُ كَثِيرَةٌ كَذَلِكَ كُنْتُمْ مِنْ قَبْلُ فَمَنَّ اللَّهُ عَلَيْكُمْ فَتَبَيَّنُوا إِنَّ اللَّهَ كَانَ بِمَا تَعْمَلُونَ خَبِيرًا

... If they withdraw from you but fight you not, and (instead) send you (guarantees of) peace, then Allāh has opened no way for you (to war against them). (Qur'ān 4:90)

فَإِنِ اعْتَزَلُوكُمْ فَلَمْ يُقَاتِلُوكُمْ وَأَلْقَوْا إِلَيْكُمُ السَّلَمَ فَمَا جَعَلَ اللَّهُ لَكُمْ عَلَيْهِمْ سَبِيلًا

Reading the treaty that the Prophet signed with all the Jewish tribes in Yathrib, it is clearly stated that all Muslims— immigrants or natives of Yathrib—shared with non-Muslims the equal rights and duties of individuals in any society. Differences of faith did not stop the Prophet from writing in the treaty that as individuals in a Muslim-ruled society, *"Jews are to be protected by Muslims against any outside aggression."* It is written in the treaty that *"the Jews can be one nation with Muslims, if they so wish,"* and that they could join them in fighting and in financing battles when either was exposed to outside aggression. The treaty says, *"Anyone (Muslim or Jew) should care just as much that no harm comes to his neighbor as to himself."* The treaty gives full *"security to whoever (Jew) accepts to stay in Medina or he who chooses to move away."*[34]

Muslims were ordered to treat conquered people with kindness and love, to be compassionate and understanding. The Prophet said,

> *"Do not kill an old man, a small child, or a woman. Do not commit acts of treachery nor make profits of the spoils of war." (PH)*[35]
>
> لا تقتلوا شيخا فانيا ولا طفلا صغيرا ولا امرأة، ولا تغلوا
>
> *"Release the captured, support whoever asks for help, feed the hungry, and visit the sick." (PH)*[36]
>
> فكوا العاني (الأسير) وأجيبوا الداعي وأطعموا الجائع وعودوا المريض

Certain treaties between the Prophet and inhabitants of the conquered lands were documented. Those treaties were similar in guaranteeing not only People of the Book but also Zoroastrians[37] and

[34]The text of the treaty is in Haikal, 239-241.
[35]Narrated by Abū Dā'ūd.
[36]Narrated by Bukhārī and Aḥmad.
[37]Worshippers of fire, which they believed to be the origin of all that exists.

other non-Muslims the freedom to practice their worship system and to choose their beliefs as long as they did not harm others. The Prophet, for instance, addressed the inhabitants of Najrān (near the border with Yemen):

> *"All archbishops, priests, with their followers, and monks have to maintain full authority over their churches and monasteries, few or many. They are to be regarded (by Muslims) as neighbors of Allāh and His Prophet. An archbishop, a priest or a monk is not to be forced to quit his faith. And none of them is to be stripped of any of his legal rights or authority as long as they perform their duties without extending any injustice to anyone, and without being treated unjustly."* (PH)[38]
>
> «««أساقفة نجران وكهنتهم ومن تبعهم ورهبانهم لهم على ما تحت أيديهم من قليل وكثير من بيعهم وصلواتهم ورهبانيتهم، وجوار الله ورسوله لا يغير أسقف عن أسقفيته ولا راهب عن رهبانيته ولا كاهن عن كهانته، ولايغير حق من حقوقهم ولا سلطانهم ولا شيء مما كانوا عليه ما نصحوا وأصلحوا فيما عليهم غير مثقلين بظلم ولا ظالمين.»»»

The Prophet would tell his companions that, in an Islamic society, people of other faiths were forever under his personal protection. He called them *Dhimmeyin*. The Prophet told his companions,

> *"If ever you hurt a Dhimmī I shall be on his side on the Day of Judgment."* (PH)[39]
>
> «««من آذى ذميا فأنا خصمه. ومن كنت خصمه خصمته يوم القيامة»»»

Regulations Regarding Tolerance

In his regulation of Islamic society, whereby non-Muslims were obliged to pay head taxes *(jizyah)*, the Prophet was eager that those

[38] Ibn Sa'd, 2: 30, 31.

[39] Narrated by As-Suyū textsubdottī. (Quoted in Ad-Dahabī, 61.)

taxes not be an indirect pressure on non-Muslims. He commanded that the tax be proportionate to the economic capacity of a non-Muslim. The *jizyah* was not forced on them as a "punishment" because they refused to convert to Islām, nor to humiliate them. On the contrary, it was intended to enhance their feelings of citizenship, since it was clear that the *jizyah* was paid to cover the expenses of protecting non-Muslims against outside attacks. As citizens, they had the right to share in their society's protection. Moreover, the poor among them were not subject to pay the *jizyah* and had the same right as Muslims to be supported by the money collected through *zakāt* (alms-giving). In short, they enjoyed the full rights of "citizenship."

Non-Muslims were not allowed to fight side-by-side with Muslims, because at that time, the danger that Muslims faced was too great. Muslims accepted martyrdom, fighting because of their faith in Allāh; they didn't fight merely to conquer or to realize worldly gains. It was not logical, therefore, to ask non-Muslims to fight in the same spirit. It would have been a way of forcing them to practice a system of worship though they did not share its basic belief.[40]

Social Tolerance

Not only do Islamic teachings advise people to be just to the People of the Book, they also push Muslims to include them as family. When a Muslim man is married to a non-Muslim woman, he considers her family as part of his. His children should invest in their relations with non-Muslim uncles to overcome sensitivities resulting from differences in belief.

In Islām, marriage is considered to be a "divine covenant." Mercy, respect, and love should infuse the relationship between husband and wife. If the wife belongs to another creed, this should not affect their relationship. The Holy Qur'ān even encourages Muslims to marry non-Muslim women, emphasizing that the relation-

[40]Later, non-Muslims in all Muslim countries joined in fighting against any outside aggression; the*jizyah* was no longer enforced. Muslim legislators clearly understood that it was a temporary solution that did not seek to humiliate non-Muslims or isolate them from the Muslim community.

ship between Muslims and others should be a relation of love and respect.

> *(Lawful unto you in marriage) are (not only) chaste women who are believers, but chaste women among the People of the Book, revealed before your time, when you give them their due dowries, and desire chastity, not lewdness, nor secret intrigues. (Qur'ān 5:5)*

الْيَوْمَ أُحِلَّ لَكُمُ الطَّيِّبَاتُ وَطَعَامُ الَّذِينَ أُوتُوا الْكِتَابَ حِلٌّ لَكُمْ وَطَعَامُكُمْ حِلٌّ لَهُمْ وَالْمُحْصَنَاتُ مِنَ الْمُؤْمِنَاتِ وَالْمُحْصَنَاتُ مِنَ الَّذِينَ أُوتُوا الْكِتَابَ مِنْ قَبْلِكُمْ إِذَا ءَاتَيْتُمُوهُنَّ أُجُورَهُنَّ مُحْصِنِينَ غَيْرَ مُسَافِحِينَ وَلَا مُتَّخِذِي أَخْدَانٍ

On the societal level, the Prophet Muḥammad called upon his followers to be friendly, considerate, and benevolent to their neighbors, regardless of belief, creed, or race. He advised his followers to exchange presents with their friends of different faiths. The Holy Qur'ān points to a sign of friendship in a verse telling Muslims that they can invite and accept the invitations of their friends to share meals.

> *The food of the People of the Book is lawful unto you and yours is lawful unto them. (Qur'ān 5:5)*

وَطَعَامُ الَّذِينَ أُوتُوا الْكِتَابَ حِلٌّ لَكُمْ وَطَعَامُكُمْ حِلٌّ لَهُمْ.

Given this very clear guidance to Muslims to live as family with people regardless of their religion, it is clear that verses in the Holy Qur'ān which seemingly convey a different message should be considered as specific cases, for they do not express the main principle of the Islamic Call. For example, the following verse came as a response to the declared enmity of Jews and Christians towards Muslims at the time of the Prophet and should not be generalized:[41]

[41] This verse was revealed at the time when the Jewish tribe of Banī Qaynuqā'in Medina was waging war against Muslims. It included criticism of a Muslim and a Christian who were allied with them, even though this was a violation of the treaty of co-existence signed with the Prophet and a clear expression of their enmity. (Exegeses of the Holy Qur'ān, 180).

O you who believe! Take not the Jews and the Christians for your friends and protectors; they are but friends and protectors to each other. And he among you that turns to them (for friendship) is of them. Verily Allāh guides not people who are unjust. (Qur'ān 5:51)

يَاأَيُّهَا الَّذِينَ ءَامَنُوا لَا تَتَّخِذُوا الْيَهُودَ وَالنَّصَارَىٰ أَوْلِيَاءَ بَعْضُهُمْ أَوْلِيَاءُ بَعْضٍ وَمَنْ يَتَوَلَّهُمْ مِنْكُمْ فَإِنَّهُ مِنْهُمْ إِنَّ اللَّهَ لَا يَهْدِي الْقَوْمَ الظَّالِمِينَ

Again, this and other holy verses refer to exceptional cases. According to Islamic teachings, the general rule regulating relationships among people recognizes a common affiliation deeper than race, nationality, color, religion, or labels of any kind. The Holy Qur'ān says that all people are brothers and sisters in humanity and are honored as coming from one Origin.

We have honored the sons of Adam. (Qur'ān 17:70)

وَلَقَدْ كَرَّمْنَا بَنِي ءَادَمَ

O mankind! Revere your Lord, who created you from one soul, created, of like nature, its mate, and from the two scattered (like seeds) countless men and women. (Qur'ān 4:1)

يَاأَيُّهَا النَّاسُ اتَّقُوا رَبَّكُمُ الَّذِي خَلَقَكُمْ مِنْ نَفْسٍ وَاحِدَةٍ وَخَلَقَ مِنْهَا زَوْجَهَا وَبَثَّ مِنْهُمَا رِجَالًا كَثِيرًا وَنِسَاءً

O mankind! We created you from a male and a female, and made you into nations and tribes, that you may know each other (not that you may despise each other). Verily the most honored of you in the sight of Allāh is (he who is) the most righteous of you. And Allāh has full knowledge and is well-acquainted (with all things). (Qur'ān 49:13)

يَاأَيُّهَا النَّاسُ إِنَّا خَلَقْنَاكُمْ مِنْ ذَكَرٍ وَأُنْثَىٰ وَجَعَلْنَاكُمْ شُعُوبًا وَقَبَائِلَ لِتَعَارَفُوا إِنَّ أَكْرَمَكُمْ عِنْدَ اللَّهِ أَتْقَاكُمْ إِنَّ اللَّهَ عَلِيمٌ خَبِيرٌ

Maintaining the Main Principles of Islām Does Not Conflict with Tolerance

Despite all the evidence of Islām's tolerance, the fact that non-Muslims were not allowed in Mecca following the spread of Islām in Arabia raises many questions. The situation of Mecca can be considered a unique case. Before the Revelation to Muḥammad, pagan tribes came to the *Ka'bah* (the symbol of the House of God) to present offerings and carry out their pilgrimage rites. Around the *Ka'bah* each tribe would place its deities and perform its worship system. Before Muḥammad's return to Mecca, the *Ka'bah* was a symbol of pagan beliefs.

Islām came with a very clear message, aiming to support man in overcoming illusions that he created and then worshipped. To allow the deities around the *Ka'bah* to remain would be completely illogical and inconsistent. It would not be a demonstration of tolerance; it would merely confuse Muḥammad's followers. On the other hand, the *Ka'bah*'s symbolic dimension was to be preserved.

When Muslims destroyed the idols inside the *Ka'bah*, they were drawing a sharp line between Truth and illusion. As a sacred symbol, the *Ka'bah* should represent holiness and purity. Within this context, we can understand Allāh's commandment in the Holy Qur'ān:

> *O you who believe! Truly the Pagans are unclean; so let them not, after this year of theirs, approach the Sacred Mosque. (Qur'ān 9:28)*
>
> يَاأَيُّهَا الَّذِينَ ءَامَنُوا إِنَّمَا الْمُشْرِكُونَ نَجَسٌ فَلَا يَقْرَبُوا الْمَسْجِدَ الْحَرَامَ بَعْدَ عَامِهِمْ هَذَا

Mecca, as it is the home of the Sacred Mosque, should be a peaceful place. No fights, conflicts, or wars should take place in Mecca. This is a reminder that Mecca is, symbolically speaking, a piece of heaven on earth. This meaning is emphasized in the discipline to which pilgrims should conform. Pilgrims are not to kill any living beings, whether insect or animal. As it was difficult to make people of other creeds abide by such rules, Mecca was restricted to Muslims alone.

This was not intended as a distinction between the followers of Muḥammad and others; it was meant only to convey the message that underlies making the *Ka'bah* the *Qiblah* (Direction). It is a constant reminder that the path that Muḥammad followed is the path of Abraham.

This rule, if understood in context, is void of discrimination against, or superiority over, non-Muslims. For instance, Muslims are allowed to live under non-Muslim political authority and to abide by its rules if they do not contradict the basic teachings of Islām. The Prophet sent early Muslims to live under the authority of the Negus of Ethiopia, a Christian ruler known for his sense of justice.[42] In doing so, the Prophet was not seeking a compromise with the emperor to gain his alliance and support; a compromise with the leaders of Quraysh, eager to offer him money and authority so that he would abandon his Call, would have been more advantageous. He refused another compromise when one of the tribes' leaders agreed to support his Call on the condition that the latter succeed him once Muḥammad dominated the other tribes. He could have accepted and then broken the agreement, but that would have violated his own ethics. He never broke a promise in his entire life.[43]

Summary

Much of the confusion concerning the Islamic Call and the relationship to be established between Muslims and followers of other creeds stems from distorted, literal, or partial readings of the Holy

---

[42]The Muslim immigrants to Ethiopia numbered 83 men and 11 women. They lived for several years under the protection of the Negus. In a position of safety, they could speak freely of their faith, without fear of oppression, but did not try to convert people to Islām. (Ibn Sa'd, 1:191, 192. Also Ibn Hishām, 1:302, 303.) The Prophet said to Muslims, *"You should leave for Ethiopia, which is governed by a king (Negus) whose subjects are not exposed to any oppression. It is a land of faithfulness. Stay there until Allāh grants you an outlet."* (Ibn Hishām, 1: 291, 292)

لو خرجتم إلى أرض الحبشة فإن بها ملكا لا يظلم عنده أحد وهي أرض صدق حتى يجعل الله لكم فرجا مما أنتم فيها

[43]See the Appendix, "The Prophet Muḥammad Used Moral Means for Spreading the Word of Truth."

Qur'ān, Prophetic *Sunnah,* and events that took place during the life of the Prophet. Consequently, some Muslim groups feel obliged to spread Islām by all means, even by violence, even though this directly contradicts the basis of the Islamic Call that the Prophet Muḥammad conveyed and lived in both Mecca and Medina. The Prophet Muḥammad's way in conveying the divine mission was characterized by respect for freedom of faith, as it perceived diversity of creeds to be part of the natural laws of creation, and an eagerness to spread peace and tolerance towards followers of previous revelations.

When he rejected paganism in Mecca, the Prophet Muḥammad was not attempting to impose his belief system on non-believers. Indeed, out of love of all and according to the Divine's commandment to him, he was inviting those who considered their economic and political power a legitimate reason for exploiting the less powerful to realize that they were worshipping false gods (money, authority, and tribal pride), which would lead to their own spiritual downfall. He was also inviting the poor to liberate themselves from fear of and submission to their exploiters. In other words, he was inviting people to become aware of the ultimate goal of their existence: to realize their human potential. Attaining such a goal implies man's striving to be spiritually free from devotion to any aspect of the transient life. That was and is the core of the Islamic Testimony, the *Shahādah,* "There is no god but God," *Lā ilāha illā Allāh.* To the People of the Book, the Islamic Call was an invitation to come to "the reconciling principle" with Muslims: to worship none but Allāh. The Prophet called upon them to share an approach to life that would make them feel that they belonged to each other, a reminder that what he called for existed already in the Revelations to Moses and Jesus. His primary aim was not that they would convert to the worship system adopted in the Revelation given to him or that they would follow the Islamic legal system; rather, he guided them to follow the pure guidance of the Prophets Moses and Jesus, drawing their attention to the essence of the Primordial Religion of Abraham that they all shared.

Spreading peace was and is the core of the Islamic Call. Peace starts from within us when we are spiritually liberated from devotion to any transient goal. This inner peace is spontaneously reflected outwards, towards all of nature and all human beings. Islamic teachings guide Muslims to give the higher Self the opportunity to express peace and to control the lower self. This is the principal battle advocated by the Islamic Call, which is referred to as the greater struggle, *al-jihād al-akbar*. During the lifetime of the Prophet Muḥammad, he and his companions were never the first to initiate a battle against an outside enemy in the lesser struggle, *al-jihād al-asghar*. In every stage of the Islamic Call, in Mecca and Medina, the Prophet exhausted all possible efforts to reach agreements with his opponents in an attempt to maintain peaceful coexistence. In Mecca, the leaders of the Quraysh initiated hostilities against the Prophet and his followers and attempted to kill him. When he migrated to Medina, they planned to cripple the newborn Muslim society and waged war against the Muslims. The Prophet's attempts to live in peace with the Jewish tribes in Medina, giving them full rights as one nation with Muslims, were also in vain. One after another, the Jewish tribes broke the treaties they had signed with the Prophet and committed many acts of treason. However, according to the guidance of the Divine in the Holy Qur'ān and the Prophetic *Sunnah*, Muslims were told never to initiate war or to lust for revenge or bloodshed. Muslims were advised to agree immediately to a cease-fire whenever there was a chance to restore peace. When fighting was unavoidable, the Prophet's guidance to his followers was to minimize losses in any new land they entered. His strict teachings were: never destroy a church, a temple, or any place of worship and never destroy a house, cut down a tree, or terrorize people.

Tolerance towards people of other creeds is firmly advocated in the Holy Qur'ān and the Prophetic *Sunnah*. People of different creeds are granted full guarantees to practice their religious rites in safety. Muslims are guided never to attempt to convert people of other faiths to Islām. Muslims are encouraged, however, to establish friendships with non-Muslims, invite them to meals, accept their invitations, and exchange presents with them as signs of love. In this way, Islamic guidance enables people of other creeds to make the "reconciling principle" a basis for peaceful coexistence and a life that reflects their oneness. Tolerance extends to all, even to non-believers, because the Islamic teachings clearly say that freedom of faith is to be fully and unconditionally guaranteed. A person is never to be rejected by a Muslim community because of his thoughts or belief system. Rather, a person is denounced, regardless of his belief, when he harms another, as he is violating the oneness of humanity.

7
General Conclusion

The Revelation to the Prophet Muḥammad (Peace be upon him) was and remains a continuation, confirmation, and clarification of the ONE MESSAGE that the Divine has sent to mankind since Father Adam. The core of that Message is a reminder to us about how to realize the ultimate goal of our existence, how to approach life from a perspective that supports us in achieving that goal. "Islām" as revealed to the Prophet Muḥammad was a rejuvenation of the Divine's Call to humanity to "surrender" to the Law of creation in both its physical and metaphysical manifestations. And because that Law is inherent in the primordial nature of man, *fiṭrah,* Islām is termed the Primordial Religion, *ad-dīn al-fiṭrah,* the religion that all Prophets conveyed and that was revealed to Abraham as *ad-dīn al-ḥanīf,* the religion of essential righteousness. As such, "Islām" as revealed to the Prophet Muḥammad emphasized the One Origin of all revelations. Accordingly, "Islām" did not—and does not— require followers of other revelations to convert to its system of worship or legislation, and it did not—and does not—ask Muslims to impose their system on others. "Islām" only guides all to come to "the reconciling principle":

> *". . .our God and your God is One; and it is to Him we bow (in Islām)." (HQ 29:46)*
>
> وَإِلَٰهُنَا وَإِلَٰهُكُمْ وَاحِدٌ وَنَحْنُ لَهُ مُسْلِمُونَ

Although the core Call of that Revelation was and is to spread love, peace, tolerance, freedom, knowledge, and justice, many misconceptions have accumulated through the years, hindering people of different cultures and civilizations from benefiting from its wisdom. Both Islamic and non-Islamic societies are susceptible to such misunderstandings. The investigation and analysis of those misconceptions are beyond the scope of this book, but deserve further research.

Our aim here was to demonstrate how Islām as revealed through the Prophet Muḥammad guided humanity to a balanced approach to life. The authors suggest that the modern world needs to learn about that "balanced path"; by discerning the original principles of the Revelation, people will lead fulfilled lives. The authors propose that such principles are of paramount significance to the modern world, which lacks balance in many respects. **First**, many conflicts in our world are rooted in people's tendency to feel somehow superior to others. Fully occupied in realizing their political, economic, military, racial, and cultural distinctions, people oppress each other. Islām guides people to realize that being human implies that they share an origin that transcends any differences of race, color, language, nationality, or even religion. It confirms that their shared goal is to be fulfilled as humans and at the same time to respect existing diversities. A balance between feelings of commonality and respect for diversity would enhance peace, tolerance, justice, and cooperation among all people. **Second**, the world has indulged itself in the superfluous aspects of life, neglecting the spiritual dimension. This lack of balance harms us in many ways. Islām guides people to realize that our earthly life should serve the spiritual dimension. The two aspects of life, the spiritual and the worldly, are complementary, not contradictory, as long as we are aware of the ultimate goal of our existence. **Third**, the modern world suffers from excessive feelings of individuality, which has led to the spread of selfishness among people, with individuals trying to fulfill their personal goals anyway they can, even if it means hurting others or damaging nature. Islām respects the individuality of each human being, rather than treating each one as an anonymous person in a crowd. At the same time, the individual is guided to feel his oneness with others on a more transcendental level. As such, one can attain balance on the two levels of existence, as an individual and in his relations with others.

Each chapter of this book examines a dimension of the Islamic Revelation that gives considerable knowledge as to how to lead such a balanced life. Here we retrace the messages discovered throughout the book and what they can offer to modern man.

The Holy Qur'ān clearly refers to Islām not as a creed, but as the Way to surrender to the Divine Order. Hence all the Prophets are deemed Muslims in the Holy Qur'ān, as each led his life in a state of surrender to the Order and each was a manifestation of what it is to be a Muslim. Their stories are narrated in a way that demonstrates that a Muslim is one who respects reason, seeks knowledge, works hard, and at the same time seeks spiritual freedom, namely, devotion to God.

Because the Religion revealed by the Divine is one, it was only natural that each Prophet came to confirm and clarify the revelation that preceded him. Jesus said that he came to fulfill the Law that Moses revealed. The Prophet Muḥammad teaches that the Revelation he conveyed confirmed the Revelations to Moses and Jesus, by reviving the origins of the Religion dating to Abraham. His confirmation of previous revelations also included clarification of misconceptions that arose through the years. The most notable deviation from the original teachings is the tendency of people to transform Religion into sets of dogmas, stagnant traditions, and ready-made shapes and forms. Limited understanding leads people to worship the images that they have made of God and to forget the Unseen aspect of life. Lacking spiritual awareness, they think of Prophets as mere historical figures; consequently, the followers of each Revelation think that their loyalty to "their" Prophet obliges them to prove that he is superior to the others. They ignore or forget the oneness of Religion and the shared path of the Prophets. Islām as revealed to Muḥammad was and remains a reminder of that oneness.

By reminding people of the shared path of the Prophets, the Revelation to the Prophet Muḥammad may rally the followers of all revelations, Prophetic or natural. It can help them to liberate themselves from the imprisonment of names and labels. It teaches them to remember the oneness of all people and to live accordingly.

We are guided to discern that everything in the universe is created and ordered according to the Divine Law. The Natural Law is but a manifestation of the transcendental Divine. Man can experience the Divine within himself. This experience reveals to us the spiritual aspect of existence, which in turn strengthens our faith in the continuation of life. The more we approach the worldly life from that dimension, the more we sense freedom. That freedom is symbolized in the Islamic Testimony, the *Shahādah;* to witness that there is no god but God *(Lā ilāha illā Allāh)* is to be devoted to nothing and to no one but Allāh. The second part of the *Shahādah,* proclaiming that Muḥammad is the Messenger of God *(Muḥammad rasūlu Allāh),* symbolizes that the freedom a person seeks is achieved through Muḥammad. In this context, Muḥammad is a symbol of all Prophets and teachers of humanity, who should be present in the hearts of the seekers, providing them spiritual support.

Because faith in the Messenger of God is not merely historical or physical, the Revelation to Muḥammad showed that the *Ka'bah,* the House of God that was revealed to Abraham, is a symbol of the Light that people can turn to when seeking guidance. That is, the holy shrine is not a mere building, but is a symbol of man's need to have a "direction," a focus in life. That direction is represented in the Islamic concept of the *Qiblah,* turning one's face towards the *Ka'bah* as a symbol of divine guidance. When a person is completely and solely devoted to Allāh and is aware of the ultimate goal of his existence, he or she is transformed into a servant of Allāh. To be a servant of Allāh is thus to be spiritually free and to have a focus in life—a goal that deserves everyone's every effort.

The Islamic teachings can guide modern man to achieve balance, drawing his attention to the link between heaven and earth. This balance saves man from the arrogance resulting from man's scientific and technological advances. Realizing that there is a higher, spiritual existence unknown to him, he can try, instead, to link what he does in this life with the Hereafter. Inventions are to be measured according to their contribution to humane purposes. Believing in the unseen aspect of life liberates us from the imprisonment of matter, allowing us to realize that life is not limited to the temporal existence. This gives us a focus and a fuller life. Still, knowledge and faith are not attained once and for all; spiritual knowledge grows as we are purified spiritually.

The spiritual training system that the Revelation to Muḥammad presented, and which exists in different forms in other revelations, supports us in our struggle for purification. It is a system that expresses the embedded meanings of the Testimony "There is no god but God, Muḥammad is the Messenger of God." Each aspect of the system is a means to spiritually liberate oneself from the constraints of matter, by exposing oneself to the grace of God throughout the day: in the ritual prayers; by living as a spirit during the month of fasting; by being a tool of charity in the hands of the Divine once a year in *zakāt*; and experiencing life as a journey in which one metaphorically travels to Allāh's House once in one's life, in pilgrimage. Ritual prayers, fasting, alms-giving, and pilgrimage are means of spiritual purification, as well as a reminder to man to pursue his goal as a servant of Allāh to achieve balance.

Spiritually purified, we can approach everything in life from a perspective that enhances love, beauty, and goodness. However, it is not only in worship that we can attain spiritual elevation. We can achieve this daily by carrying out every activity from the perspective of witnessing our oneness with everything. Islām guides us to the way to become aware of the oneness of life. Because the One expresses His existence through everything that He created, everything points to Him. Life then follows one order and everything is linked to the whole. When we perceive things as fragmented, we risk creating conflict with our surroundings; when we feel the Oneness deep inside our hearts, we sense and seek harmony. In short, the oneness of Allāh should be reflected in the realization of the oneness of life. With this realization, we can lead a just and balanced life within ourselves, with nature, and with our fellow human beings. The Islamic *Sharīʿah* (the Divine path to Truth) introduces us to principles that make daily life spiritually rewarding. The principles of the Islamic *Sharīʿah* are not ready-made forms or rules; rather, they are basic principles that can inspire humans with the means to live a balanced life on both the individual and the societal levels. The *Sharīʿah* guides us to respect the original oneness on a practical level. All aspects of the Islamic *Sharīʿah* support us in striking a balance between our needs and the conditions for justice.

The principles inherent in the Islamic *Sharīʿah* can assist us in readjusting our approach to our personal needs, to nature, and to others. We can respect the natural environment rather than seeking to dominate it. We can learn to satisfy our physical needs without harming our spiritual growth. We can seek to build our human relations from a perspective that guarantees justice for all. People can develop political and economic systems that help human beings fulfill themselves spiritually through cooperation, not conflict. International relations can be designed in such a way that each country would examine how it could help others rather than seek growth through exploitation and domination. The invitation to discern the oneness of humanity through relationships with people of other faiths is shows the approach of the Islamic teachings.

Spreading peace was and remains the core goal of the Islamic Call. The Prophet never attempted to impose the knowledge revealed to him on non-believers or followers of other revelations. As a Messenger of God, he drew their attention to a way of life in which no one should dominate or exploit others, as everyone's devotion should be to Allāh alone. Fearing that the Call would limit their oppression of others, his opponents in Mecca and Medina not only rejected the Call, but also initiated wars against him and his followers. In his approach to the followers of Jesus and Moses (the People of the Book), he invited them to share "the common principle," also found in their Revelations. All revelations advocated the common principle: to be devoted to Allāh and to manifest that devotion by expressing love to humanity.

A Revelation that calls for spreading peace within and without is eager to guide its followers to the means by which they can realize their goal. To be worthy of what the Revelation to the Prophet Muḥammad epitomizes and to be true followers of Muḥammad implies living as an exemplar. Such a person, by their very existence, radiates a light that, unsurprisingly, attracts searching souls and spreads peace, love, tolerance, and knowledge wherever he or she may be. "Let there be no compulsion in religion" is a basic principle that followers of the Islamic Revelation should embrace. From the believers' loving hearts, they should invite themselves and others to seek the common path in all revelations, recognizing that *all* should seek the better way. The Islamic Call suggests dialogue as a mechanism for humanity to spread all types of knowledge and wisdom, old and modern. The distinction between true and false does not depend on names or temporal goals, but on the degree to which any new knowledge aids people in recognizing how to live according to the Divine Law. In this way they can grow spiritually and they will see clearly the path of Truth.

In today's world, the scene of endless fighting and feelings of enmity that spread terror, the Islamic Call for peace is needed more than ever. The Call that the Prophet Muḥammad conveyed more than 1400 years ago is valid and vital now.

Appendix

This appendix refers to certain events and verses of the Holy Qur'ān and Prophetic *ḥadīths* related to them, in an attempt to clarify further the approach presented in this book. To include the entirety of events and holy sayings is beyond the scope of this appendix; rather, a few examples are offered, inviting those who seek the truth to read, with deep insight, the history of the Islamic Revelation, presented in hundreds of books, avoiding being distracted by seemingly contradictory episodes scattered here and there. There is a clear, well-defined pattern of events, which appear as a mosaic demonstrating the consistency of the way the Prophet presented and lived the Islamic Call.

The Islamic Call Should Be Free of any Earthly Aspirations

The Prophet Muḥammad (Peace be upon him) illustrated this principle in all his acts, throughout his life, both when he lacked any political or economic power and when he ruled a state in Arabia. His guidance to his followers was to retain that purity and not to confuse their struggle to spread the word of truth with any temporal ambitions.

The Prophet Muḥammad Uwho was sed Moral Means for Spreading the Word of Truth

Noting the increasing number of Muslims in Mecca, among them the Prophet's uncle Hamza, one of the city's most honorable citizens, the Qurayshi leaders became wary and tried to remove the "threat" of the Islamic Call by proposing to the Prophet what they thought was a very tempting offer. They said,

> *"If the aim of all you are doing is to gain much money, we shall gather enough and give it to you so that you will be the richest*

among us. If you are after tribal pride, we shall bestow upon you due esteem, and will never make a decision without your permission. If you seek to be king, we shall make you our king. If what is happening to you is a type of obsessive vision that you cannot stop by yourself, we shall seek your cure sparing no money until you are fully recovered."

The Prophet reacted:

"I am not at all what you are saying. What I am conveying does not imply the pursuit of your money, tribal honor, or authority over you. It is only that God sent me among you as His messenger. He revealed to me a Book, and commanded me to be a carrier of good tidings and a harbinger. I have conveyed to you the messages of my Lord, advising you (to the straight path). If you accept what I have conveyed to you, it will be your reward in this life and in the coming one. If you reject it, I shall patiently submit to Allāh's determination until He judges between you and me."

ما بي ما تقولون، ما جئت بما جئتكم به أطلب أموالكم ولا الشرف فيكم ولا الملك عليكم، ولكن الله بعثني إليكم رسولا وأنزل علي كتابا وأمرني أن أكون لكم بشيرا ونذيرا، فبلغتكم رسالات ربي ونصحت لكم، فإن تقبلتم مني ما جئتكم به فهو حظكم في الدنيا والآخرة، وإن تردوه علي أصبر لأمر الله حتى يحكم بيني وبينكم.

At the end of their dialogue with Muḥammad, they said,

"We shall never surrender after all you have done to us. Either we shall destroy you or you will destroy us." (Ibn Hishām, 1:268, 269)

The same purity is seen in an incident that followed the deaths of the Prophet's wife Khadījah and his uncle Abū Ṭālib, his leading supporters since the start of the Revelation. It is well known that in the tribal life, individuals were obliged to be under the protection of the leaders of a tribe; otherwise they could be subject to aggression from a rival tribe, with no means of defense, as there were no laws other than the decisions of tribal leaders. Thus the Prophet sought the protection of other Arab tribes so that he might avoid the Quraysh's continuous aggression against him and his followers. A majority of the tribes of Mecca rebuffed him, as they had no interest in provoking the enmity of the Quraysh. However, a member of the Bani Amer tribe named Baihara bin Feras, anticipating that the Prophet would gain more and more power, thought that in an alliance with him his tribe might dominate all the Arabs. Baihara thus told the Prophet that his tribe was ready to support him on the condition that his successor would be chosen from their tribe if, with their support, he became "king." The Prophet refused and continued to seek the support of other tribes who might listen to the Call, believe it, and back him. (Ibn Hishām, 2:26)

The Path of Allāh is an Inner Struggle for Purification

Stressing the meaning of struggle, *jihād,* as a person's sincere and persistent attempts to be pure of the taints of the lower self, the Prophet guided his followers to maintain high moral standards when forced to enter into battle against aggressors. He clarified that to be on the path of Allāh means that a Muslim is never preoccupied by what he will receive for any action he performs. Their primary and ultimate preoccupation should be to demonstrate devotion to Allāh when doing anything. Several *ḥadīths* of the Prophet explain that when a fighter seeks egoistic desires, it is a sure sign that he is not on the path of Allāh.

> *One of the Prophet's companions asked him, "Some fighters might seek to profit from the spoils of war, gaining fame or high status. Which of those is on the path of Allāh?" The Prophet said, "Only the one who fought for raising the word of Allāh higher."*[1]
>
> «جاء رجل إلى النبي فقال: الرجل يقاتل للمغنم، والرجل
> يقاتل للذكر، والرجل ليرى مكانه، فمن في سبيل الله؟ قال من

[1]Narrated by the five great scholars of *ḥadīth*.

قاتل لتكون كلمة الله هي العليا فهو في سبيل الله»»»

In another *ḥadīth*, an individual asked the Prophet,

> *"If someone joined a fight for the sake of profiting from the spoils of war or to gain fame, what would he attain (spiritually)?"*

The Prophet said,

> *"Simply nothing."*

The man repeated the question three times and the Prophet gave the same answer:

> *"He would gain nothing, because God accepts deeds only when they are motivated by purity and when one wants nothing but Allāh's Face."*[2]

«««قال رجل: يا رسول الله أرأيت رجلا غزا يلتمس الأجر والذكر، ما له؟ فقال: لا شيء له. فأعادها ثلاث مرات، فقال: لا شيء له إن الله لا يقبل من العمل إلا ما كان له خالصا وابتغى به وجهه.»»»

The Prophet also clarified that being a martyr is more an inner spiritual state than an outward eagerness to fight. He said,

> *"He who prayed to God sincerely for attaining martyrdom (dying in the path to Allāh), God takes him up to the status of martyrs, even if he died in his bed."*[3]

«««من سأل الله الشهادة بصدق بلغه الله منازل الشهداء وإن مات على فراشه»»»

A Muslim Never Initiates Aggression

[2]Narrated by Nasā'ī and Abū Dā'ūd.
[3]Narrated by the five great scholars.

The history of the Islamic Revelation to the Prophet Muḥammad clearly shows that his opponents, not the Prophet, were responsible for initiating wars.

The Quraysh and Other Arab Tribes in Mecca Chose To Be Hostile to the Prophet Muḥammad

As soon as the Qurayshi leaders were certain that the Prophet Muḥammad would not be tempted by money or tribal power to stop spreading the divine message with which he was charged, they openly announced their enmity to him and his followers. They initiated the hostilities by announcing that they aimed to assassinate the Prophet Muḥammad (Ibn Saʿd, 1:188). They exerted pressure on other tribes by severing relations with them if they allowed Muḥammad or any of his followers into their homes. They also prevented them from receiving any goods from Mecca or elsewhere, in an attempt to weaken them to the point that they were faced with starvation. In the meantime, they ordered the physical torture of Muḥammad's followers (Ibn Saʿd, 1: 193, 194; Ibn Hishām, 1:287, 288, 317). The siege was imposed not only on Muslims, but on all members of the Banī Hāshim (the family of the Prophet) in an attempt to force them to surrender Muḥammad to them so that they could kill him (*A Selection of the Holy Qur'ān Exegeses*, 43, 44). When a number of Muslims, approximately 100, migrated to Ethiopia to escape oppression, the Quraysh sent two envoys to the Negus of Ethiopia to persuade him to send the Muslims back to Mecca, where they would be tortured (Ibn Hishām, 1:303). Muslims were commanded by the Divine to be patient and to avoid the non-believers. God told them,

> *Forgive and overlook, until Allāh accomplishes His purpose, for Allāh has power over all things.* (*Qur'ān* 2:109)
>
> فَاعْفُوا وَاصْفَحُوا حَتَّى يَأْتِيَ اللَّهُ بِأَمْرِهِ إِنَّ اللَّهَ عَلَى كُلِّ شَيْءٍ قَدِيرٌ

When the Prophet sought to migrate to Yathrib (later called Medina), a city sympathetic to the Islamic Call, and leave Mecca, which rejected it, the Qurayshi leaders plotted to assassinate him. When they failed and he succeeded in leaving Mecca, they followed him out of the city, but again failed, a sign of Divine support guiding the Prophet to Yathrib.

In time, Muslims were given permission to defend themselves against those who initiated hostilities against them. The first verse that allowed Muslims to fight explains it as follows:

> *To those against whom war is made, permission is given (to fight), because they are wronged, and verily, Allāh is Most Powerful to aid their victory. (Qur'ān 22:39)*
>
> أُذِنَ لِلَّذِينَ يُقَاتَلُونَ بِأَنَّهُمْ ظُلِمُوا وَإِنَّ اللَّهَ عَلَى نَصْرِهِمْ لَقَدِير

The verse that follows specifies the type of oppression and injustice to which they were exposed:

> *(They are) those who have been expelled from their homes in defiance of right, (for no cause) except that they say, "Our Lord is Allāh." (Qur'ān 22:40)*
>
> الَّذِينَ أُخْرِجُوا مِنْ دِيَارِهِمْ بِغَيْرِ حَقٍّ إِلَّا أَنْ يَقُولُوا رَبُّنَا اللَّه

The latter part of the verse speaks of another kind of injustice:

> *Did Allāh not check one set of people with another, monasteries, churches, synagogues, and mosques, in which the name of God is commemorated abundantly, would surely have been destroyed. (Qur'ān 22:40)*
>
> وَلَوْلَا دَفْعُ اللَّهِ النَّاسَ بَعْضَهُمْ بِبَعْضٍ لَهُدِّمَتْ صَوَامِعُ وَبِيَعٌ
> وَصَلَوَاتٌ وَمَسَاجِدُ يُذْكَرُ فِيهَا اسْمُ اللَّهِ كَثِيرًا

These two verses outline the basic reason for *jihād*: Muslims were wronged and oppressed and the injustice against them was overwhelming. The wealthy and powerful in Mecca did not want to grant slaves freedom or rights. They did not want the poor to ask for fair reward for their work. Even when Muslims wanted to emigrate, they tried to prevent them (Haikal, 220).

Note, also, that in every verse containing a commandment for Muslims to go into battle, the objective and the limits are explicitly mentioned.

> *And fight against them until there is no more tumult or oppression, and there prevails justice and faith in Allāh altogether and everywhere; but if they cease, verily Allāh sees all that they do. (Qur'ān 8:39)*
>
> وَقَاتِلُوهُمْ حَتَّىٰ لَا تَكُونَ فِتْنَةٌ وَيَكُونَ الدِّينُ كُلُّهُ لِلَّهِ فَإِنِ انتَهَوْا فَإِنَّ اللَّهَ بِمَا يَعْمَلُونَ بَصِيرٌ

> *Nor will they cease fighting you until they turn you away from your faith if they can. (Qur'ān 2:217)*
>
> وَلَا يَزَالُونَ يُقَاتِلُونَكُمْ حَتَّىٰ يَرُدُّوكُمْ عَن دِينِكُمْ إِنِ اسْتَطَاعُوا

One can safely conclude that battles were never intended to impose faith in Islam on others, but were meant to stop outside aggression. A clear commandment was given: with the end of aggression and oppression should come an end to fighting.

The Quraysh Tribe Extended its War Against Muslims Following their Emigration to Medina

The Prophet Muḥammad's enemies in the Quraysh tribe sought to exert economic pressure to weaken the Muslims' position in Medina, before attacking them there. To do so, they sought the collaboration of Bedouin gangs, located near Medina, who would attack the city's pastures, steal sheep, and block trade coming from ash-Sham to Arabia and vice-versa. The Quraysh paid the Bedouin in exchange for full control over the trade route. The Prophet attempted to neutralize those gangs and avoid their attacks. In this he succeeded and Muslims were able to control the trade route (Mo'nes, 137-139). The Muslim immigrants, who had left their homes and possessions behind when they were forced to leave Mecca for Medina, finally had the opportunity to retrieve some of their possessions and to be compensated for what they had lost. Controlling the trade route, the Muslim immigrants went to Mecca while the merchant caravan of Quraysh leader Abū Sufyān was returning there. Muslims wanted to stop them and declare their rights; they were not seeking to fight, being committed to the Prophet's strict commandment never to initiate a war. The Qurayshi leaders, however, decided to fight Muḥammad and his followers and destroy the newborn power. They prepared an army of 1,000 soldiers; the number of Muslims able to fight was little more than 300. Aware of the Qurayshi preparations for war, the Muslims had no choice but to defend themselves. When the adversaries clashed, near a well called Badr, the Muslims unexpectedly beat the Qurayshi troops and returned to Medina miraculously victorious. This took place after the second year of emigration, the *Hijrah*. The defeat made the Quraysh even more determined to conquer Muḥammad and his followers. Following their defeat in Badr, and before departing for Mecca, their leader said to the Prophet,

> *"O Muḥammad, there will be war. Until next year in Uḥud!" (A Selection of the Holy Qur'ān Exegeses, 43, 44).*

It was the Quraysh, then, who initiated, in Uḥud, the second battle the following year, when 3,000 troops left Mecca to attack the Muslims in Medina. The same is true of the battles in Badr (a second time) and As-Suwaiq. The battle al-Aḥzāb, in the fifth year of the *Hijrah*, was again initiated by the Quraysh, now allied with the Ghaṭafān (another Arab tribe), Jews, and some Muslim "hypocrites." They invaded Medina with 10,000 troops, against only 3,000 Muslims. Despite their numerical superiority, however, they were not able to achieve their goal and were again defeated.

The Prophet Accepted a Peace Treaty with the Quraysh

Now that Muslims were aware of how dear to them was the holy shrine of the *Ka'bah*, they longed to go to Mecca to perform the small pilgrimage, the *'umrah*. The Prophet Muḥammad sent an envoy to the Quraysh, asking them to allow some Muslims to go to Mecca and assuring its leaders that the Muslims had no intention of causing any troubles or of attacking anyone; indeed, because they did not want to shed blood in the holy city, they would come unarmed. The Qurayshi leaders, however, did not trust Muḥammad and instead of merely refusing his request, they felt provoked and tried once more to attack him. This led to the battle at Ḥudaybiyyah.

In spite of the Muslims' overwhelming victory in that battle, the Prophet offered a ten-year peace treaty to the Quraysh, accepting conditions onerous to Muslims because he would not exclude any chance for spreading peace and avoiding more bloodshed. Those conditions were as follows:

First, Muslims should return to Medina without performing the small pilgrimage, *'umrah*, that year. However, the following year they could perform it; the Quraysh would leave Mecca to them for three days.

Second, there were to be no battles for ten years, and the two parties committed to put an end to acts of treason and robbery.

Third, if anyone migrated from Mecca to Medina, Muḥammad should send them back to Mecca; while if anyone living in Medina decided to abandon Islam and return to Mecca, Muḥammad should not stop them.

Fourth, each of Arabia's tribes should choose to be under the protection of either Muḥammad or the Quraysh and, accordingly, abide by the commitment of the party it chose (Abū Ẓahra 1993, 2: 749-751).

The Prophet was fully committed to the treaty he had signed. When Abū Baṣīr, an inhabitant of Mecca who converted to Islām, managed to escape to Medina, where he professed his faith before the Prophet, the Quraysh sent two envoys to retrieve him. The Prophet agreed to this, telling him,

> *"O Abū Baṣīr, we have given those people the promise you know, and according to our religion we should not be treacherous. Be sure that Allāh will prepare for you and all the weak a way out." Abū Baṣīr said, "Messenger of God, would you give me back to those non-believers who will force me to quit my faith!" Again the Prophet responded, "Go ahead, Abū Baṣīr, God Almighty will prepare for you and the other oppressed a way out."*
>
> يا أبا بصير إنا قد أعطينا هؤلاء القوم ما قد علمت ولا يصلح لنا في ديننا الغدر وإن الله جاعل لك و لمن معك من المستضعفين فرجا ومخرجا. قال أبوبصير: يا رسول الله أتردني

إلى المشركين يفتنونني في ديني؟ قال الرسول: يا أبا بصير انطلق فإن الله تعالى سيجعل لك و لمن معك من المستضعفين فرجا ومخرجا

However, Abū Baṣīr and other Muslim converts sent back to Mecca on the Prophet's orders announced their rejection to the Quraysh, causing many problems. The Quraysh then asked the Prophet to take them back and announced the abrogation of the clause in the Ḥudaybiyyah treaty that committed the Prophet to return to Mecca anyone who migrated to Medina (Ibn Hishām, 3: 158-169; Abū Ẓahra 1993, 2: 760-762).

Opening Mecca Served to Spread Peace

Several events quickly followed the signing of the Ḥudaybiyyah treaty, leading to the opening of Mecca just before the end of the year. According to one of the treaty's clauses, the Banī Khuza'a tribe chose to be under the protection of the Prophet Muḥammad, while the Banī Bakr chose to be under the protection of the Quraysh. These two Arab tribes had always been hostile towards one another, with the Quraysh always supporting Bani Bakr. It was only logical, then, that the Bani Khoza'a sought the protection of the Prophet. Accordingly, the two tribes had to abide by the clause that stipulated an end to hostilities for ten years. Both the Quraysh and the Prophet Muḥammad were responsible for supervising the tribes under their protection. Nevertheless, the Bani Bakr initiated confrontation with the Bani Khuza'a. The Quraysh supplied the Bani Bakr with weapons and some of its members secretly participated in the conflict, a direct violation of the Ḥudaybiyyah treaty. When the news reached the Prophet, he was sure that the Qurayshi had broken the truce. He decided to invade the Quraysh, making it clear to his companions and followers that he did not seek war and bloodshed but an end to the battles taking place in holy Mecca.

With approximately 10,000 troops, the Prophet departed for Mecca, giving strict orders to Muslims not to kill anyone, but only to defend themselves when attacked. In the end, the holy city of Mecca was opened peacefully. Seeing the Muslims arriving in such great number and fearing annihilation, the Qurayshi people surrendered the city to them. The Prophet thus returned to his native city victoriously, facing no resistance, and seeking neither vengeance against those who had conspired to destroy him completely, nor forced converts to his beliefs. Upon entering the city, he assuaged people's fears by saying,

> *"Everyone is safe if he simply enters Abū Sufyān's house, his own house, or the holy mosque."*
>
> من دخل دار أبي سفيان فهو آمن ومن أغلق عليه بابه فهو آمن ومن دخل المسجد فهو آمن

The Prophet then went directly to the Holy *Ka'bah*, where he circumambulated the Holy Shrine while crowds gathered to see what was happening. He faced the masses and said,

> *"O people of Quraysh, what do you think I shall do with you?"*
>
> يا معشر قريش ما تظنون أني فاعل فيكم

They told him,

> *"We have not known you but as a generous brother and cousin."*
>
> أخ كريم وابن أخ كريم

In his position of power, he told them,

> *"Go, you are set free."*[4]
>
> فاذهبوا فأنتم الطلقاء

Hence was an amnesty granted to all of Mecca's inhabitants (Haikal, 426). Even though the Quraysh, the most powerful tribe in Arabia, surrendered, several other, smaller tribes near Mecca initiated hostilities against Muslims, leading to battles—at Banī Muṣṭaliq, Najrān, Ḥunayn, Ghaṭafān, Aṭ-Ṭa'īf and Dawmat Al-Jandal—but they lost each successively (Al-Abed, 588-603).

---

[4]The whole story of the opening of Mecca is in Ibn Hishām, 3:223-245 and Abū Ẓahra 1993, 3: 878-889.

The Prophet Extended His Love to the Surrounding World

Love and caring always filled the heart of the Prophet when he spread the message that the Divine had commanded him to convey.

The Jews in Medina Refrained from Living in Peace with the Prophet Muḥammad

The Jewish tribes could have lived peacefully with the Muslims, enjoying full guarantees of rights and duties equal to the Muslims. According to the treaties that they signed with the Prophet, they were to cooperate with Muslims in confronting outside aggression directed against any of them. Yet the Jewish tribes, one after another, violated the treaties that they had signed. One of the Jewish tribes, the Bani'n-Naḍīr, made secret agreements with the people of Quraysh, who were planning to attack the Muslims and kill the Prophet (in the second year following the *Hijrah*). Its leader not only eschewed supporting Muslims as agreed to in the signed treaty, but also told the Quraysh about the Muslim army's weaknesses. The following year, when the Muslims faced the Quraysh at Uḥud, the Jews attempted to discourage Muslims from joining the army; they also tried to assassinate the Prophet (Al-Abed, 244-246). The Muslims, inevitably, fought the Bani'n-Naḍīr, in the fourth year of the *Hijrah*. When the Bani'n-Naḍīr were conquered, they asked the Prophet to allow them to leave Medina in safety. They were permitted to go with all of their property excepting their armor (Al-Abed, 257). The Qur'ān revealed verses regarding these historical facts.

> *It is He Who drove the deniers among the People of the Book from their homes at the first gathering (of the forces). Little did you think that they would go; and they thought that their fortresses would defend them from Allāh! But the (Wrath of) Allāh came to them from quarters from which they little expected, and cast terror into their hearts, so that they destroyed their dwellings with their own hands and the hands of the faithful. Take warning, then, O you with eyes (to see)! (Qur'ān 59:2)*

هُوَ الَّذِي أَخْرَجَ الَّذِينَ كَفَرُوا مِنْ أَهْلِ الْكِتَابِ مِنْ دِيَارِهِمْ لِأَوَّلِ الْحَشْرِ مَا ظَنَنْتُمْ أَنْ يَخْرُجُوا وَظَنُّوا أَنَّهُمْ مَانِعَتُهُمْ حُصُونُهُمْ مِنَ اللَّهِ فَأَتَاهُمُ اللَّهُ مِنْ حَيْثُ لَمْ يَحْتَسِبُوا وَقَذَفَ فِي قُلُوبِهِمُ الرُّعْبَ يُخْرِبُونَ بُيُوتَهُمْ بِأَيْدِيهِمْ وَأَيْدِي الْمُؤْمِنِينَ فَاعْتَبِرُوا يَاأُولِي الْأَبْصَارِ

Jews are here deemed "deniers among the People of the Book," not to generalize about People of the Book, but to highlight the fact that among them there existed a number of deniers. Otherwise they would not seek to kill the word of Truth and combine with its enemies to fight it.

When the Banu'n-Naḍīr left Medina for Khaybar, they wanted to take vengeance against the Prophet and Muslims. They thus began to urge the Arab tribes to fight the Muslims, succeeding in rallying the troops of the Quraysh and another Arab tribe named the Ghaṭafān. Their 10,000 troops camped near Medina, directly threatening the Muslims. They initiated the war in a battle called al-Aḥzāb, "the clans," referring to the various tribes collaborating against the Muslims. During that battle, which took place in the fifth year of the *Hijrah*, another Jewish tribe, the Banī Qurayẓah, was tempted to join al-Aḥzāb by the leader of the Banu'n-Naḍīr. Following negotiations, they agreed and their leader Kaʿb ibn Asad tore the treaty that they had signed with the Prophet into pieces (Al-Abed, 404-417). About that collaboration, the Holy Qur'ān says:

> *Have you not observed the hypocrites say to their denying brethren among the People of the Book, "If you are expelled, we too will go out with you, and we will never hearken to any one in your affair; and if you are attacked (in fight) we will help you." But Allāh is witness that they are indeed liars. (Qur'ān 59:11)*

أَلَمْ تَرَ إِلَى الَّذِينَ نَافَقُوا يَقُولُونَ لِإِخْوَانِهِمُ الَّذِينَ كَفَرُوا مِنْ أَهْلِ الْكِتَابِ لَئِنْ أُخْرِجْتُمْ لَنَخْرُجَنَّ مَعَكُمْ وَلَا نُطِيعُ فِيكُمْ أَحَدًا أَبَدًا

وَإِنْ قُوتِلْتُمْ لَنَنْصُرَنَّكُمْ وَاللَّهُ يَشْهَدُ إِنَّهُمْ لَكَاذِبُونَ

The verse exposes part of a dialogue between certain Jews and Muslim hypocrites before the battle of al-Aḥzāb. It clarifies the common interest of the parties in the alliance they formed; certain Arab tribes, Jewish tribes, and hypocrite Muslims agreed to band together to attack Muslims.

It is worthy of note that whenever a Jewish tribe violated its treaty with the Prophet, he confronted it without expanding the dispute to another tribe simply because it might be Jewish. He kept his promises with those who kept theirs.

Confrontation with the Romans Was Unavoidable

Persia and Rome were the two superpowers competing for political influence over Arabia, Iraq, Egypt, Palestine, Syria, and other countries of the region. Yemen and Iraq fell into the Persian sphere of influence, while Egypt and ash-Sham (now Lebanon, Syria, Jordan, and Palestine) were under Roman rule. The Arabs were economically dependent on trade with Yemen and ash-Sham. At the time, the Arabs formed scattered tribes, with frequent disputes among them; they had no common bonds that would make of them one political bloc. Hence the Arabs could not contemplate challenging either of the superpowers. The tribes on the borders of Arabia and ash-Sham were forced to submit to Roman authority to avoid being attacked by them (Haikal, 389, 290). Nevertheless, Islam was slowly spreading in the lands surrounding Arabia that were then under Roman influence.

The Prophet sent envoys to the Roman ruler, Heraclius, who, after inquiries were made, appeared to believe that Muḥammad was truly a Prophet. However, Heraclius was not ready to accept the Revelation, thinking:

> *"He (Muḥammad) will definitely usurp my power" (Abū Ẓahra 1993, 3:858-860).*

He thus wanted to put a stop to this perceived threat and to prevent Islam from spreading among his people. He gave orders to kill a number of Muslims in Syria who had learned of Islam from the trade caravans that traveled between Arabia and ash-Sham. Heraclius gave orders to kill one of the Prophet Muḥammad's envoys to the ruler of Baṣra, then a governorate of the Roman Empire (Abū Ẓahra 1993, quoting Ibn Taymiyyah, 3:846).

When the Prophet learned of this, he was terribly saddened and certain that the Romans were determined to prevent the mission from penetrating the area under their influence. Muḥammad thus sought a just response to the killing, a way to protect other Muslims there, and to break the barriers put in place by the Roman Empire to curb the Islamic Mission. These were the reasons behind the first battle that Muslims under the rule of the Prophet fought against the Romans, which took place in Mu'ta, a town south of Damascus. In the eighth year following the *Hijrah*, approximately 3,000 Muslim troops went to face the Romans, who numbered up to 100,000 and were supported by 100,000 Arab Christian troops (Abū Ẓahra 1993, 3: 847). The Muslims were only supported by their faith, which reminded them:

> *How often, by Allāh's will, has a small force vanquished a big one? Allāh is with those who steadfastly persevere. (Qur'ān 2:249)*
>
> كَم مِّن فِئَةٍ قَلِيلَةٍ غَلَبَتْ فِئَةً كَثِيرَةً بِإِذْنِ اللَّهِ وَاللَّهُ مَعَ الصَّابِرِينَ

The three leaders whom the Prophet nominated were courageous enough not to be frightened by the vast numerical superiority of the Romans and their allies. Standing fast courageously, they were killed one after another. The surviving troops elected a new commander without surrendering or retreating. The new leader, Khālid ibn al-Walīd, seeking to save the remaining Muslim troops honorably, organized the troops in such a way that the Romans thought that reinforcements had arrived. Despite their greater number, the Romans felt great fear in their hearts and would not follow the Muslim troops trying to withdraw with honor.

The second battle fought against the Romans—and the last in the Prophet's lifetime—was an extension of the first one. The Prophet knew that the Romans were preparing to invade Medina and destroy it. The Romans were increasingly angry, as many tribes under their influence sought the protection of the Prophet Muḥammad; that is, their power was on the wane while that of the Muslims was expanding. The Prophet knew that they would launch their invasion from Tabūk, a town in the south of ash-Sham, near the northern border of Arabia. He decided to confront them there rather than wait until they reached Medina. However, when he reached Tabūk with his army, he found no Roman troops. Consequently, he decided to return to Medina rather than penetrate ash-Sham, demonstrating that his aim was not to invade any land with the goal of occupying it. The Prophet was applying a general principle:

> *(O deniers!) . . . if you desist (from doing wrong), it will be best for you, but if you return (to the attack), so shall we. (Qur'ān 8:19)*
>
> وَإِنْ تَنْتَهُوا فَهُوَ خَيْرٌ لَكُمْ وَإِنْ تَعُودُوا نَعُدْ

While the Muslim troops were still in Tabūk, certain Arab Christian tribes, formerly allied with the Romans against the Muslims in Mu'ta, came to the Prophet Muḥammad and proposed that they come under his *Dhimmah* protection (Abū Ẓahra 1993, 3: 958-960). He thus signed treaties with them in which they promised not to support the Romans against Muslims and the Prophet promised to protect them against any Roman aggression.

Glossary

ʿAbdullāh: A servant of God, a person who is spiritually free from devotion to any illusion or transient aspect of life.

Allāhu Akbar: Allāh is Greater, ever Greater.

Al-amānah: The Trust; the divinity within man that distinguishes him from the other creatures of Allāh. It also refers to the "responsibility" or the "mission" that man shoulders as God's representative on Earth.

Al-amr al-wasaṭ: The balanced state between two extremes. It can refer to the state of man in which he is steady and consistent in his relations with himself and his surroundings. It can also refer to man as a point where heaven and earth meet and integrate; spirit and matter are well balanced in his existence

ʿArafat: A holy mountain in Mecca. Derived from the verb *ʿarafa*, "to know." Spending time on the holy mountain praying and expressing devotion to Allāh is a basic ritual of pilgrimage. Symbolically speaking, devotion to Allāh implies that man should seek greater heights through knowledge.

ʿAṣabīyyah: Tribal pride, whereby a tribe member defends another or others merely because they belong to a certain tribe, regardless of whether that person or group is right. Islam adamantly denounces *ʿaṣabīyyah*, considering it a sign of ignorance, *jāhiliyyah*.

Baghyan: (adv.) Oppressively, unjustifiably, by transgressing.

Al-bāṭil: Falsehood or illusion; anything void of truth.

Baytullāh: The House of God. (See *Al-Kaʿbah.*)

Dayn: Loan. The word implies that the Divine loans man his life, which is thus a Trust that man should keep safely and honestly.

Dīn: Religion.

Ad-dīn al-fiṭrah: The Religion that is stamped on man's primordial and pure nature (*fiṭrah*). (See *Al-fiṭrah.*)

Ad-dīn al-ḥanīf: The religion of righteousness. The term refers to the Religion of the Prophet Abraham in particular and connotes "Islam" in the broad sense of the word.

Dhimmeyyin: Followers of other faiths living in a Muslim society. *Dhimmah* means "responsibility" or "protection." The Prophet Muḥammad told his followers that non-Muslims were under his protection or responsibility, as a way of persuading them to be just and kind to them.

Dhikrullāh (Dhikr Allāh): Remembrance of Allāh. It refers both to a person's awareness of Allāh within and beyond everything in his life and to all aspects of worship and meditation.

Dhu'l-Ḥijjah: The last month of the *Hijrī* Calendar, that of Pilgrimage.

'Eīd al-aḍḥā': the feast of the sacrifice, commemorating the Prophet Abraham's willingness to sacrifice his son if Allāh required it.

Al-Fātiḥah: "the opener," referring to the first *sūrah* in the Holy Qur'ān. It is also the opening prayer recited at the beginning of each *rak'āh* of ritual prayers.

Al-fiqh: Understanding, discernment. Long used to refer to the dynamically accumulated knowledge that scholars of Islam elaborated as a result of their attempts to understand the layers of meanings embedded in the Holy Qur'ān and Prophetic *Sunnah.* This understanding was then presented in the form of guidance and regulations as to how to make of everything in life a means for living in harmony with the Divine Law. (See also *al-Ijtihād.*)

Al-fiṭrah: The innate, pure nature of man as originally created by the Divine, containing the Law within its very fiber. Not to be confused with "instinct," which is related to the attributes of the physical body, *al-fiṭrah* is the primordial nature of the soul that contains spiritual awareness.

Fiṭratullāh: The Way Allāh conceived His creation according to the Divine Order.

Furqān: That which allows those who seek truthfulness to distinguish between what is true and what is false. Used in the Holy Qur'ān to refer to Divine wisdom generally and to the Qur'ān specifically.

Furūḍ: The plural of *Farḍ*, a religious duty. It does not imply the use of force or that certain persons have the authority to compel others to comply to these rules. *Furūḍ* allows man to be in harmony with the Divine Law.

Al-Ghayb: The Unseen, referring to everything that is beyond the known and the knowable, exceeding man's reach.

Ḥadīth: A Saying of the Prophet Muḥammad.

Ḥajj: Pilgrimage.

Ḥanīf: The state of righteousness or the person who seeks it.

Ḥanīfiyyah: The name given to the Religion revealed to the Prophet Abraham and reinvigorated by the Revelation to the Prophet Muḥammad.

Al-ḥaqq: The truth.

Al-Ḥaqq: The Truth or the Real; one of the beautiful names of Allāh.

Al-hawāh: Aany human desire or inclination that stems from the lower self. It generally constitutes a barrier between a person and his inner *fiṭrah*, the higher self that has the potential to live in submission to the Law of Life.

Al-hijrah: The emigration of the Prophet Muḥammad from Mecca to

Yathrib, later named *al-Madīnah al-Munawwarah*, the illuminated city (Medina). The date of *al-Hijrah* was later made the beginning of the *Hijrī* Calendar.

Ḥudūd: "Limits," as in those that are transgressed. The Holy Qur'ān refers to *Ḥudūd Allāh,* implying teachings that reveal to people how to attain the law of spiritual growth. It also refers to legal punishments according to the Islamic *Sharī'ah.*

Iblīs: The Adversary; originally the fallen Angel who refused to bow down to Adam, when ordered to do so by Allāh. A common symbol of man's lower self.

Al-iḥrām: The state of sanctification associated with Pilgrimage. It symbolizes man's full surrender to Allāh and the fact that once he begins his journey to Him, it is as if he already belonged to Heaven and, accordingly, he halts all deeds related to everyday life.

Al-ijtihād: The effort that goes into creative thinking and purification of the heart in order to better understand the *Sharī'ah.* This leads to the creation of new means for living in harmony, with divine guidance, in new situations as an individual or as a society.

Islām: Surrender (to Allāh).

Al-jihād: The struggle taking place within, for purification, and outwardly, when one strives to make one's every action an expression of purity.

Al-Ka'bah: The holy shrine in Mecca that is said to have existed since the time of Father Adam and which was made a symbol as God's House by the Prophet Abraham. It is the focal point which Muslims face when performing ritual prayer, and it is their destination in Pilgrimage.

Kāfir: A denier or one who does not have faith; one who is ungrateful (to Allāh's graces).

Al-kalimah as-sawā': This is translated variously as the reconciling principle, the common principle, or common terms. This is the expression used in the Holy Qur'ān to rally followers of different Revelations to come together and feel their unity by discussing the core of all Revelations, which is the belief in the oneness of God. This belief leads to a path of spiritual liberation for man, by guiding him to be devoted solely to Allāh. This devotion helps him realize his humanness and approach life from a proper perspective.

Al-Kitāb: The Book, referring not only to the Holy Scriptures but also to the Law of Life expressed within man and in nature.

Khalifāh: Representative; used in the Holy Qur'ān in reference to Adam at the moment when God bestowed upon him His trust.

Lā ilāha illā Allāh, Muḥammad rasūlu Allāh: "There is no god but God, Muḥammad is the messenger of God." This is the Islamic testimony by which a Muslim expresses his faith in the oneness of Allāh and in the Prophet Muḥammad as His messenger. It is more than a verbal expression, as it must be experienced. When one's heart declares that testimony, it implies that one is spiritually ready to start down the path of spiritual freedom. (See *ash-Shahādah*)

Laylat al-Qadr The Night of God's Grace, when the revelation to the Prophet Muḥammad began, on the 26th day of the holy month of *Ramaḍān*.

Mount Marwa: One of two holy mountains in Mecca. *Marwa* signifies the state of a person who has suffered from a great thirst, which is now quenched. It is considered holy as Hagar, the wife of the Prophet Abraham, went back and forth between it and Mount Ṣafā in search of water for her small child, Ismā'īl. Pilgrims to Mecca now tread the same path as one of their rituals.

Mount Ṣafā: One of two holy mountains in Mecca. *Ṣafā* means "purity." It is considered holy, as it is from here that Hagar, the wife of the Prophet Abraham, began her trek between it and Mount Marwa. She walked between the two points seven times. Symbolically, her trek implies that when a person searches for a source of life, he or she starts in a state of purity (*ṣafā*), then gains spiritual satisfaction (*marwa*). However, that journey is not done only once, but is repeated continually, as the more one becomes pure, the more one searches for satisfaction.

Al-qiblah: The direction or focus. It refers to the holy shrine of the *Ka'bah,* which Muslims face when performing ritual prayer. Symbolically speaking, it refers to the Light of God expressed in all His Prophets and messengers. (See *al-Ka'bah.*)

Rak'āh: The set of movements performed and words spoken or internally repeated during ritual prayer.

Ramaḍān: The ninth month of the *Hijrī* Calendar, the month of fasting.

Ar-Rūḥ: Spirit.

As-ṣadaqa: Voluntary charity, of any size, which one gives out of love. It may be a physical object or moral support to the needy.

Salām: Peace.

Aṣ-Ṣalāt: "Calling" Allāh devotedly and seeking connection with Him and His Messenger; i.e., the five ritual prayers that Islam as revealed to the Prophet Muḥammad prescribed each day for Muslims.

Sallama: (v.) To surrender.

Ṣawm: Fasting.

Ash-Shahādah: The testimony "there is no god but God, Muḥammad is the Messenger of God," *Lā ilāha illā Allāh, Muḥammad rasūlu Allāh.* The first part of the *Shahādah* emphasizes man's awareness of his devotion to Allāh only, not to any transient objective in life. With that awareness, man becomes conscious of his need of a higher source of guidance. As such, he seeks manifestations of Light on earth—the messengers of Allāh—of whom Muḥammad is a symbol.

ash-Shahr al-Karīm al-Mubārak: The blessed month of the annual fast (*Ramaḍān*). *Shahr* means "month" and is also associated with the verb "to proclaim" or "to declare." Symbolically speaking, *shahr* refers to the state of living as a spirit or a totally divine being, renouncing any attachment to physical life. Thereby a person "declares" the divinity within, the realization of his or her origin as spirit.

Shākir: Grateful, thankful.

Sharīʿah: The Divine path revealed in the Holy Book of the Qur'ān and clarified in and exemplified by the Prophetic *Sunnah;* basic "principles" that inspire man with ever new means to live according to the Divine Law. The *Sharīʿah* is a living spirit that emerges in pure hearts and expresses itself in constantly innovative ways.

Shaykh: A scholar in Islamic Fiqh or a teacher of a Sufi order.

Ṣirāṭ: Path.

Aṣ-ṣirāṭ al-mustaqīm: The straight and righteous path.

As-sujūd: Prostration; in ritual prayer, the last posture in a *rakʿāh,* after which one begins a new *rakʿāh*. It symbolizes full surrender to Allāh.

Sunan: The plural of *Sunnah*.

Sunnatullāh: The "Way" of Allāh, the Divine Law.

As-sunnah: The "Way" that the Prophet Muḥammad lived and expressed the divine teachings. It has come to refer to his tradition—his sayings and deeds as documented in canonical works. It also refers to the Divine Law when rendered as *Sunnatullāh,* the "Way" or the "Law" of Allāh.

Sūrah: Aa section of the Holy Qur'ān, which is comprised of 114 *sūrahs*.

At-taḥiyyāt: Salutations; the words that a Muslim pronounces while sitting, after completing two *rak'āhs* of ritual prayer, and at the end of the prayers. A Muslim testifies his or her faith in the Prophet Muḥammad, saying

> *"Peace be upon you, oh Prophet. Peace be upon us and on all good servants of Allāh. I witness that there is no god but God and Muḥammad is the Messenger of God."*

There are variations of *At-Taḥiyyāt*, derived from Prophetic *Sunnah*, but all of them include these phrases.

Taslīm: Living in full submission to the Law of Allāh.

Ṭawāf al-qudūm: *Ṭawāf* means "circumambulation." *Qudūm* means "arrival." Combined, it is the ritual of circumambulating the house of God, the *Ka'bah*, upon arriving in Mecca on pilgrimage.

Ṭawāf al-ifāḍa: *Ifāḍa* means "great radiance" or "brightness." *Ṭawāf al-ifāḍa* refers to the circumambulation of the *Ka'bah* that a pilgrim performs once he is purified of his lower nature and thus ready to receive the divine Light. It is one of the basic rituals of pilgrimage.

Az-zakāt: Alms-giving; one of the five pillars of Islām. Originally meaning "purification" and also "growth," it is the pillar that links man's zeal for spiritual elevation with his role in building a society based on social integration. *Zakāt* is an expression of man's faith in the oneness of Allāh by means of giving the poor "their right" to a part of his property. Islamic teachings not only purify man spiritually, freeing him from greed and selfishness, they make *zakāt* a tool for social cohesion.

Zakka: (v.) To cause something to be purified or to grow.

References

Al-ʿAbed, Abū Badr Muḥammad Bin Bakr, *Ḥadīth Al-Qur'ān Al-Karīm An Ghazawāt Ar-Rasūl Ṣalah Allāhu Ạlayhi Wa Sallam (The Holy Qur'ān on the Battles of the Messenger, Peace Be upon Him)*. Beirut: Dār Al-Gharb Al-Islāmi, 1994.

حديث القرآن الكريم عن غزوات الرسول صلى الله عليه وسلم. أبو بدر محمد بن بكرآل عابد. دار الغرب الإسلامي. بيروت. ١٩٩٤م

Abū Ẓahra, Muḥammad, *Ad-Daʿwa Ila Al-Islām (The Call to Islām)*. Cairo: Dār Al-Fikr Al-ʿArabī, 1992.

الدعوة إلى الإسلام. الإمام محمد أبو زهرة. دار الفكر العربي. القاهرة. طبعة جديدة ١٩٩٢م

Abū Ẓahra, Muḥammad, *Khātam An-Nabiyyīn (The Seal of Prophets)*. Cairo: Dār Al-Fikr Al-ʿArabi, 1993.

خاتم النبيين. الإمام محمد أبو زهرة. دار الفكر العربي. القاهرة. ١٩٩٣م

Abū Ẓahra, Muḥammad, *Al-ʿIlāqāt Ad-Dawlīa fīl Islām (International Relations in Islām)*. Cairo: Dār Al-Fikr Al-ʿArabi, 1995.

العلاقات الدولية في الإسلام. الإمام محمد أبو زهرة. درا الفكر العربي. القاهرة. طبعة جديدة. ١٩٩٥

Ad-Dahabī, Edward Ghalī, *Muʿāmalat Ghayr al-Muslimīn fī al-Mujtamʿ al-Islāmī (The Treatment of Non-Muslims in a Muslim Society)*, first edition. Cairo: Gharīb Bookshop, 1993.

معاملة غير المسلمين في المجتمع الإسلامي. الدكتور إدوارد غالي الدهبي. مكتبة غريب .الطبعة الأولى. القاهرة. ١٩٩٣

Al-Ghazālī, al-Imām Abū Ḥāmid, *Iḥyā' ʿUlūm ad-Dīn*, Second edition, Dār al-Ghad al-ʿArabi, Cairo, 1987.

إحياء علوم الدين، الإمام أبو حامد الغزالي، (مضاف إليه تخريج الحافظ

العراقي)، الطبعة الثانية، دار الغد العربي، القاهرة، ١٩٨٧.

Haikal, Muḥammad Ḥusayn, *Ḥayāt Muḥammad (The Life of Muḥammad)*, 16th ed. Cairo: Dār Al-Ma'ārif, 1981.
حياة محمد • محمد حسين هيكل • دار المعارف • القاهرة • الطبعة السادسة عشرة • ١٩٨١

Al-Himṣī, Muḥammad Ḥassān, comp. 1984. *Tafsīr wa Bayān al-Qur'ān al-Karīm ma'a Asbāb an-Nuzūl li's-Suyū textsubdottī (Exegeses of the Holy Qur'ān, with "Occasions of the revelation of some verses by As-Suyū textsubdottī")*. Damascus, Beirut: Dār Ar-Rashīd, 1984.
تفسير وبيان القرآن الكريم مع أسباب النزول للسيوطي، إعداد محمد حسن الحمصي، دار الرشيد، دمشق - بيروت، ١٩٨٤

The Holy Bible, King James Version.

The Holy Qur'ān (Electronic Version 7.01). Cairo: Harf Company for Information Technology, 1998.
القرآن الكريم (طبعة إلكترونية باللغة العربية والإنجليزية) لشركة حرف لتقنية المعلومات • الإصدار ٧,٠١ مصر ١٩٩٨

Ibn Hishām, Abi Muḥammad 'Abdil Malik *Ṣirāṭ an-Nabiyy 'Alayhi aṣ-Ṣalāt Wa as-Salām (The Biography of the Prophet Peace Be Upon Him)*, first edition. Cairo: Al-Khairyia, 1911.
سيرة النبي عليه الصلاة والسلام للشيخ الإمام محمد عبد الملك بن هشام • المطبعة الخيرية بمصر • الطبعة الأولى • ١٣٢٩ هجرية •

Ibn Sa'd, Muḥammad, *Aṭ-Ṭabaqāt Al-Kubrā L'Ibn Sa'd (The Great Layers of Ibn Sa'd)*. Cairo: Ath-Thaqāfa Al-Islāmia, 1939.
الطبقات الكبرى لابن سعد • محمد بن سعد • مطبعة لجنة نشر الثقافة الإسلامية • القاهرة • ١٣٥٨ هجرية

Mawsū'at al-Ḥadīth ash-Sharīf (Encyclopedia of Sharīf Ḥadīths). Cairo: Ṣakhr Software Co., 1995.
موسوعة الحديث الشريف لشركة صخر لبرامج الحاسب • القاهرة • ١٩٩٥م

Mu'nes, Ḥussayn. *Dirāsāt Fis-Sīrah An-Nabawiyya (Studies in the Prophet's Biography)*, first edition. Cairo: Az-Zahrā for ʿArab Information, 1984.
دراسات في السيرة النبوية • الدكتور حسين مؤنس • الزهراء للإعلام العربي •
الطبعة الأولى • ١٩٨٤م

Al-Muntakhab fī Tafsīr al-Qur'ān al-Karīm (A Selection of the Holy Qur'ān Exegeses), compiled under the supervision of the Supreme Council of Islamic Affairs, 11th edition, vol. 11. Cairo, 1985.
المنتخب في تفسير القرآن الكريم • المجلس الأعلى للشئون الإسلامية •
الطبعة الحادية عشرة • القاهرة • ١٩٨٥م

Nāṣef, Mansūr, *At-Tāj Al-Jāmiʿ Lil-Uṣūl fī Aḥādīth Ar-Rasūl Ṣalla Allāhu ʿAlayhi Wa Sallam (The Crown that Gathers Original Sayings of the Prophet, Peace Be upon Him)*. Cairo: Isa Elias Al-Halabi & Partners, 1934.
التاج الجامع للأصول في أحاديث الرسول صلى الله عليه وسلم • الشيخ
منصور علي ناصف (من علماء الأزهر الشريف) • مطبعة عيسى إلياس الحلبي
وشركاه بمصر • ١٩٣٤م

As-Suyū textsubdottī, Jalāl ad-Dīn ʿAbdar-Raḥmān Ibn Abī Bakr (D 911 HC), *Al-Jāmiʿ Aṣ-Ṣaghīr Fī Aḥādīth Al-Bashīr An-Naẓīr*, Fourth edition, Dār al-Kutub al-ʿilmīa, Beirut, Lebanon, 1954.
الجامع الصغير في أحاديث البشير النذير، جلال الدين عبد الرحمن ابن أبي
بكر السيوطي (متوفي ٩١١ هـ)، الطبعة الرابعة، دار الكتب العلمية، بيروت،
لبنان ١٩٥٤.

At **The Book Foundation** our goal is to express the highest ideals of Islam and the Qur'an through publications, curricula, and other learning resources, suitable for schools, parents, and individuals, whether non-Muslims seeking to understand the Islamic perspective, or Muslims wanting to deepen their understanding of their own faith. Please visit our website: **thebook.org**

The Book of Revelations

A Sourcebook of Themes from the Holy Qur'an,

Edited by Kabir Helminski

$33 £16.95 6 x 9" 508pp

1-904510-12-4

This book invites us to recognize and reflect upon the essential spiritual themes of the Qur'an. It offers 265 titled selections of ayats, presented in a fresh contemporary translation of high literary quality, with accompanying interpretations by Muhammad Asad, Yusuf Ali, and others. It is an essential sourcebook for Muslims and non-Muslims alike.

The Book of Character

An Anthology of Writings on Virtue from Islamic and Other Sources

Edited by Camille Helminski

$33 £16.95 6 x 9" 484pp

1-904510-09-4

A collection of writings dealing with the qualities of our essential Human Nature: Faith and Trust; Repentance and Forgiveness; Compassion and Mercy; Patience and Forbearance; Modesty, Humility, and Discretion; Purity; Intention and Discernment; Generosity and Gratitude; Courage, Justice, and Right Action; Contentment and Inner Peace; Courtesy and Chivalry. From the Prophets Abraham and Moses, to the sages Confucius and Buddha, to the Prophet Muhammad, his wife, Khadija, and his companions Abu Bakr and 'Ali, through great saints like Rumi, and humanitarians like Florence Nightingale, Mother Theresa, and Martin Luther King, and even in the personal story of the bicyclist Lance Armstrong, we find stories and wisdom that will help us toward spiritual well-being.

The Book Foundation *has embarked on an important effort to develop books and teaching tools that are approachable and relevant to Muslims and non-Muslims.* ~**Shabbir Mansuri**, *Founding Director, Council on Islamic Education (CIE)*

The Book of Essential Islam

The Spiritual Training System of Islam
Ali Rafea,
with Aisha and Aliaa Rafea
$21 £10.95 6 x 9" 276 pp
1-904510-13-2

This book examines the main teachings and practices of Islam with lucidity and depth. It is a corrective to the distortions and misconceptions of Islam that abound. It can serve equally well to introduce non-Muslims to Islam, as well as to enhance Muslims understanding of their own faith. This book presents Islam as a spiritual training system that supports us in harmonizing ourselves with the Divine Order and thus with each other and our environment. It reveals the intent and inner significance of practices like ablution, ritual prayer, fasting, and pilgrimage.

The Fragrance of Faith

The Enlightened Heart of Islam
Jamal Rahman
$15.95 £9.95 6 x 9" 176pp
1-904510-08-6

The Fragrance of Faith reveals the inner Islam that has been passed down through the generations. Jamal is a link in this chain, passing along the message, just as he received it from his grandfather, a village wiseman in Bangladesh. We need reminders of this "enlightened heart of Islam" in our lives, our homes, and our schools. In Jamal Rahman's book Islam is alive and well. ~**Imam Feisal Abdul Rauf**, Author *Islam: A Sacred Law* and *What's Right With Islam*.

This heartfelt book is perfect for the classroom, whether in a Muslim context, or outside of it. It conveys a tradition of compassion and humor passed through one family that represents the best Islam has to offer. And Mr. Rahman is highly entertaining. ~**Michael Wolfe**, *The Hadj: An American's Pilgrimage to Mecca*, Producer of the PBS Documentary: *Muhammad: The Legacy of a Prophet*.